THE
BELGIC
CONFESSION
A COMMENTARY

THE BELGIC CONFESSION

A COMMENTARY

———

VOLUME 1

DAVID J. ENGELSMA

REFORMED
FREE PUBLISHING
ASSOCIATION
Jenison, Michigan

Reformed Free Publishing Association
1894 Georgetown Center Drive
Jenison, Michigan 49428
616-457-5970
www.rfpa.org
mail@rfpa.org

Cover design by Christopher Tobias/tobiasdesign.com
Interior design by Katherine Lloyd/theDESKonline.com

ISBN: 978-1-944555-33-7 (hardcover)
ISBN: 978-1-944555-34-4 (ebook)
LCCN: 2018936104

To Ruth

CONTENTS

PREFACE

Both the members of the Protestant Reformed Churches and the Reformed community of churches worldwide need a commentary on the Belgic Confession of Faith. Regarding the former, their theologians have published commentaries on the Heidelberg Catechism and on the Canons of Dordt. But a commentary on the Belgic Confession is lacking. This commentary intends to supply this lack.

Regarding the Reformed churches throughout the world, to the best of my knowledge there is no commentary in English on the Belgic Confession in print today.

There is, almost certainly, no full-scale commentary on the Confession in print that does full justice to the sound Reformed doctrine of the creed. Such a commentary not only would not blur, or even corrupt, the doctrines of the creed, under the pressure of false doctrines that are at home today even in churches that are reputed to be "conservative." But such a commentary would expose, refute, and condemn the contemporary departures from, or corruptions of, the Reformed, Christian orthodoxy of the Belgic Confession, as the Confession itself requires and enables the Reformed church to do.

The Confession itself requires this exposure, refutation,

and condemnation of doctrines that depart from the truths it teaches inasmuch as the Confession is an official, authoritative, binding standard of gospel truth for Reformed churches everywhere. It is one of the three forms of unity that function as official creeds of almost all Reformed churches everywhere. By an instrument known as the Formula of Subscription (adopted by the Synod of Dordt in 1618–19), all officebearers in Reformed churches vow that they will "refute and contradict" and "exert [themselves] in keeping the church free from…errors [that militate against the doctrines taught in the Belgic Confession.]"[1]

I specify.

This commentary defends the Confession's confession that holy scripture is "infallible," or inerrant (art. 7); that regarding origins God created the universe "of nothing" (art. 12); that the origin of the human race is God's creating man "out of the dust of the earth" (art. 14); that the explanation of the wickedness and death of the human race is this first man's "giving ear to the words of the devil" (art. 14); that the depravity of the fallen sinner is total (art. 14); that the source of salvation is unconditional election, accompanied by sovereign reprobation (art. 16); that Christ's death was substitutionary atonement and that, as such, it was a death for some only, not for all (art. 20–21); that faith is a gracious gift of God, not a condition fulfilled by the sinner (art. 22); that justification is by faith alone, to the exclusion of all works of those who are justified (art. 22–24); that sanctification and the doing of good works do not qualify ("moderate") the truth of justification (art. 24);

---

1 Formula of Subscription, in *The Confessions and the Church Order of the Protestant Reformed Churches* (Grandville, MI: Protestant Reformed Churches in America, 2005), 326.

that there are true church institutes, and false (art. 28–29); and that the return of Christ will be according to the amillennial teaching of the last things (art. 37).

These doctrines and others, a commentary on the Belgic Confession must not only explain, but also defend.

Calvin insisted on the necessity of defending the faith by condemning errors, and that in connection with his approval of the Belgic Confession:

> We do not see, however, how it would be hard for anyone who wants to be counted among the household of the church to sincerely be enlisted under Christ its head. This is impossible unless he clearly assents with upright piety, and honestly condemns errors by which the sincerity of the religion is corrupted.[2]

Significantly, Calvin added that the church and her confessions must take note of and contend against *new, contemporary* errors: "Now the rejection of errors often depends on the circumstances. For, as Satan thinks up new ways to cause disturbances, it is necessary to counteract wisely."[3]

Directly against the foolish thinking of the present time, that the peace of the church requires the tolerance of false doctrine and the demonizing of controversy, Calvin remarked that the biblical commendation of "the unity of the spirit in the bond of peace (Eph. 4:3)...would be ineffective unless everyone would clearly denounce both heretical and corrupt teachings."[4]

---

2   Nicolaas H. Gootjes, *The Belgic Confession: Its History and Sources* (Grand Rapids, MI: Baker Academic, 2007), 69.

3   Ibid.

4   Ibid.

Nevertheless, as the Belgic Confession itself is not chiefly polemical, neither is this commentary. Its purpose, like that of the Confession, is mainly instruction. It explains all the leading doctrines of the Reformed faith to the Christian reader, as these doctrines are taught in the Bible. Should the commentary fall into the hands of an unbeliever, which is heartily to be desired, it can serve the end of witness and evangelism. The enemy that the commentary envisions is not so much false doctrine as it is ignorance. This enemy, within the camp, is by no means imaginary.

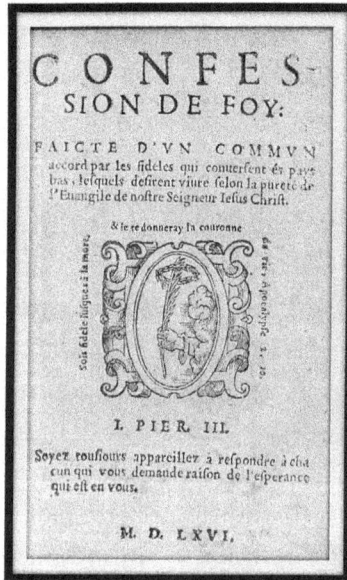

An explanatory word is in order concerning the cover of this commentary. It is a replica of the cover, which was also the title page, of the original edition of the Belgic Confession in 1561. The French title at the top is translated as "Confession of Faith. Made with common consent by the believers who are scattered throughout all the

Netherlands, who desire to live according to the purity of the holy gospel of our Lord Jesus Christ." At the bottom of the title page is the date of publication in Roman numerals: MDLXVI. The date is 1566 since this title page is the cover of a 1566 edition of the original 1561 edition. The 1566 edition, which was virtually unchanged from the original 1561, was officially adopted by the Reformed synod of Antwerp.

In the center of the reproduction of the cover and title page of the Confession of 1566 is a symbolic design, or printer's mark, surrounded by a quotation of Revelation 2:10: "Be thou faithful unto death, and I will give thee a crown of life." This text was especially pertinent since thousands in the Lowlands of Belgium and the Netherlands were being killed, and would be killed in the near future, for their belief of and witness to the faith that is the content of the Belgic Confession. Indeed, the author of the creed would soon be among those martyrs.

The symbol on the cover is powerful. A strong arm extending from the cloud holds a palm branch topped by a crown. The strong arm of God himself assures the triumph of the truth of the gospel that is taught and defended by the Belgic Confession, regardless of the strong opposition to this gospel at the time of its publication and, one may add, at the present time. Both palm and crown are biblical symbols of victory. The arm of God is almighty.

Under the printer's mark is a partial quotation of 1 Peter 3:15: "Be ready always to give an answer to everyone that asks you a reason of the hope that is in you."[5] This

---

5   For much of this information concerning the cover and its meaning, I am indebted to Gootjes, *The Belgic Confession.* Explanation of

citation on the cover page of the Belgic Confession speaks for itself.

The question of the Protestant Reformed reader of this commentary concerns the identity of the edition used by the Protestant Reformed Churches (PRC).[6] It is substantially the English translation of the original Confession of 1561. Changes and revisions of the Confession by various Reformed synods over the years are negligible. None involves doctrine.

Almost certainly the Confession that is current in the PRC is the translation of the Latin edition that was approved, regarding the content, by the Synod of Dordt. This was the source of the translation into English that was approved by the English-speaking churches in the Netherlands. This English translation was published in the Netherlands in 1689. In 1792 the Reformed Dutch Church in the United States (today's Reformed Church in America) adopted that English translation of the Belgic Confession. In the beginning of its history, the Christian Reformed Church carried along this edition of the Confession into its new church formation.

The PRC did the same when they were expelled from the Christian Reformed Church in 1924. That the PRC simply took with them the edition of the Belgic Confession that was used in the Christian Reformed Church prior to 1924 is evident from the footnote appended to article 36 of

---

the cover of the 1566 edition of the Confession is found on pages 117–18.

6 *Confessions and Church Order*, 23–80. See also *The Psalter with Doctrinal Standards, Liturgy, Church Order, and added Chorale Section*, reprinted and revised edition of the 1912 United Presbyterian *Psalter* (Grand Rapids, MI: Wm. B. Eerdmans Publishing Co., 1927; rev. ed. 1995), 37–54.

the Confession. This article concerns the civil magistracy. The note speaks of the dissent to an element of the article on the part of the "Christian Reformed Church."[7]

Schaff judges this translation of the Belgic Confession into English to be "excellent": "the excellent English version in use in the Reformed Dutch Church of America."[8]

A careful comparison of the original English translation adopted by the "Reformed Dutch Church in America" as found in Schaff's *Creeds of Christendom*[9] and the version of it used by the PRC reveals that the differences even in insignificant wording are few and slight. For example, whereas the original English translation has "eternal power and Godhead" in article 2, the version in use by the PRC has "power and divinity." There is one instance of a more significant difference. In article 36, concerning the magistrates, Schaff has the Reformed believer detesting "the *error* of the Anabaptists" (emphasis added).[10] The psalter used by the Protestant Reformed Churches has "detest *the Anabaptists*" themselves (emphasis added),[11] which does not necessarily apply to the Baptists of the present day. Insertion of the words "error of" was a later revision of the original text of the Confession to avoid offending contemporary Baptists.[12]

---

7 *Confessions and Church Order*, 74.

8 Philip Schaff, ed., *The Creeds of Christendom with a History and Critical Notes*, 6th ed., 3 vols. (New York: Harper and Row, 1931; repr., Grand Rapids, MI: Baker Books, 2007), 3:507.

9 Ibid., 3:383–436.

10 Ibid., 3:433.

11 *Psalter with Doctrinal Standards*, 54.

12 An English translation of the original text of the Belgic Confession is "We detest all those who want to reject the Superiors and Magistrates." In 1566 a Reformed synod inserted the word "Anabaptists," explicitly naming the objects of detestation. This edition is regarded as authoritative. The texts changed and adopted by Dordt in 1619

All quotations of the Belgic Confession in this commentary are from the third volume of Schaff's *Creeds of Christendom* (pages 383–436). This English translation of the Belgic Confession is the edition that was published in the United States in 1767; that was adopted by the Reformed Dutch Church in the United States in 1792; and of which Schaff judged that it is "excellent."

Regrettably, the size and substance of the Belgic Confession make publishing the commentary in one volume unsatisfactory. God willing, the second volume will appear shortly.

---

changed the wording to "error of the Anabaptists," thus moderating the condemnation. Later, the Reformed Dutch Church in America adopted the English version that had "error of." The creed in the Protestant Reformed psalter is closer to the original. The creed in *Confessions and Church Order* follows Dordt's softening.

INTRODUCTION

THE AUTHOR OF THE CONFESSION

Just as the Belgic Confession itself tends to be slighted, in comparison with the Heidelberg Catechism, which is preached regularly in Reformed churches, and with the Canons of Dordt, which is always the object of intense study on account of its controversial content, including double predestination, so also the author of the Confession seldom receives his due, even from Reformed believers.

Guido de Bres was a genuine, outstanding hero of the Reformation on behalf of the Reformed, Christian faith. His authorship itself of the Belgic Confession raises him to the highest pinnacle of honor. By his Confession and his diligent preaching, he was responsible for the gathering and establishment of Reformed churches throughout the Lowlands and in the western part of France. Then his courageous martyr's death, with its attendant moving circumstances, puts him in the ranks of the greatest heroes of the Reformed faith in all of history, indeed of the Christian religion. De Bres deserves to be mentioned and honored with Luther, Calvin, Beza, and the other worthies of Protestantism. He was a Netherlander highly honored by God.

De Bres was born into the Roman Catholic Church

and raised in the Roman religion. Sometime before he was twenty-five years old, De Bres was converted to the Reformed faith, mainly by his reading of the Bible and of Reformed materials that were flooding the Lowlands. Almost as soon as he was converted, he taught others, as he had opportunity. This public teaching of the Reformed faith brought down upon him the rage of the Roman Catholic authorities in the southern Lowlands. Several times he had to flee the country. He spent many years of his brief life in exile. On one occasion, although he escaped his foes, the high price he paid for his confession of the gospel was the burning of his house, of his library, and of himself in effigy.

In the providence of God, his flights from his persecutors, especially to Great Britain and Switzerland, brought him into contact with leading reformers, including John a Lasco, Martin Bucer, Petrus Dathenus, Martinus Micronius, and John Calvin. In fact, one of De Bres' periods of exile was spent largely in Switzerland, where he studied for some three years under Calvin. Undoubtedly, these contacts deepened his grasp of the Reformed faith and thus enabled him to write the Confession. These contacts with prominent, learned reformers served also as a kind of seminary training for De Bres, making him a more capable preacher.

De Bres met with William of Orange, the political hope of the Netherlands in its bondage. The meeting was useful to William as he planned his deliverance of the Lowlands from Spanish and Roman oppression.

In 1559 De Bres married Catherine Ramon. This godly young woman agreed to marry De Bres despite his warning that she was marrying a man with a price on his head, so that she could expect bereavement and widowhood at any time. Catherine was one of the unsung heroines of the Reformation. With Catherine, De Bres had five children, all of whom were left fatherless at a young age when Rome murdered De Bres.

Even though he was often forced to flee on account of persecution, De Bres would again and again bravely return to what is now Belgium in order to preach and teach. He pastored large congregations, if only for a short time. He engaged also in field preaching, preaching to thousands in the open fields, because of the threats of the civil authorities. Armed men protected the gatherings. Thus De Bres was used by God for the salvation of many. Thus also, in spite of the eventual crushing of the Reformed churches in the southern Lowlands, his ministry bore lasting and abundant fruit in the spread of the Reformed faith and in the establishment of Reformed churches in the northern Lowlands, present-day Holland.

De Bres was a dedicated, indefatigable worker on behalf of the Reformed faith, Reformed churches, and his Lord, Jesus Christ. "Tirelessly working, shrinking back from no danger, he has made himself extraordinarily serviceable for the extension of the Reformation in the southern Netherlands and in the present-day north of France."[1]

A physical description of De Bres has come down to us. He was tall. He had a pale, thin, long face. He shoulders were high. He was bearded.[2]

The end—the *earthly* end—of this man of God was as

---

1 *Christelijke Encyclopaedie* [*Christian Encyclopedia*], ed. F. W. Grosheide, J. H. Landwehr, C. Lindeboom, and J. C. Rullmann (Kampen: J. H. Kok, 1925), 1:378. All quotations from this work are my translation of the Dutch. The work has not been translated.
2 Ibid., 377–78.

heroic and grand as his life. Christ privileged De Bres to die a martyr, an especially godly and courageous martyr. In July 1566, De Bres returned from exile in France, where he had been preaching, to the Lowlands. This extremely dangerous move was at the urging of Reformed believers, who desired De Bres' preaching. De Bres became pastor of a large congregation in Valenciennes. In the short time in 1566 between his return from exile and his capture, De Bres attended the first synod of the Reformed churches in the Lowlands, the synod of Antwerp. So dangerous were the circumstances of the meeting of this synod that attendance required the use of a password. The password was "the Vineyard." This synod adopted the Belgic Confession as the creed of the Reformed churches.

The next year, De Bres was finally captured by his Roman Catholic adversaries. They treated the reformer cruelly and abominably. For two weeks he was imprisoned in heavy chains in a dungeon cell in the castle over the walls of which he had earlier thrown a copy of his Confession. De Bres remained undaunted. To a visitor who remarked the heavy chains, De Bres responded, "It is guilt that makes a chain heavy. Innocence makes my chains light. I glory in them as my badges of honor."[3]

De Bres was then transferred for seven weeks to a prison in Valenciennes. Here he was tortured in a small, foul dungeon known as the Black Hole. For the most part he was kept in chains that bruised and cut his flesh and bones. Somehow, in these miserable, painful circumstances, De Bres managed to write a large treatise on the Lord's supper

---

3   Thea B. Van Halsema, *Three Men Came to Heidelberg and Glorious Heretic: The Story of Guido de Brès* (Grand Rapids, MI: Baker, 1982), 130.

and moving letters to his wife and to his mother. These letters, written as it were with the last drops of his life's blood, are a moving testimony, not only to the spiritual heroism of their author, but also to the spiritual experience that characterizes the Reformed faith.

To his beloved wife of merely seven years, the mother of his five young children, De Bres said his farewell in the following words:

> I call on you with all urgency that you not grieve beyond measure, so as to offend God. You have always known well, that when you married me, you have taken a mortal mate, who was uncertain of his life from moment to moment. Nevertheless, it pleased the good God to allow us to live together about seven years and to give us five children. If the Lord had willed to let us live together longer, he certainly had the means for this. But it did not please him. Wherefore let his good pleasure be realized, and may this be to you as a conclusive reason [for my imprisonment and death, and your widowhood].[4]

As part of his letter to his wife, De Bres also wrote the following:

> O God, thou hast caused me to be born at the time and at the hour that thou hadst ordained. During my entire life thou hast preserved and protected me in threatening dangers and completely delivered

---

4 A. D. R. Polman, *Onze Nederlandsche Geloofsbelijdenis* [*Our Netherlands (Belgic) Confession*] (Franeker: T. Wever, n.d.), 1:105. All quotations from this work are my translation of the Dutch. The work has not been translated.

me from them. Thus today my hour has come, in which I must leave this life in order to go to thee. Thy good will be done. I cannot escape thy hand, and even if I could, I would not will [to do so], for my highest salvation consists in this, that I conduct myself according to thy will. All these considerations have made my heart very joyful and cheerful, and they do this still. And I call on you, beloved, faithful companion, that you rejoice with me and thank the good God for what he has done...Here is not the place of our dwelling, but in heaven. Here is our pilgrim-journey. Therefore, we must long for the real land, that is, for heaven, in order to be received there in the house of my heavenly Father so that we may see our brother, head, and savior, Jesus Christ, and so that we may see the very noble fellowship of patriarchs, prophets, apostles, and so many thousand martyrs, into whose fellowship I hope to be received, when I shall have completed the course of my service. I beseech you then, my dearly beloved, that you comfort yourself in the consideration of these things. Consider with full consciousness the honor God grants you by having given you a husband who is not only a minister of the Son of God, but also so esteemed by God, and valued, that he deems him worthy to have a share in the crown of the martyrs. Such an honor God does not give even to his angels. I am overjoyed. My heart is aroused. In my trials, nothing is lacking to me. I am filled to overflowing with the abundance of the riches of my God...I experience today the faithfulness of my Lord Jesus Christ. I bring now into practice what I have preached to others. Certainly, I must confess this, namely, that I, when I preached, spoke as a blind man about colors, if I compare it with what I now feel by experience. I have made progress and learned more in my imprisonment than in all my life. I find myself at a very good school. I have the Holy Ghost, who continually inspires me and who instructs me to handle the weapons in the conflict. On the other hand, Satan encircles me, the opponent of all children of God, who is as a roaring lion in order to devour me. But the one who has said to me, "Fear not, I have overcome the world" [John 16:33], causes me to conquer...He comforts and strengthens me in an unbelievable manner. I am more comfortable than the enemies of the gospel. I eat, drink, and sleep better than they do. I have been put in the strongest and gloomiest prison, which itself allows [one] to think...I receive no air or light than through a small opening, through which one throws the filth. I have rough and heavy chains on my hands and feet, which are a continual torment to me. But despite all this, my God does not forsake his promise and comforts my heart and gives me a great contentment.[5]

From his harsh and gloomy prison, with death looming, the soon-to-be martyr wrote to his mother (still a Roman Catholic?).

I have now served Christ already for more than twenty years, and never has he caused me to lack

---

5 Ibid., 105–7.

anything. Always he has shown me a love far above human understanding... What now? Shall I forsake the Living One in order to hide with the dead? Shall I forsake heaven in order to obtain the earth? Shall I give up the eternal things for the temporal things? Shall I say farewell to the eternal life for the sake of bodily death?...I have more than enough reason greatly to rejoice when I see that my Lord Jesus Christ does me the honor of causing me to sit at his table and to drink from his cup. Is it a little thing to follow such a Lord? He has made the heaven and the earth simply by his mighty word. Before his face angels and archangels cover their faces with their wings and bow before him. Behold, me, an earthen vessel, full of weakness, me, he calls his friend and not merely his servant. O, what an honor! Even the angels he does not grant the honor of suffering for his name. And who am I, that to me this honor is bestowed? Indeed, I am enraptured above heaven when I consider these things. And if this were still not enough, he comforts me without ceasing in my struggle. He is here imprisoned with me. I hear Jesus my Lord. I see him, so to speak, locked up in my fetters and bonds. I see him with the eyes of my spirit locked up in my obscure and dark prison, as he has promised me in his absolutely true word to be with me always to the very end...He is here with me with an innumerable host of angels, comforting and strengthening me, and this very sweet melody of words from his mouth he causes to resound in my ears: "To him that overcometh will I give to eat of the tree of life, which is in the midst of the paradise of [my] God" [Rev. 2:7]. "I know thy trouble and poverty, but thou art rich" [v. 9]. O, what a comfort! My heart leaps within me, when these words sound in my ears. It is no liar, no deceiver, who speaks thus, but it is the Son of God, the mouth without deceit, the infallible truth.[6]

At his sentencing to death, this invincible, glorious man of God and hero of the faith exclaimed for all to hear:

I am exceedingly gladdened and had never supposed that God would give me such honor. I feel that my countenance changes and am joyful on account of the grace that increases in me more and more. I am strengthened from moment to moment...The time of my departure is at hand...It seems to me that my spirit has wings to fly to heaven. There, today, I have been invited to the wedding feast of my Lord, the Son of God.[7]

Philip Schaff remarked that De Bres "met his death as if it were a marriage-feast."[8] It was.

On May 30, 1567, his Roman Catholic persecutors hanged De Bres for his witness to the gospel of Jesus Christ, very much including the witness of the Belgic Confession. He was only forty-five years old. A reliable report has it that, not content with killing De Bres, his haters then burned his body and scattered his ashes in the great river that flows through the southern Lowlands into the sea. No matter! With his dying breath, De Bres was brought in honor in the

---

6   Ibid., 107.

7   Ibid., 108.

8   Schaff, *Creeds of Christendom*, 1:504.

soul into heaven to be seated on a throne with the other martyrs, to reign with the exalted Christ (see Rev. 20). As for his ashes, God has his eye on them and preserves them with a view to De Bres' resurrection in the body at the coming of Jesus Christ. In the words of article 37 of his own Confession,

> the faithful and elect shall be crowned with glory and honor; and the Son of God will confess their names before God his Father, and his elect angels; all tears shall be wiped from their eyes; and their cause, which is now condemned by many judges and magistrates as heretical and impious, will then be known to be the cause of the Son of God. And, for a gracious reward, the Lord will cause them to possess such a glory as never entered into the heart of man to conceive.[9]

The same article of the same confession warns the wicked persecutors of De Bres and his fellow martyrs that those whom they persecuted:

> shall see the terrible vengeance which God shall execute on the wicked, who most cruelly persecuted, oppressed, and tormented...in this world; and who shall be convicted by the testimony of their own consciences, and, being immortal, shall be tormented in that everlasting fire which is prepared for the devil and his angels.[10]

---

9 Ibid., 3:435–36.
10 Ibid., 3:435.

THE CONFESSION ITSELF

The Belgic Confession of Faith is one of the creeds, or confessions, of Reformed churches worldwide, along with the Heidelberg Catechism and the Canons of Dordt. As a creed, it expresses what the Reformed churches and their members believe to be the teachings of holy scripture, the inspired word of God. As a confession, the creed is the public declaration by these churches and their members of the truths, or doctrines, of holy scripture as these doctrines are known by the Reformed churches and live in the hearts of the members of these churches. The Belgic Confession is an aspect of the conformity of Reformed churches and believers to the spiritual reality taught by the apostle in Romans 10:10: "For with the heart man believeth unto righteousness; and with the mouth confession is made unto salvation."

In order to function as a creed and confession of Reformed churches, the Belgic Confession had to be officially adopted by the Reformed churches at their authoritative gatherings, or synods. This happened soon after the writing of the Confession in 1561.[11] As early as 1566 a national synod of Reformed churches adopted the Belgic Confession as an authoritative statement of the faith of these churches. The international synod of Reformed churches, the Synod of Dordt (1618–19), adopted the Belgic Confession, with the Heidelberg Catechism and the Canons of the Dordt Synod, as the official, binding expression of the faith of holy scripture as known and confessed by

---

11 For the names, places, and dates of the early Reformed synods that adopted the Belgic Confession, see Schaff, *Creeds of Christendom*, 3:505.

the Reformed churches. The Synod of Dordt also adopted a Formula of Subscription, by which the Belgic Confession and the other two creeds are made binding upon all office-bearers in Reformed churches and thus upon the churches themselves.[12]

Even though the members of the Reformed churches do not sign the Formula of Subscription, the implication is that the three creeds are binding also upon them. The members are not at liberty to oppose the creeds or any of their content. They are bound to submit to preaching and teaching that are in harmony with the creeds. They are bound to learn the faith contained in the Belgic Confession as fully as possible. Therefore, all members of Reformed churches are bound to know the Belgic Confession and its teachings. It is the purpose of this commentary on the Belgic Confession that it enables the members of Reformed churches to carry out this sworn, solemn, and bounden duty. Ignorance of their creed by Reformed believers is dereliction of duty, dangerous, and disgraceful.

As the official, authoritative creed of Reformed churches worldwide, how great is the importance of the Belgic Confession! It authoritatively defines the truth of scripture. Explicitly and by implication, it also authoritatively defines heresies. It identifies true churches of Christ

---

12 For this Formula of Subscription, see *The Confessions and the Church Order of the Protestant Reformed Churches* (Grandville, MI: Protestant Reformed Churches in America, 2005), 326. The Formula has all officebearers affirm that they are convinced that "all the articles and points of doctrine contained in the [Belgic] Confession...do fully agree with the Word of God"; that they therefore will "diligently... teach and faithfully...defend the aforesaid doctrine, without...contradicting the same, by [their] public preaching or writing"; and that they will "refute and contradict" all errors that militate against the teaching of the Confession, as of the other two creeds.

in the world. It constitutes the authoritative witness of these churches to other churches and to the world outside the church. On the title (front) page of the original publication of the Confession was a quotation of 1 Peter 3:15: "Be ready always to give an answer to every man that asketh you a reason of the hope that is in you."[13] It is a document to instruct the members of Reformed churches in the biblical truth that they profess, especially the children of Reformed believers. It is the guide of Reformed preachers concerning the doctrines they must teach and defend. It is the defense of the Reformed faith against errors by which the faith is threatened, whether by heretics within the churches (always a danger, to all churches) or by the winds of false doctrine blowing upon the true church from without.

By no means the least of the functions of the Confession, with the Catechism and the Canons of Dordt, is its preservation of the unity of the Reformed congregation, of a Reformed denomination, and of whatever ecumenical federation may be a reality. For good reason, the Confession, the Heidelberg Catechism, and the Canons of Dordt are commonly called the three forms of unity. The unity of the church of Christ is precious, indeed essential, as is the confession of the Nicene Creed, itself one of the confessions of the universal church of Jesus Christ: "I [believe] one Holy Catholic and Apostolic church."[14] The confession of the church's unity is based, in part, on Ephesians 4:4: "There is one body." This oneness is "the unity of the Spirit," as verse 3 explains. But the Spirit works and

---

13 J. N. Bakhuizen van den Brink, *De Nederlandsche Belijdenisgeschriften* [*The Dutch Confessional Documents*] (Amsterdam: Uitgeversmaatschappij, Holland, 1940), 48–49.

14 Nicene Creed, in Schaff, *Creeds of Christendom*, 2:59.

preserves the church's unity by means of agreement in the one, pure doctrine of scripture. Introduction of false doctrine into the church is schismatic, divisive, and destructive of the precious unity of the church. With the Catechism and the Canons, the Belgic Confession is the vigilant, effective guard against schism in the Reformed churches.

Ignorance or disregard of the Belgic Confession by the Reformed churches that formally have the Confession as their creed makes the churches vulnerable to a host of evils that are destructive of the churches, including their unity in the true doctrine of him whom scripture calls the Word of God and the Truth (John 1:1; 14:6). This commentary purposes the living, thorough knowledge of the Confession that not only the church's officebearers, but also all the church's members ought to have.

The Belgic Confession is the statement and brief explanation of all the leading doctrines of the Christian faith in logical order. In this regard, the Confession is unique, and of the greatest significance, among the three creeds that constitute the confessional treasury of the Reformed churches. The Canons of Dordt does not confess all the leading truths of the Christian and Reformed religion. It limits itself to the specific doctrines that were opposed by the Arminian party in the Reformed churches in the Netherlands in the early seventeenth century. These are the truths that ascribe salvation to the sovereign, particular grace of God, the so-called doctrines of grace or the five points of Calvinism.

The Heidelberg Catechism does contain all the leading doctrines of scripture, but not in logical order. Rather, it rather presents and considers the truths of scripture in light of their comfort of the believer. Therefore, the Catechism's treatment of many of the doctrines is relatively scanty. It concentrates on the comfort that particular doctrine affords the believer. For example, all that the Catechism says about predestination—certainly a fundamental doctrine of the gospel—is that there is "a chosen communion," which is saved by the Son of God.[15]

Uniquely among the Reformed creeds, the Belgic Confession sets forth the whole of the Christian and Reformed faith, beginning in articles 1–11 with the doctrine of God as revealed in the inspired scripture and concluding in article 37 with the last judgment. Also, for the most part the Confession's explanation of the doctrines is more complete than that of the same doctrines by the Heidelberg Catechism.

The Confession is polemical. One implication of the polemical nature of the Confession is that Reformed office-bearers, especially ministers and professors of theology, are required by their signing of the Formula of Subscription also to be polemical in their preaching, teaching, and writing. A polemical ministry on the part of a Reformed minister is not merely the personal style of the man (increasingly viewed as a deplorable weakness), but confessional.

At crucial points in its defense of the faith, the Confession exposes and condemns fundamental errors of the Roman Catholic Church (without ever mentioning that church by name). For example, in article 6, the Confession rejects Rome's apocryphal books. In article 14, the Confession condemns Rome's doctrine of "the free will of man." In article 15, the Confession denies that baptism abolishes original sin. Article 21 denies Rome's doctrine

15 Heidelberg Catechism Q 54, in Schaff, *Creeds of Christendom*, 3:325.

that there are "other means" of reconciliation with God than the suffering and death of Christ. Articles 22–24 carry on an extended polemic with Rome's doctrine of justification by faith *and works*. Article 26 denies that there is any other "advocate" with God, including Mary, than Jesus alone. Article 29 plainly has the Roman Catholic Church in view when it describes "the false church." When article 35 affirms that in the supper the believer receives the body and blood of Christ "by faith," it is repudiating Rome's doctrine that all participants at the supper eat and drink Christ with the physical mouth. Yet even here, where the controversy of the Reformed churches with Rome was the sharpest, the Confession does not name the Church of Rome.

The liveliest, and most explicit, controversy of the Confession is with that strange and troublesome sect known to the reformers, as to the Belgic Confession, as the "Anabaptists."[16] These were a religious group that broke with the Roman Church during the Reformation but refused to join either the Lutheran or the Reformed churches. The Protestant churches called them Anabaptists because, refusing to recognize infant baptism, they insisted on the necessity of baptizing again, as adults, those who had been baptized as infants. *Anabaptist* means "baptizing again." In respect of the doctrine that the sacrament of baptism may only be administered to adult believers, they were the ancestors of the contemporary Baptists.

But the original Anabaptists were guilty of more than only the denial of the validity of the baptism of the infants of believers. They were a revolutionary lot. Regarding

---

16 Belgic Confession 36, in ibid., 3:433.

themselves as the biblical kingdom of God and expecting the return of Jesus Christ at any moment, to establish them as his carnal kingdom on earth (thus showing themselves as millennialists), the Anabaptists despised and rejected all earthly magistracy. They revolted against the civil rulers. With disastrous consequences for themselves! In addition, they were grossly immoral. The leaders were sexually depraved, practicing polygamy, taking other men's wives for themselves as they pleased, and appearing nude in public. They left the distinct impression that the kingdom of Christ was mainly debauchery.

It was of great concern to Guido de Bres that the Belgic Confession differentiate the Reformed churches from the Anabaptists. The tactic of the Roman Catholic enemies of the Reformed churches was to identify the Reformed people as Anabaptist revolutionaries. This, of course, would bring down upon the Reformed churches the fear and fury of the civil magistrates.

Regarding its controversy, the Confession contends more against the Anabaptists than it does against Rome, at least in its explicit references to its ecclesiastical and doctrinal adversaries. The Confession mentions the Anabaptists several times, distinguishing the Reformed churches from them (see art. 18, 34, and 36). Article 36 is at pains both to confess the Reformed belief that submission to the magistrates is "the bounden duty of every one" and strongly to condemn the "Anabaptists" as "seditious people."[17]

This controversy of the Reformed churches with Anabaptism accounts for an intriguing aspect of the early history of the Belgic Confession. Soon after he had written

---

17 Belgic Confession 36, in ibid., 3:433.

the Confession, De Bres threw a copy of the Confession, with an explanatory letter, over the wall of a castle in which the Roman Catholic rulers of the country were living. The result was rage on the part of the rulers, an intense hunt for De Bres in order to kill him, and the flight of the author of the Confession, to escape. But the purpose of the act of throwing a copy of the Confession over the castle wall and into the possession of the civil authorities was not at all to provoke the magistrates. De Bres wanted to assure the civil magistrates that the Reformed churches and believers were not revolutionary Anabaptists, but good citizens of Belgium, who were submissive to the authority of the civil government. It was De Bres' purpose that the rulers read article 36 of the Belgic Confession. At the same time, the Confession would acquaint the rulers with the biblical nature of the Reformed faith. The act was comparable to Luther's "here I stand" at Worms.

The instrument used by Jesus Christ to write the Belgic Confession was Guido de Bres. But De Bres was strongly influenced by John Calvin. During one of his exiles, when fleeing from his persecutors in the Lowlands (what now is Belgium) De Bres studied under Calvin in Switzerland for some two or three years. Also, De Bres benefited from Calvin's *Institutes*. In addition, it is evident that De Bres patterned the Confession after the Gallican Confession, which is also known as the French Confession of Faith (1559) and which was largely the work of Calvin. In the Belgic Confession, therefore, the influence of John Calvin upon Reformed churches is strong.

De Bres wrote the Belgic Confession in 1561 in French. The Confession is the earliest of the three creeds that constitute the three forms of unity of the Reformed churches.

Within a year of its original composition the Confession was translated into Dutch. A little later, it appeared also in Latin. The English translation found in Schaff's *Creeds of Christendom* is generally regarded as faithful to the French original, and "excellent": "The excellent English version in use in the Reformed Dutch Church of America is made from the Latin text of the Synod of Dort."[18]

The Belgic Confession has authority for the faith of Reformed churches and believers. As soon as 1566, a territorial synod of Reformed churches adopted it as the faithful expression of the doctrine of holy scripture. Several subsequent synods also adopted it as a creed of Reformed churches. The international Synod of Dordt (1618–19) adopted it, with the Heidelberg Catechism and the Canons of Dordt, as the authoritative confession of the faith of Reformed churches worldwide and as binding upon officebearers in these churches. This authority is effected by the Formula of Subscription, which officebearers must sign.

Like the other two creeds, the Belgic Confession is binding upon officebearers and churches, not "insofar as" it agrees with the inspired scripture, but "because" it agrees with scripture. The authority of the three creeds is that of the word of God itself, of which word they are the faithful summary and expression.

Not being inspired scripture itself, and therefore not possessing the inherent authority of scripture, the Confession is subject to amendment. The process of such amendment is carefully prescribed in the Formula of Subscription. The process entails the judgment of the church regarding the proposed amendment. No individual,

18 Schaff, *Creeds of Christendom*, 1:507–8.

though a minister of the gospel or a professor of theology, is at liberty to revise or contradict the Confession on his own. By signing the Formula of Subscription, the office-bearer promises never to teach contrary to the creeds, but always to be sure that the content of his preaching and writing is the doctrine of the creeds.

If the truth itself that is the content of the Confession were not enough to make it exceedingly precious in the estimation of Reformed Christians, the bloody history of the creed would serve this end. Within a few years of his writing of the creed, De Bres gave his life, a martyr, on behalf of the creed and its gospel. The Roman Catholic civil rulers, at the behest of the Roman Catholic Church, imprisoned, tortured, and then hanged De Bres for writing the Confession and for preaching the Christian faith that is the content of the Confession.

Soon after De Bres' death, the Roman Catholic emperor, Philip II, unleashed a brutal, barbaric, and bloody persecution upon those in the Lowlands (the Netherlands and Belgium), men, women, and children, who believed, confessed, and worshiped God according to the Belgic Confession. In his great history, John Lothrop Motley states that more than one hundred thousand Reformed Christians died in the persecution that was already ongoing when De Bres wrote the Confession and that intensified soon after De Bres' death. More Reformed Christians were killed in the Netherlands in the sixteenth and early seventeenth century than were killed in all the persecutions of the early church by the Roman empire.

> The number of Netherlanders who were burned, strangled, beheaded, or buried alive...for the offences of reading the Scriptures, of looking askance at a

graven image, or of ridiculing the actual presence of the body and blood of Christ in a wafer, have been placed as high as one hundred thousand by distinguished authorities.[19]

Inasmuch as both De Bres himself and the Netherlands (Lowland) Reformed who died in the persecution that was taking place during De Bres' life and that intensified after his death were killed on account of their confession of the faith embodied in the Belgic Confession, it may truthfully be said that the Belgic Confession has been sealed with the blood of a host of martyrs. If Reformed churches and their members today permit themselves to become ignorant of the Belgic Confession, much more to corrupt the truths of the Confession, they despise the blood of Christ's martyrs— blood shed so that the truth of the word of God confessed in the Belgic Confession might come down to us and our children.

That the Confession is the faithful expression and summary of holy scripture implies that it is never outdated. The Confession does not need continual revision so that its doctrines may remain relevant to contemporary religious belief and life. All clamor that the Belgic Confession is out-of-date and in need of revision is, in reality, a plea for corrupting certain doctrines under the pressure of some current heresy, whether a fallible Bible, evolution, a cross that did not satisfy the justice of God, or salvation conditioned by the will of the sinner. Already in the early seventeenth century, the Arminians in the Reformed churches in the Netherlands contended for a change in article 16 of the

---

19 John Lothrop Motley, *The Rise of the Dutch Republic: A History*, 3 vols. (Philadelphia, PA: David McKay, n.d.), 1:122.

Confession, the article on predestination. Their contention for revision was, in fact, opposition to the article's confession of biblical predestination in the interest of their heretical doctrine of salvation by the free will of the sinner.

It is not out of the question, however, that Reformed churches might amend the Confession by making it fuller and clearer regarding certain doctrines. This might be the case with article 37, the Confession's treatment of eschatology, or the doctrine of the last things. The sixteenth century did not see extensive development of eschatology. Also, since the writing of the Confession grievous millennial errors have risen to plague the Reformed faith, against which confessional exposure and condemnation would be helpful. But it is doubtful that Reformed churches in all the world, or even in North America, are doctrinally strong enough to accomplish such amendment. It is a wonder that there are still Reformed churches that hold the Belgic Confession without reservation, the officebearers of which sign the Formula of Subscription without their tongues firmly and obviously in their cheeks.

Regarding the worth of the Belgic Confession, Philip Schaff has judged that the Confession is "the best symbolical statement of the Calvinistic system of doctrine, with the exception of the Westminster Confession."[20]

---

20 Schaff, *Creeds of Christendom*, 1:506. There are good reasons for the Reformed believer to take exception to Schaff's exception.

Chapter One

THE NATURE OF GOD
(ARTICLE 1)

ART. I. THERE IS ONE ONLY GOD.

We all believe with the heart, and confess with the mouth, that there is one only simple and spiritual Being, which we call God; and that he is eternal, incomprehensible, invisible, immutable, infinite, almighty, perfectly wise, just, good, and the overflowing fountain of all good.

Our Reformed confession begins with God. The very first article expresses our faith concerning God. We open our mouth to utter what lives in our heart, and the first word that comes out is "God." Not even what we believe about scripture precedes, even though it is through scripture that we know God.

That the Reformed confession begins with God is significant. God *is* first, not merely as though the truth concerning God is then followed by other important topics, but so, that all that follows in the Confession only serves to reveal and magnify God. The one object of faith, according to the Reformed religion, is God. The sole confession of the Reformed believer is: "God!" The Reformed faith is God centered. Its motto is "*soli Deo gloria*," that is, "to God alone the glory." Implied is that to corrupt any article in the Belgic Confession is adversely to touch the truth of God, that is, to bedim the glory of God.

This opening article about God consists of three truths concerning God. The first is the truth of his being: "one only simple and spiritual Being." The second is the truth of his name: "which we call God." The third is the truth of his attributes, or better, his perfections: "that he is eternal," and what follows.

In addition to the truths that are expressed in the article, there is also a truth that is implied: God exists; God lives; God is reality. As Hebrews 11:6 teaches, faith believes "that he is." How we know this will be explained in the articles that follow, on holy scripture. It is not the case that we believe merely that there is a god—some higher power or supreme being—but rather that God exists—the God who is "one only simple and spiritual Being," and what follows in article 1.

We do not try to prove this. There is no preliminary article in which we try to prove to unbelievers that there is a god, perhaps by arguing that man has an idea of the greatest of all possible beings in his mind, or that the universe must have a first cause, or that history and creation show design and purpose, or that all peoples worship some deity or other. Proving to unbelievers by rational arguments that God exists cannot be done. This cannot be done because the problem with unbelievers is not their ignorant minds, but their depraved, hard hearts. The problem with the unbeliever is not intellectual, but spiritual.

The fact is that all men *do* know that God exists. "That which may be known of God is manifest in them; for God hath shewed it unto them. For the invisible things of him from the creation of the world are clearly seen, being understood by the things that are made, even his eternal power and Godhead; so that they are without excuse: Because that, when they knew God, they glorified him not as God" (Rom. 1:18–21). But because they are spiritual fools, they deny the God whom they know to exist and some of whose divine perfections they know also. "The fool hath said in his heart: no God!" (Ps. 14:1; literal translation).

Agnostics and atheists are liars, including the educated agnostics and atheists of contemporary Western society, the learned, degreed liars in the state schools who teach the children and young people the big lie—the biggest lie of which humans can be guilty. The agnostic claims that he does not know whether God exists. The atheist denies the existence of God. Both rebelliously shout into God's face, "No God!" that is, "We refuse to acknowledge you as God." It does enter into their denial of God that confessing God would require them to serve God in a holy life. They, however, "are corrupt, they have done abominable works," and are slavishly committed to their filthy way of life (Ps. 14:1–3).

Scripture itself does not begin by proving the existence of God; rather, it simply confronts the human race with God: "In the beginning God..." (Gen. 1:1).

Confession of God is a matter of faith, not of intellectual ascent to rational evidence, as denial of God is a matter of unbelief, not of lack of intellectual evidence. The truth that confession of God is a matter of faith bears on the theological issue of apologetics, that is, the right defense of the faith to the unbeliever. One ought not engage the unbeliever in rational, nonbiblical argumentation. No unbeliever can be argued into faith. The believer should witness to the unbeliever on the basis of and in light of the word of God, holy scripture. The opening salvo in the debate is not "Your arguments against God are self-contradictory," but "You are a guilty sinner exposed to the wrath of God, and Jesus Christ revealed in the Bible is the only way of escape from this wrath," or "You have no hope in the face of death and judgment; the death and resurrection of Jesus are the reason for my hope, as they are the only hope for humans in the face of the terror of death."

Good apologetics, therefore, is not the specialty of a few brainy theologians, but the calling and ability of every Christian. The calling to give "an answer to every man that asketh you a reason of the hope that is you" (1 Pet. 3:15), where "reason" is literally "apology" (referring to a defense of the Christian's hope), comes to every believer. What is important for a good defense of the faith is not that we give the defense, or engage in this apologetics, with shrewd arguments, but that we boldly give the defense of the Christian hope "with meekness and fear" (v. 15).

It belongs to the existence of God that he is personal. More about this will be said when the doctrine of the Trinity, in articles 8–11, is treated. But already here it is clearly implied that God is a conscious, knowing, willing being, an "I" not an "it." God is the conscious subject of his existence. According to article 1, "*he*, a personal being, is eternal, incomprehensible," and so on. Nor can an impersonal substance be "perfectly wise, just, good, and the overflowing fountain of all good."

The Reformed faith, as the sound confession of the

Christian faith, rejects pantheism. Pantheism is the belief that God is the universe—all things—or a vague spirit of the universe, but in either case impersonal. It is more accurate to describe pantheism as the notion that the universe is God. This has been the religion of some of the most highly regarded philosophers, for example, Baruch Spinoza. In the form of the notion that God is the vague spirit of the universe, pantheism is a popular religion of the masses in Western society.

This religion manifests itself in the trust of the masses that the evolutionary process, to which they are committed, largely through the educational efforts of the agnostic and atheistic liars who taught them in the state schools, works toward a happy outcome for mankind, as though by the beneficent purpose of a deity—an impersonal, blind deity, but a deity. Or, although committed to sheer materialism, having ruled the Creator out of his creation, nevertheless the masses still pray on occasion of some happy event in their lives or in the face of impending disaster either to thank the spirit or to beseech it to ward off the threat. How ready is the unbeliever in Western society to assure his grieving compatriot, "You are in our prayers." To what is he praying, if he prays at all? Not to God! Surely, not to the earth, water, atmosphere, and planets of the material universe! But to some vague spirit that is supposed to be abroad in the material universe and that, contrary to the rejection of the personal God by Western society, pays attention to prayers!

Pantheism is idolatry. It is the worship of the universe rather than the worship of the Creator of the universe. Or it is the worship of some vague, impersonal spirit, rather than the worship of the personal God who is a spiritual being.

Pantheism is a form of the wickedness of changing "the truth of God into a lie" and worshiping "the creature more than the Creator, who is blessed for ever" (Rom. 1:25). The only difference between pantheism, which worships the creation, and the worship of Baal is that pantheism has a bigger idol.

The being of the true God confessed in article 1 of the Belgic Confession is one. God is one being and one "only" being. God is one numerically. There is no other divine being. There is, as God repeatedly declares in the Old Testament against the idolatry of Israel, no other god besides him. All other alleged deities besides the God known and confessed by the Reformed faith are idols. They are non-existent figments of the depraved imaginations of their worshipers.

What nominal Protestants and Reformed Christians must hear in our day about the oneness of God is that the other, purported gods of the pagan religions are not manifestations of the one, true God, but idols. Contemporary ecumenism, which is the uniting of the nations as prophesied by Revelation 13, advances by the concession on the part of Rome and the leading apostate Protestants that the gods of the pagans, although perhaps inferior forms of the one, true God, nevertheless represent genuine revelations of the one, true God. The God of Christianity is the highest and best form of the Godhead. The gods of the heathen religions are forms of this God in his as yet imperfect, inadequate development. Essentially, however, God and the gods are one and the same. Such an explanation of God and the gods not only serves the ecumenical program well, but also applies the evolutionary theory, which has Western society by the throat, to religion. On this popular view of God and the gods, God has been evolving with the world.

The highly regarded Christian apologist C. S. Lewis gave expression to this conception of the relation of God and the gods in his acclaimed Narnia series. At the very end of *The Last Battle*, which is also the end of the Narnia series, Lewis has Aslan, the symbol of Christ Jesus, say to a worshiper of the idol god Tash that "all the service thou hast done to Tash, I account as service done to me." Although the lion representing Christ denies that Tash and he are one and the same, he does insist that "I take to me the services which thou hast done to him [Tash]...Therefore if any man swear by Tash and keep his oath for the oath's sake, it is by me that he has truly sworn, though he know it not, and it is I who reward him." When the lifelong idolater objects that he has been seeking the idol Tash "all my days," Aslan replies that "unless thy desire had been for me thou wouldst not have sought so long and so truly."[1]

God is one. He is not the highest and best deity, accompanied by lesser and inferior deities. If he were the highest and best deity, he would not be one God, but many. He is God alone. Baal, Zeus, Allah, and Tash are not gods, nor inferior, lesser developed manifestations of the true God, but idols. Fundamental to the oneness of God is that he alone is to be worshiped, and worshiped as the one and only God. This is the first commandment of his law: "Thou shalt have no other gods before me" (Ex. 20:3). If the worship of Tash were acceptable to God as a form of worship of himself, Tash would be a god, and God would not be one. Lewis was a delightful author, but a wretched apologist on

---

1   C. S. Lewis, *The Last Battle* (London: The Bodley Head, 1956), 166.

behalf of the Christian faith. The first article of the faith is that God is one, so that all other gods are despicable idols, and the worship of them, damnable idolatry.

Therefore, the ecumenical project of our time is, among its other evils, idolatrous.

With the apostle, we Reformed believers, who confess article 1 of the Belgic Confession, "know that an idol is nothing in the world, and that there is none other God but one. For though there be that are called gods, whether in heaven or in earth, (as there be gods many, and lords many,) but to us there is but one God, the Father, of whom are all things, and we in him; and one Lord Jesus Christ, by whom are all things, and we by him" (1 Cor. 8:4–6).

Closely related to the numerical oneness of the being of God is a truth about God's being that is strange to modern ears, little taught by the churches, and difficult to understand, but fundamentally important for all that. This is the truth of God's simplicity, which also characterizes the being of God: "one only simple…Being." Negatively, simplicity denies that God's being is composed of parts. Positively, simplicity affirms that all of God's perfections have their source in his very being, so that these perfections are identical with the being of God.

If God's being were composed of parts, for example, love as a part of his being and justice as another part of his being, each part would be God, so that there would be as many gods as there are parts: the god love, the god justice, and as many other gods as there are perfections of the divine being. Likewise, if God's perfections were not identical with his being, but only elements, or parts, of his being, each perfection would be a god. The identity of all the perfections with his being itself is an aspect of the oneness of the divine being.

The simplicity of God is an aspect of the truth of Deuteronomy 6:4: "The LORD our God is one LORD." First John 4:8 reveals that God is his perfection of love. He does not merely *possess* love. He does not merely *exercise* love. But he *is* love: "God is love."

Simplicity implies that the denial of one of the perfections of God is, in fact, the denial of God himself. For example, modernism's denial of the justice of God, by its denial that the cross of Christ was, and had to be, the satisfaction of the justice of God on behalf of guilty sinners, is not only the denial of the perfection of the justice of the being of God, but also the denial of the being of God himself. For the being of God is justice, or righteousness. To deny justice is to deny God. In denying the justice of God, modernism not only denies one of the perfections of God, which is serious enough, but it also denies God.

Further, simplicity rules out any discord or friction in God's being. Love and justice harmonize perfectly in God, for God is both of these perfections. There is distinction between the two perfections. Love is God's blissful delight in himself as the glorious, divine, triune being of fellowship. Righteousness is the splendid conformity of the being of God with all his thoughts, will, and actions to the standard of his own goodness. Between these two perfections is harmony grounded in the oneness of the being. It is sin, therefore, nothing less than the sin of assault upon the oneness of God's being, that theologians appeal to the love of God in support of their denial of the justice of God.

They do this by their doctrine of salvation that denies the cross of Christ as satisfaction of God's justice. For them, love and justice are at odds. The love of God banishes the righteousness of God. Divine love saves, not in the way of the satisfaction of the justice of God, but by ignoring, and even despising, the justice of God. The guilt of sinners goes unpunished. Because the being of God is simple, such a denial of the justice of God is, in fact, the denial of God himself. The result is a modernistic idol, as much an idol as Baal.

This comparison of the god of modernistic theology, a god of a love that has annihilated justice, with old Baal is evident in the features of both. Old Baal delighted in murderous human sacrifices as an aspect of the worship of himself (itself, really), especially the sacrifice of children (see Jer. 7:31). Similarly, the god of modernism delights in the murderous sacrifice of unborn and partially born infants, in the murder that is known as abortion. The officiating priests at the modern sacrifice of unborn and partially born infants are not only the brutal doctors who execute the murders, but also the suave, modernist preachers and theologians who justify the murders in the name of their god, or goddess, love—purported love for the woman who hates her unborn child and consigns the child to the cold steel of the doctor's knife.

The theological rejection of simplicity, therefore, has bloody consequences in abounding abortion in Western civilization (barbarism, really), as it also has consequences in the refusal to execute criminals worthy of this punishment, again with the approval, if not at the instigation, of the modernist churches and theologians. God is justice, as well as love, and love does not rule out justice. Justice demands the death penalty for murder, and it demands the death penalty in the love of God for himself, who originally made humans in his own image.

The being of God is also spiritual. This description of God is not a reference to the third person of the holy

Trinity—the Spirit. But it describes the entire substance of God as a spiritual substance. God's being is nonmaterial. It is not any kind of bodily substance. Therefore, God has no shape or form. Jesus taught this truth about God's being when he declared, "God is a Spirit" (John 4:24).

This quality of the being of God requires that the worship that is due him be a spiritual worship. This is the implication that Jesus drew from God's spirituality in John 4:24: "They that worship him must worship him in spirit and in truth." True worship that is alone acceptable with God may not be merely formal and external—going through the motions on a Sunday—but must be the inner activity of the spirit of the worshiper. Only such worship is worship "in truth." All merely formal worship is false worship.

The spirituality of God forbids also that anyone worship him by means of images. This is the prohibition of the second commandment of the law of God: "Thou shalt not make unto thee any graven image, or any likeness of any thing that is in heaven above, or that is in the earth beneath, or that is in the water under the earth: Thou shalt not bow down thyself to them, nor serve them: for I the LORD thy God am a jealous God" (Ex. 20:4–5).

Denial of the spirituality of God was the sin of Israel by its worship of God under the (material) form of the golden calf. This was a total corruption of the worship of God and a denial of God himself, as the wrathful response of God to this illicit worship made abundantly plain (see Ex. 32).

The Roman Catholic Church sins against the spirituality of God by its worship of God under the form of (material) images, whether images of Mary, or the (material) bread of the Eucharist, or other material substances. In addition,

Rome creates an obviously unspiritual worship by all the (external) formalities that Rome has invented and that it has bound upon both officiating priests and compliant congregation. Endless are the outward ceremonies that make up Roman Catholic worship. One such ceremony that is supposed to please God and obtain his blessing, still today as in the days of the Reformation, is the obtaining of indulgences by various outward acts of penance, including the payment of money. Rome also blesses acts of worship that are merely formal and external, a mere performance of the outward rite. These are religious acts that in the words of Jesus are not done "in spirit and in truth" (John 4:24). Rome's worship, therefore, is false worship. Its falsity and wickedness are not only that the contrived acts of worship are not pleasing to God. But the god worshiped in this nonspiritual manner is not the spiritual God of scripture. It is another god.

This searing judgment upon Roman worship is that of the Reformed creed the Heidelberg Catechism. Explaining the second commandment of the law of God, forbidding image worship, the Catechism forbids that we "make any image of God," adding that "God may not and can not be imaged in any way." This includes that "God forbids the making or keeping any likeness of them [creatures], either to worship them, or by them to serve himself." Against the Roman argument that pictures, or images, may "be tolerated in churches as books for the laity," the Catechism responds that God "will not have his people taught by dumb idols, but by the lively preaching of his Word."[2]

2 Heidelberg Catechism Q&A 96–98, in Schaff, *Creeds of Christendom*, 3:343.

Jesus' application of the spirituality of God in John 4:24 is still wider. For one thing, it condemns the notion that one can worship God, or worship God supremely, only in a certain, specified location, whether Jerusalem (v. 21), or Rome, or Mecca, or Geneva, or Grand Rapids. To limit the location of the possibility of the right worship of God is, evidently, to limit God and thus to deny his spirituality. For another thing, the requirement that God be worshiped "in spirit and in truth" condemns all progressive, innovative worship of God. God may only be worshiped in the "way [that] he has commanded in his Word."[3] The rule of right worship is not merely that his people not worship him in ways forbidden in his word. But the rule is that they may worship God only in the way that he has commanded in his word. Not only does God require that he alone be the object of worship. He also determines *how* he is to be worshiped.

This implication of the spirituality of God is known as the regulative principle of worship. It is a distinctive characteristic of Reformed worship. The thought of the principle is that if humans are free to invent ways of worshiping God, they will invariably invent methods of worship that transgress the spirituality of God, which is fundamental to the glory of God. The truth of this fear is evident in the manner of worship now prevailing in nominally Protestant, and even Reformed, churches in the twenty-first century. Churches sing Arminian hymns and silly ditties, instead of the psalms; they worship God with lascivious dances, to the detriment of reverence in worship; instead of preaching sound doctrine, they show movies. So far have Reformed

---

3 Heidelberg Catechism Q 96, in ibid.

churches developed in violating the second commandment of the law, as explained by question 96 of the Heidelberg Catechism, that they have "worship committees" devoted to the invention of new and different modes of worship.

John Calvin indicated the relation between God's spirituality and the regulative principle of worship: "His spiritual nature forbids us to indulge in carnal or earthly speculation concerning Him."[4] In his commentary on John 4:24, which text teaches that "God is spirit," Calvin contended against those who "contrive many things in the worship of God which are full of display, but have no solidity [in that they are not commanded by God]." In Calvin's day, the application of this charge was to Roman Catholicism. In our day, the application is as truly to much of Protestant worship. The ground of the charge was the doctrine of John 4:24, namely, the spirituality of God: "Christ simply declares here that his Father is of a spiritual nature, and, therefore, is not moved by frivolous matters, as men, through the lightness and unsteadiness of their character, are wont to be."[5] Progressive worship consists of "frivolous matters." The worship committees that invent these frivolities are composed of men (and women) of "lightness and unsteadiness of...character."

This "one only simple and spiritual Being...we call God." His name is God. The Hebrew, Old Testament form of this name is *Elohim*. The Greek, New Testament is *Theos*. Both words identify and describe the named as the one who alone possesses the majesty and deserves the honor of Godhead.

---

4 John Calvin, *Institutes*, 1.13.1:109.
5 John Calvin, *Commentary on the Gospel according to John*, trans. William Pringle (Grand Rapids, MI: Eerdmans, 1956), 1:164.

We "call" this being God because he has made known that this *is* his name and that he wills us to use this name in speaking to him and about him. He has named himself God. He has done this in his own, inspired self-revelation, holy scripture. We call him God, but we have not named him. It is not our right to name him. For people to name God as they please, for example, Mother or Allah, is gross sacrilege, apart from the wickedness of the particular names themselves. God has not named himself "Mother" or "Allah" in sacred scripture.

It is not sacrilege, however, to call Jesus God. In fact, it is the essential uniqueness of the Christian, Reformed religion that, as the Holy Spirit moved the apostle Thomas, so also does he move all the genuine disciples of Jesus Christ (rightly) to call *Jesus* "God" (John 20:28). The man Jesus is the simple and spiritual being, whom we call God, inasmuch as his person is the second person of the Godhead, the eternal Son.

This being, whose name is God, possesses and displays several perfections that manifest the glory of his divine being. Article 1 of the Belgic Confession mentions some of the most outstanding perfections of God, which all Reformed Christians must confess. God is "eternal." Not only is he without beginning and without end, but also he is exalted above time and history. God is not time-bound or part of the historical process. He is not limited or affected by time. Indeed, time is his creature. In the beginning, God created time, as he created all else. God does not *become* but *is*.

This is one of the truths about God that is expressed in the outstanding name of God in the Old Testament: Jehovah. Although the name occurs in this form in the Authorized Version only infrequently, it appears often in the form LORD. The name means "I Am That I Am" (see Ex. 6:1–8). In contrast to all creatures, God does not become but is. Implied is that he has his being of himself. He is self-sufficient and independent. The saving import of God's eternality, as revealed in his name Jehovah, is that he is unchangeable in his love toward his people. He is faithful to them in the covenant of grace.

The movement of time, or history, with its unfolding events, does not sweep God along with itself. It does not constrain, disappoint, or surprise the eternal God. On the contrary, history is the unfolding of the counsel of God, which counsel decrees, controls, and guides history along its appointed course to its appointed end, or goal. To the consternation of the ungodly world, but to the comfort of the church, the one now governing the unfolding of the counsel of God as history is the risen Jesus Christ (Rev. 5), as he also at his coming is the goal toward which all of history infallibly moves. The meaning of history is Jesus the Christ.

In the language we time-bound, historical creatures can understand, Psalm 90:2 confesses the eternality of God: "Before the mountains were brought forth, or ever thou hadst formed the earth and the world, even from everlasting to everlasting, thou art God." Peter applies the eternity of God to the problem that believers have with the apparent delay of the coming of Christ and the reaching finally of the end of history and the last chime on the clock of time. "Be not ignorant of this one thing, that one day is with the Lord as a thousand years, and a thousand years as one day" (2 Pet. 3:8). If 2 Peter 3:8 accounts for what seems to a longing church to be the delay of the coming of Christ in terms of God's eternity, verse 9 explains the redemptive reason. God will save all the members of the elect church:

"The Lord is not slack concerning his promise, as some men count slackness; but is longsuffering to us-ward, not willing that any should perish, but that all should come to repentance."

The divine being is also "incomprehensible." God cannot be fully searched out or exhaustively known by any creature, including the saved, Spirit-filled human creature. This attribute of the being of God is due to the infinity of his being and of all his perfections. As God, God is infinitely great. He is infinitely wise. No human creature, not even the saved human creature, who is finite, or limited, is able fully to grasp God's greatness. He cannot fully understand the wise way of God in saving the church, or in saving one of his children. He certainly cannot fathom the wise way of God in governing all things to bring about the glorification of himself in the day of Christ.

How often does the believer struggle with the seeming lack of divine power to save someone or to bless the church, delivering the church from her sore distress! How often does the believer wonder at the ways of God in his own burdened life and in the miserable plight of the church in history! If God is almighty, why is not my child delivered from the power of sin, or even from a grievous sickness? If God is all-wise, why does his church go through such distressing circumstances, whether of apostasy or of persecution?

Like scripture, the Reformed faith does not attempt to answer such questions and quiet such struggles with an explanation of the ways of God. It cannot, for God is incomprehensible. "Great is the LORD, and greatly to be praised; and his greatness is unsearchable" (Ps. 145:3). The New Testament intensifies the believer's confession of the incomprehensibility of God: "O the depth of the riches both of the wisdom and knowledge of God! how unsearchable are his judgments, and his ways past finding out!" (Rom. 11:33).

Only God can search out and comprehend God. "The Spirit searcheth all things, yea, the deep things of God... The things of God knoweth no man, but the Spirit of God" (1 Cor. 2:10–11).

The confession that God is incomprehensible is not to say that God cannot be known by us, or that he cannot be known truly, as he really is and as he really acts in history. This is the explanation of incomprehensibility that is given by some Presbyterian theologians. They maintain that the knowledge Christians have of God is merely analogical. It is only a kind of approximation to the truth itself of God's being and acts. It is knowledge that is merely similar to the truth itself of God. Such a conception of the knowledge of the believer presents itself as an honoring of the incomprehensibility of God. In fact, it is no such thing. It is, rather, a dishonoring of the divine work of revelation, God's act of making himself known to his people. It is also a disparagement, indeed a calling into question, of the believer's knowledge of God. If the believer's knowledge of God is not true knowledge, knowledge that is the same as God's knowledge of himself, except that God's knowledge is comprehensive whereas the believer's is limited, the believer's knowledge is not genuine knowledge at all. If it is not knowledge, it is ignorance.

Revelation of God to the believer, by the Spirit's making God known through holy scripture, gives the believer real knowledge of God, the very knowledge of himself that God has, except that the knowledge that God has of himself is infinite, whereas the knowledge of the believer is limited. The thoughts of the believer concerning God are true, but God is greater than the believer's thoughts—not different from the believer's thoughts, but greater. The end of the believer's thinking about God is not doubt about the reality of the thoughts, but adoration and wonder: "O the depths."

This spiritual being is invisible. He cannot be seen and never will be seen by any mere creature. This is due in part to the spirituality of his being. It is due also to the enveloping of his being in the dazzling glory of his being: "dwelling in the light which no man can approach unto; whom no man hath seen, nor can see" (1 Tim. 6:16). One could easier look into the blazing sun. Even the privileged Moses could not see the face of God at Sinai: "Thou canst not see my face: for there shall no man see me, and live" (Ex. 33:20). Sheltered from the full force of the effulgence of the glory of God in "a clift of the rock," and covered from the killing rays by God's own hand as God passed by, Moses saw only God's "back parts" (vv. 21–23).

One day, believers will see God, will see his front parts, and this sight of God will be the quintessence of their bliss in the new world. But they will not see him directly, by looking upon the Godhead himself. Rather, they will see God face to face by looking upon Jesus Christ, who is the "brightness of [God's] glory, and the express image of his person" (Heb. 1:3), so that, as Jesus himself said, "He that hath see me hath seen the Father" (John 14:9).

This glorious God is "immutable." He does not change. He *cannot* change. This assures the believer that God will be faithful to his promises of salvation to the believer, as Malachi 3:6 applies immutability: "I am the LORD [Jehovah], I change not; therefore ye sons of Jacob are not consumed."

Upon this perfection of the being of God is founded the Reformed confession of the unchanging love of God toward, and faithfulness to his promise to, elect, believing sinners. On the other hand, the teaching that God's love toward, and God's covenantal promise to, sinners can change to hatred and the revocation of the promise is guilty of denying the perfection of immutability. In the words of Malachi 3:6, such a deity changes, and therefore at least some sons of Jacob are consumed; all are in constant danger of being consumed. Such a god is essentially different from the God of holy scripture and of the Belgic Confession.

What would change in God imply? Certainly, lack of perfection. Perfection certainly cannot change for the better. The only change of perfection would be for the worse. The possibility of change in God would imply the possibility of God's deterioration. Such a possibility is, all by itself, imperfection. Likely, change in God would mean a lack of knowledge. Some happening in history takes God by surprise. He must change his purposes accordingly. But a lack of knowledge is imperfection. Or God might change because he is dependent on others—on humans or on the development of his world. Dependency for Deity is imperfection.

Scripture denies the imperfection of divine mutability. "The Strength of Israel will not lie nor repent: for he is not a man, that he should repent" (1 Sam. 15:29). Change is the weakness of humans. The strength of Godhead consists of unchangeableness. In God is "no variableness, neither shadow of turning" (James 1:17).

Texts in scripture that speak of God's repenting, or changing his mind, for example regarding King Hezekiah's sickness (2 Kings 20), are instances of representing God and his dealings with humans in language that is familiar to humans. In reality, God planned Hezekiah's recovery from his illness. He never intended the king's death. This event in sacred history indicates the role of prayer in God's fulfillment of his unchangeable plan regarding his children. God unchangeably purposed the recovery of Hezekiah from his illness, and he purposed the recovery in the way of Hezekiah's prayer for this recovery. Prayer, therefore, is not an irrelevancy. God did not purpose Hezekiah's recovery regardless whether the king prayed or did not pray. The recovery of the king was an answer to his prayer. So much is this so, that had Hezekiah not prayed, he would not have recovered. But God unchangeably planned both the prayer and the recovery in answer to the prayer.

Much of Protestantism denies the immutability of God. In fact, denial of God's immutability is one of the outstanding sins of much of contemporary Protestantism. Pantheistic, philosophical Protestants affirm God's development along with the evolving world. Modernists teach a god who is always reacting to the decisions of humans and therefore changing his mind and his actions daily. So-called evangelicals boast of their power, in large gatherings characterized by emotional, insistent prayer, to change the will of God to conform to their will, which alleged power not only opposes the third petition of the model prayer, but also ought to fill a Christian with terror. Arminians proclaim a god who is changeable regarding his attitude toward humans in the matter of divine love and salvation. If the sinner wills salvation, God loves him and works at his salvation. If the same sinner changes his will, God's love changes into hatred and God works at his damnation. Only the Reformed orthodoxy of article 1 of the Belgic Confession confesses the perfection of the immutability of God and thus the God of this perfection.

God is also "infinite," that is, without any limitation. This perfection applies to the being himself, particularly regarding space. This is God's omnipresence. God is everywhere present with all his being. The thought is not that he fills all space and then spills over beyond the boundaries of space. Rather, just as his eternality is his exaltation above time, so also his infinity is his exaltation above space. Space does not contain and confine him. Space too is a creature of his. Solomon confessed God's infinity regarding space, at the dedication of the temple, in wonderment at the grace of the infinite God in willing to dwell in the confines of that building for the benefit of Israel: "But will God indeed dwell on the earth? behold, the heaven and heaven of heavens cannot contain thee; how much less this house that I have builded?" (1 Kings 8:27).

The reality of the grace displayed by God's dwelling in that Old Testament building is God's dwelling in the confined space of the man Jesus. "In him [Jesus Christ] dwelleth all the fulness of the Godhead bodily" (Col. 2:9). In the days of the earthly ministry of Jesus, the grace of God shone most brightly in that the infinite God dwelt in the confined space of the *weakened* man Jesus. So, so much, in Jesus Christ did the infinite God humble and empty himself, on behalf of finite, sinful humans. How this grace of God exposes and shames the unwillingness of finite humans to humble themselves, that is, to undergo a little more diminishing of their finitude, both before the infinite God and before their fellow, finite creatures. The name of this unwillingness is pride.

That infinity is fundamental to God's incomprehensibility has already been demonstrated. In keeping with the rule that God is his perfections so that all harmonize with the others, the infinity of God characterizes all of his perfections. God is not merely mighty, but he is "*al*mighty." He is not merely wise and just, but he is "*perfectly* wise [and] just." He is not merely good, but he is "the overflowing fountain of all good."

The Reformed believer who knows and confesses the infinity of all the perfections of God will not question the perfections of God. He will not doubt them regarding their application to the wicked, for example, the perfection of his being almighty when the wicked world seems to triumph over God's cause, church, and kingdom in history, as will especially be the case in the days of the supremacy of the antichrist over all the earth. But even more importantly, he will not doubt the infinite power of God when all things seem to go against him personally—in times of debilitating sickness; of troubles in the family; and even of persecution at the hands of that which has the name of church. Psalm 73 is the passionate cry of the godly over this problem, this severe trial: the wicked prosper in the world; the godly are plagued.

Arising to his comfort and encouragement is the truth that God is infinitely powerful, wise, and good in his dealings with the believer personally. Often, the church and the believer do not *see* this, do not *understand* this, do not *feel* this. Often God's dealings with his church and with the believer individually seem to indicate the very opposite of God's being almighty, wise, just, and good. In this life, the truth of the infinity of God's perfections is strictly a matter of faith. As article 1 of the Confession begins, "We all *believe with the heart*" the infinity of God's perfections, specifically, his might, wisdom, justice, and goodness in his dealings with the church and her members.

We *believe*! This means that the believer's knowledge and confession of the perfections of God are founded upon God's revelation of himself in Jesus Christ. In the incarnation, lifelong suffering, atoning death, and resurrection of Jesus, as the revelation of the perfections of God at work for the church and the elect believer, is proved beyond all doubt the infinity of the might, wisdom, justice, and goodness of God on behalf of the church and the believing member of the church. In the face of the worst afflictions and bitterest disappointments, the heartfelt confession of the believer is faith's rhetorical question: "He that spared not his own Son, but delivered him up for us all, how shall he not with him also freely give us all things?" (Rom. 8:32). That is to say, "He that spared not his own Son, how can I doubt his infinite power, wisdom, justice, and goodness on my behalf, regardless of the evidence to the contrary in my troublous experiences?"

The divine being believed with the Reformed heart and confessed with the Reformed mouth is almighty. So much is this a perfection of the divine being that it is his name. God calls himself "Almighty God." When he appeared to father Abraham, in order to establish his covenant with Abraham and his seed, God named not only Abraham, but also himself. "I am the Almighty God" (Gen. 17:1). The name reveals a twofold perfection of God. He is the sovereign over all, having all authority in heaven and on earth: the *right* to do as he pleases. In addition, he is the possessor of actual strength to perform whatever he wills. In Isaiah 46:10, God himself declares his sovereignty: "My counsel shall stand, and I will do all my pleasure." Verse 9 prefaces this declaration of sovereignty with the affirmation that sovereignty is the (essential) perfection of Godhead: "I am God, and there is none else; I am God, and there is none like me." The divine power unfailingly to accomplish the divine will is the testimony of Luke 1:37, with specific reference to the wonder of all wonders, the incarnation and virgin birth of Jesus: "With God nothing shall be impossible."

In believing and confessing that God is almighty, the soundly Reformed faith distinguishes itself from all other purported forms of the Christian religion, as well as from the apostate forms of the Reformed faith. All the others teach that God desires, or wills, the salvation of all humans without exception, but fails to save in the case of many because their will is contrary. This is the theology in non-Reformed churches of a kind of universalism. In the Reformed churches, this theology takes the form of the theory of the well-meant offer. The god of this theology is not almighty, as even a child can perceive. Neither is he sovereign, inasmuch as evidently he does not decree the reprobation of some, nor is he strong enough to accomplish his desire to save all humans without exception.

Popular as this denial that God is almighty in salvation may be, it is serious error, indeed, heresy. Since God is his perfections, to deny that he is almighty is to deny his Godhead. The god of a universal will for the salvation of sinners is not the God who identifies himself in Genesis 17:1 as "Almighty God." It is an idol. What is really god in the matter of salvation and damnation is the will of the sinner.

The last three perfections of God that are confessed in article 1 of the Belgic Confession are known as "communicable." The explanation is that God shares these perfections, in a creaturely measure, with his children. Regarding "wisdom," "justice," and "goodness," the spiritual reality is, "like Father, like son." Even these perfections, however, characterize the being of God uniquely. For God alone is *perfectly* wise and just, and only God is the *overflowing fountain* of all good.

God is wise. He knows how to direct all things to the best and highest end, namely, his own glory through the salvation of his church in Christ Jesus. First Timothy 1:17 praises God as "the only wise God." God's wisdom exposes the wisdom of the world as foolishness, especially in that the wisdom of God ordains the salvation of sinners by the foolishness of the preaching of the cross of Jesus Christ (1 Cor. 1:17–24). Christ crucified is the "wisdom of God" (v. 24).

God has wisdom of himself; it is the very perfection of his being. He learned it from no one. "Who hath directed the Spirit of the LORD, or being his counsellor hath taught him? With whom took he counsel, and who instructed him, and taught him in the path of judgment, and taught him knowledge, and shewed to him the way of understanding?" (Isa. 40:13–14).

Contemporary Christendom has a hard time with seeing the wisdom of God, even in things natural. It challenges the wisdom of God in ordaining marriage as the lifelong union of one man and one woman. It doubts the wisdom of God even regarding recognizing marriage as the union of a male and a female. It supposes that there is a better way of rearing children than that of God's institution, the family. It fails to observe that educating a population on the theory of man's evolving from the beast has the effect of society's living by the law of the jungle.

To the wisdom of God in things spiritual, contemporary Christendom is blind. It questions the validity of every one of the ten commandments of the law of God as wisdom for holy and blessed Christian life. Above all else, much of Christendom denies that supreme wisdom is the preaching of the cross of Jesus Christ for the salvation of guilty, depraved sinners and for the enjoyment of eternal life. To the learned theologians, the preaching of the cross is foolishness. Thus today as in the time of the apostle, the foolishness of God is wiser than men (1 Cor. 1:25).

God is just. If the perfection of wisdom is misconceived, the perfection of justice is hated. Like the ungodly world, the apostate churches hold the justice of God in contempt in things natural and civil. They rage against the justice of God that requires the death penalty for the murderer. They hold the justice of God that decrees that if a man will not work, neither shall he eat, in contempt, approving rather a civil society in which the man who will not work eats off the labor of others—the welfare state. They applaud judges who deliberately ignore and even contravene the established laws of the land, which more or less clearly reflect the justice of God, pleading for laws and judicial decisions that rather reflect the opinions and feelings of the lawless (liberals) of the land.

In things spiritual, the apostates know no shame in stripping the God of holy scripture, the God of the historic Christian faith, of his perfection of justice. The cross of Christ was not the satisfying of the justice of God regarding guilty sinners. Sin is not guilt but sickness. The catastrophes that strike the human race—disease, earthquakes, war, and death itself—are not judgments even upon the worst of sinners or societies developed in depravity, but unfortunate natural disasters. There is no hell for impenitent rebels against the righteousness of God. As for a decree of reprobation that serves to manifest the justice of God, defense of the decree even in the sphere of Reformed Christianity, where the doctrine is a matter of creedal confession, meets with the scornful charge of hyper-Calvinism.

In the face of this opposition, the Belgic Confession has the truly Reformed believer confess that "God...is... just." All of God's thoughts, will, and deeds accord with the goodness of his own being. Fundamental to the confession of God's justice is that his justice is not decided by the conformity of his counsel and actions to some standard outside himself and therefore above himself. There is no such standard. If there were a standard of right outside himself and above himself, that standard would be God. The standard that determines the justice of God is certainly not the imperfect judgments of humans, much less sinfully foolish humans, as to what is right. For humans, including theologians, to judge the will and works of God made known in scripture as unjust is an aspect of man's determination to deify himself. The good being of God himself is the sole standard of justice. God himself affirms his justice in scripture: "He is the Rock, his work is perfect: for all his ways are judgment: a God of truth and without iniquity, just and right is he" (Deut. 32:4).

The gospel of Jesus Christ determines the righteousness of God regarding guilty sinners. Not only, or even mainly, is this the determination that everyone who does not believe in Jesus perishes under the punitive wrath of God in time and in eternity, although it is this determination. But it is especially the truth that everyone who believes in Jesus Christ is righteous before the just God with the righteousness of God himself, which was worked out for sinners in the cross of Jesus. The glorious justice of God is the righteousness that declares guilty sinners just for the sake of the suffering and death of Christ Jesus. "To declare, I say, at this time his righteousness: that he might be just, and the justifier of him which believeth in Jesus" (Rom. 3:26). Therefore, enemies of the justice of God invariably and necessarily show themselves foes of the cross of Christ.

The sum total of all of God's perfections is his goodness. His goodness is the ethical perfection of his being. Another name for the goodness of God is holiness. This goodness exposes all human creatures, including the elect by nature, as evil. Jesus proclaimed the sole goodness of God in Luke 18:19: "None is good, save one, that is God." Implied is that whatever seeming goodness in humans leaves God out of consideration, is not attraction to the goodness of God, that is, to God himself, and does not radiate all the communicable perfections of the divine being in holiness of life is not goodness at all, no matter how the seeming goodness glitters in the estimation of humans, but evil. Implied too is that all genuine goodness in saved, sanctified humans is derived—"communicated"—from the goodness of God, for God is the source of all good: "Every good gift and every perfect gift is from above and cometh down from the Father of lights" (James 1:17).

The radiation of all these perfections is God's glory. More or less clearly do these perfections radiate in the creation and in the history of the human race, especially that element of the history that directly concerns the gathering and preservation of the church. Brilliantly, these perfections shine forth in the person and work of Jesus Christ. Indeed, Jesus *is* the glory of God. To see the radiation of the perfections—whether in the creation and history or in Jesus Christ—requires that the blinding scales of unbelief be removed from one's eyes. This has been accomplished in those who confess article 1 of the Belgic Confession: "We...believe..."

Believing, they confess.

Their confession in article 1 is a doxology.

Chapter Two

GOD'S REVELATION OF HIMSELF

(ARTICLES 2–4)

ART. II. BY WHAT MEANS GOD IS MADE KNOWN UNTO US.

We know him by two means: first, by the creation, preservation, and government of the universe; which is before our eyes as a most elegant book, wherein all creatures, great and small, are as so many characters leading us to contemplate the invisible things of God, namely, his eternal power and Godhead, as the Apostle Paul saith (Rom. i. 20). All which things are sufficient to convince men, and leave them without excuse.

Secondly, he makes himself more clearly and fully known to us by his holy and divine Word; that is to say, as far as is necessary for us to know in this life, to his glory and our salvation.

ART. III. OF THE WRITTEN WORD OF GOD.

We confess that this Word of God was not sent nor delivered by the will of man, but that holy men of God spake as they were moved by the Holy Ghost, as the Apostle Peter saith. And that afterwards God, from a special care which he has for us and our salvation, commanded his servants, the Prophets and Apostles, to commit his revealed Word to writing; and he himself wrote with his own finger the two tables of the law. Therefore we call such writings holy and divine Scriptures.

ART. IV. CANONICAL BOOKS OF THE HOLY SCRIPTURES.

We believe that the Holy Scriptures are contained in two books, namely, the Old and New Testaments, which are canonical, against which nothing can be alleged. These are thus named in the Church of God.

The books of the Old Testament are: the five books of Moses, viz., Genesis, Exodus, Leviticus, Numbers, Deuteronomy; the book of Joshua, Judges, Ruth, two books of Samuel, and two of the Kings, two books of the Chronicles, commonly called Paralipomenon, the first of Ezra, Nehemiah, Esther; Job, the Psalms of David, the three books of Solomon, namely, the Proverbs, Ecclesiastes, and the Song of Songs; the four great Prophets: Isaiah, Jeremiah, Ezekiel, and Daniel; and the twelve lesser Prophets, viz., Hosea, Joel, Amos, Obadiah, Jonah, Micah, Nahum, Habakkuk, Zephaniah, Haggai, Zechariah, and Malachi.

Those of the New Testament are: the four Evangelists, viz., Matthew, Mark, Luke, and John; the Acts of the Apostles;

*the fourteen Epistles of the Apostle Paul, viz., one to the
Romans, two to the Corinthians, one to the Galatians, one
to the Ephesians, one to the Philippians, one to the Colos-
sians, two to the Thessalonians, two to Timothy, one to
Titus, one to Philemon, and one to the Hebrews; the seven
Epistles of the other Apostles, viz., one of James, two of
Peter, three of John, one of Jude; and the Revelation of the
Apostle John.*

INTRODUCTION

Articles 2–4 of the Confession are the explanation of *how*
we have the knowledge of God that believers confess in
article 1. The explanation is revelation. The word *revelation* does not occur, although article 3 does speak of the
"*revealed* word." Article 2 also speaks of God's *making himself
known*, and this divine act is revelation.

The clearest and fullest revelation of God is holy scripture. Articles 2–4 begin the Belgic Confession's treatment
of scripture. Continuing in articles 5–7, this is the most
complete treatment of the doctrine of scripture in the
three forms of unity. Indeed, it is one of the fullest and
finest treatments of the doctrine of scripture in all of the
Reformed confessions or in any creed.

Article 2 introduces the doctrine of scripture, describing it as revelation and pointing out the superiority of
scripture as revelation to the revelation in creation: clearer,
fuller, saving, and more glorifying of God. Article 3 teaches
the author, origin, and nature of the Bible, all of which are
involved in the doctrine of inspiration. Article 4 lists the
rightful books of the Old and New Testaments, thus bringing to our attention the canon of scripture.

This Reformed confession concerning scripture is of

extraordinary importance and must be considered carefully. The significance of these articles on scripture is, first, the importance of scripture. Scripture is the origin and basis of our knowledge of God and of all the truths of the Christian faith. This knowledge is spiritual and saving, so that with the knowledge of scripture is involved our salvation. Article 2 declares that the knowledge of scripture is necessary for "our salvation."

The importance of these articles is, second, that in our day there is a concerted and fierce attack on scripture. This attack is found in many churches, including Reformed churches. Such is the attack that the theologians and churches deny that scripture is God's "holy and divine Word," as the Confession declares that it is. This amounts to a denial of divine revelation in its entirety. The effect of the denial is rejection of many, if not all, of the doctrines of the Bible, as well as of whatever of the history that does not square with the unbelieving minds of the contemporary theologians.

Third, God's glory is bound up with the doctrine of scripture. Article 2 states that God has made himself known in scripture "as far as is necessary for us to know in this life, *to his glory* and to our salvation."

Although articles 2–4 introduce the doctrine of scripture, article 2 also acknowledges a revelation of God "in the creation, preservation, and government of the universe." This revelation is commonly referred to as "general revelation" in distinction from the "special" revelation of scripture. The articles themselves do not indicate any controversy over the confession of God's revelation of himself in creation. But in the twenty-first century there is controversy. For one thing, the influential German theologian Karl Barth denied the general revelation of God in creation. For another, modernist theologians teach that general revelation is, or can be, saving. These controversies lend urgency to the belief of the Reformed confession of "general revelation" in the Belgic Confession.

GOD'S REVELATION OF HIMSELF IN CREATION (ARTICLE 2)

God makes himself known to every human by the creation, that is, what is often called "nature." The universe that God made in the beginning makes known its creator. God's revelation of himself by means of his handiwork—the marvelous universe—cannot strike anyone as strange. Even human artisans reveal themselves in their works. Beethoven's profound symphonies make Beethoven known to the listener. Rembrandt's paintings reveal the Dutch master, make known his astounding gift, and are readily recognizable as distinctively his art. If this is true of human artists, how much more would this not be true of the divine artist.

Article 2 of the Confession itself suggests the comparison of the artistry of God with the artistry of humans in that it describes the universe as "a most elegant book," the content of which is the unmistakable power and Godhead of God. When the brilliant scientist expresses that he cannot read the deity of God in the aspect of the creation he studies, he shows himself both an ignorant fool and a damnable liar. The musician who attributes Beethoven's Ninth Symphony to a child just beginning his music lessons is less culpable. Attributing the universe to chance is more foolish that attributing Handel's *Messiah* to the fortuitous coming together of the words and sounds of the grand piece, without the composer Handel, or any composer at all.

Article 2 confesses that creation makes God known

altogether apart from the Bible or preaching, for the article distinguishes God's revelation of himself by creation from his revelation of himself "by his holy and divine Word." General and special revelation are two distinct and different forms of revelation.

God's revelation of himself "by the creation, preservation, and government of the universe" is his act upon the mind of every human by means of each creature, for example, the sun, the earth, the animals, and the human himself, and by the creation as a whole with all its relationships and order. Every creature and the creation as a whole plainly and powerfully, indeed irresistibly, testify to and show forth the reality and the glory of their creator. This revelation of God is due, first, to the work itself of creation. Every creature is a living word of God, testifying necessarily to its maker, upholder, and governor. The revelation is due, second, to the almighty work of the Spirit of God in and with the creature and the whole creation irresistibly binding the testimony of the individual creature and of the universe upon the soul of every human. Every creature, including the human himself, is a character in the elegant book that is the creation, and every character declares, "God is!" To escape the powerful testimony of the creation to its creator, a human would have to escape the creation. Indeed, he would have to escape himself.

The result of this revelation is that every human knows God. He knows God in the sense that he knows that the true God described in article 1 of the Belgic Confession exists. He also knows very important things about this true God, namely, "his eternal power and Godhead." He knows also that he must worship and serve this God. Since creation reveals the "Godhead" of the creator of the universe, it necessarily makes known also that this God must be worshiped and served. As God, he must be honored as God.

Creation does not merely make known that there is a god of some kind or other, about whom various religions may theorize and differing theologians may debate. But creation makes known that the one, true God, who is more fully revealed in scripture, exists, lives, and governs.

There is therefore no atheist. Nor is idolatry merely a pitiable ignorance. Rather, it is deliberate, damnable rebellion. Having established, in Romans 1, that all the heathens "knew God" by the revelation in creation, the apostle immediately goes on to explain their universal idolatry: "They glorified him not as God, neither were thankful; but became vain in their imaginations, and their foolish heart was darkened. Professing themselves to be wise, they became fools, and changed the glory of the uncorruptible God into an image made like to corruptible man, and to birds, and fourfooted beasts, and creeping things" (Rom. 1:21–23). Rather than that the heathen are excusable in their idolatry, verse 25 charges that they deliberately changed the truth of God into a lie (the idol) and worshiped and served the creature rather than the Creator, who is blessed forever. Lest anyone challenge this analysis of the idolatry of the heathen, the apostle concludes his judgment of them with the emphatic "Amen" (v. 25).

The church's work of missions, therefore, does not excuse, much less approve, the idolatry of the nations and peoples of the world, trying to build on the foundation of the idolatry. Rather, having proclaimed the one, true God made known in Jesus Christ, according to the scriptures, it calls the idolatrous nations and peoples to repent of their inexcusable worship and service of idols and turn in faith to the living God. This was the nature of the missionary preaching of the apostle, as he states in 1 Thessalonians 1:9: "For they themselves shew of us what manner of entering in we had unto you, and how ye turned to God from idols to serve the living and true God." That the revelation of the true God in the preaching of the apostle was the making known of him in Jesus Christ the apostle goes on to declare in verse 10: "And to wait for his Son from heaven, whom he raised from the dead, even Jesus."

Real and important as this general revelation is, there are certain things that it cannot do and is not intended by God to do. It cannot save. The reason is, first, that there is no knowledge of Jesus Christ in this revelation of God, nor any knowledge of God as gracious to sinners. The outstanding passage in the Bible concerning general revelation begins with the statement that in general revelation "the wrath of God is revealed from heaven against all ungodliness and unrighteousness of men" (Rom. 1:18). Not grace, but wrath!

The second reason why general revelation does not, and cannot, save is that salvation is not God's purpose with this revelation of himself. On the contrary, his purpose is to leave all humans "without excuse" (v. 20). "So that" in the text expresses not merely result, but also purpose—the purpose, the *sole* purpose, of general revelation. The Confession captures the doctrine of Revelation 1:18–32 perfectly when it gives expression to the purpose and result of general revelation: "All which things are sufficient to convince men, and leave them without excuse." In keeping with the purpose of God with general revelation and in accordance with the truth that there is no revelation of Jesus Christ the savior in creation, there is no work of the

Spirit with and by means of the revelation of God in creation to convert the sinner who has only this revelation, softening his hard heart, illuminating his darkened mind, and liberating his bound will, so that he repents, believes, is saved, and worships the Creator rightly.

In keeping with the truth that general revelation cannot save, neither does it give to the unbelieving sinner any true, positive, profitable knowledge of God. There is no natural theology. This is because the curse upon the creation and sin in the mind of the unbeliever dim the testimony of the creation to God. This is also because the heart of the sinner is depraved, so that the sinner at once opposes the knowledge of God that creation does give and corrupts it by changing the truth of God into a lie by some form of idolatry. Or, as is increasingly the case, he shakes his fist in the face of God and lives a life of avowed rebellion.

The revelation of God "by the creation" differs radically, therefore, from that of scripture and the preaching of scripture. Scripture is much clearer and fuller in revealing God. In addition, scripture is a saving revelation to elect humans. Scripture makes known Jesus Christ and the grace of God in him. With scripture and by means of it, the Spirit of Christ works in elect sinners to convert them, so that they repent, believe, and worship God rightly. Only in connection with its reference to God's "holy and divine Word" does the Confession proclaim the possibility and reality of "our salvation."

Those whose hearts have been regenerated by the Spirit and whose minds have been enlightened by the gospel *do* see the revelation of God in the "creation, preservation, and government of the universe." "*We* know him by two means," according to the opening words of article 2 of the Confession. The believers' knowing of God by means of general revelation is important especially for the great calling and cause of Christian education. Unbelievers cannot educate the covenantal children in the truth of the creation, preservation, and government of the universe, because they deny God the creator, upholder, and ruler of the universe. They change the truth of God into a lie. They do this with the purpose of making the children under their tutelage fools like themselves. This is the condemnation of the state schools in our day.

In the good, Christian school, believing teachers instruct the children to read rightly the "most elegant book" of "the creation, preservation, and government of the universe." Fundamental to this right reading of the book of general revelation is that the children view all the creatures, "great and small...as so many characters leading" the children to contemplate the Creator in his power, wisdom, and Godhead.

True as it is that the believer knows God in two ways, corresponding to the twofold revelation of himself by God, scripture governs and interprets general revelation. General revelation, that is, the perversion of general revelation by the ungodly, does not, and may not be allowed to, govern and even criticize scripture, for example, regarding the creation of the universe in six days; the historical reality of the fall into sin on the part of the human race in a historically real individual man, Adam; the worldwide flood; or, for that matter, the virgin conception and birth of Jesus. John Calvin rightly asserted that the Christian is to view and understand the creation, including its history, through the spectacles of scripture.

Scripture is the clear, complete, and saving revelation

of God, and it is this revelation of God by the wonder of inspiration. This is the subject of article 3 of the Belgic Confession.

THE INSPIRATION OF SCRIPTURE (ARTICLE 3)

The inspiration of scripture was God's moving, directing, and controlling certain men to write down his word. In many cases, he first inspired the speaking of his word by these men, but he then inspired the writing of it. The writing of scripture is the concern of article 3 of the Confession: "God, from a special care which he has for us and our salvation, commanded his servants...to commit his revealed Word to writing."

The result of inspiration was that what his servants, the prophets and the apostles, wrote down was the very word of God, and only the word of God, as much as if he had written it with his own finger. Exactly this is the force of the Confession's relating the inspiration of all scripture to God's writing "with his own finger the two tables of the law." Because the work of inspiration of all of scripture is, regarding authorship, the same as God's writing part of scripture with his own finger, scripture is "holy and divine." It is "the Word of God" written.

Scripture is *only* holy and divine. It is not at all common and human. It is *only* the word of God. It is not at all the words of men. Striking in this regard is the Confession's exclusion of the will of man from the gift of the word of God as later the Confession will also exclude the will of man from the gift of the salvation that the word proclaims: "This Word of God was not sent nor delivered by the will of man." The will of man did not give holy scripture. The will of man does not give the salvation that the word of God reveals. The Reformed faith is jealous on behalf of all of salvation's originating in, depending exclusively upon, and being accomplished by the will of God. This great gospel truth runs throughout the entire Confession.

Contrary to a clever, contemporary attempt to evade the force of the confession of the inspiration of scripture, the Confession does not teach that the writers of scripture were inspired, but that the book itself was inspired. The inspiration of the writers would merely mean that they were ecstatically moved to write down grand religious thoughts, which thoughts may or may not be true and all of which would be subject to the critique of contemporary scholars. Confession of the inspiration of the writing itself demands that the content of the Bible, in whole and in part, is the very word of God. The Bible is not subject to the thinking of moderns, whether theologians or laity, but stands in judgment upon the thinking of all humans.

Implied by the inspiration of scripture, as confessed in article 3, are fundamental aspects of inspiration. Inspiration was "plenary," or full. All of scripture was inspired, not merely parts, or leading ideas, or ideas and thoughts that moderns consider important, for example, that God is love. Concerning the entirety of scripture, the Confession states that it is the "revealed Word," which God had "commanded his servants...to commit...to writing," so that concerning all of scripture it is as if God "himself wrote [it] with his own finger."

Inasmuch as the "writings" that constitute the scriptures were inspired, or *God breathed*, inspiration was *verbal*. It extended to the very words of the Bible. Since the Bible is words arranged in definite order to reveal God, his perfections, and his works, inspiration of the Bible expresses that

God's work of giving scripture extended to, indeed consisted of, the very words of scripture in their precise order. If inspiration of the book is not verbal, it is not inspiration. Rejection of this or that word in its context, therefore, is rejection of inspiration. For instance, when the Reformed theologian who opposes predestination rejects the word "hardens" in Romans 9:18, in its context of contrast with God's eternal will to have mercy on some humans, that theologian denies the inspiration of scripture as much as does the openly modernistic theologian.

The truth of the inspiration of scripture itself settles the issue of the infallibility of scripture. Unbelief concerning scripture as the word of God, which appears also today in reputedly Reformed churches as in the liberal Protestant churches, alleges that scripture can and does err. Bolder critics of the Bible instance this alleged weakness of the Bible in such Old Testament doctrines as the fall of the human race into sin and the entrance of death into the world by the disobedience of Adam, which necessarily calls into question the teaching of the apostle in Romans 5 of the New Testament; the watery death of all of mankind except Noah and his family in a universal flood, which necessarily calls into question the teaching of the apostle in 2 Peter 2:5; and the swallowing of the prophet Jonah, alive, by a great fish, which necessarily calls into question the teaching of Jesus in Matthew 12.

This bold, indeed brazen, criticism today calls into question fundamental teachings of the Christian faith as clearly taught in the New Testament, including the incarnation and virgin birth of Jesus; the nature of Jesus' suffering and crucifixion as the satisfying of the justice of a righteous God; the bodily resurrection of Jesus from the dead; the eternal election by God of a church out of the reprobate world of ungodly men and women; and the inspiration itself of scripture. This bold criticism of the Bible makes plain that all criticism of scripture, even the mildest, is unbelief that will not, indeed cannot, stop until all the doctrines of scripture, indeed the doctrine itself of scripture's inspiration, are denied.

Milder critics reject the doctrine of Genesis 1 that God made the universe in six days, subjecting the wisdom and authority of scripture to those of contemporary, evolutionistic science in the teaching that God made the universe over a period of millions, if not billions, of years. This criticism of the biblical teaching of days necessarily implies also that the Bible errs in its account of the origin of humanity in the creation of Adam from the dust and in the creation of the woman from Adam's rib. The rejection of the biblical teaching of creation in six days involves also the rejection of the biblical revelation concerning the manner of the creation of the various creatures. The biblical account has each creature coming into existence by a distinct, creative word of God. The theory, now popular in nominally Reformed churches, has the various creatures coming into existence by development from previously existing creatures.

Similarly, the milder critics in Reformed churches set aside the teaching of the Bible in Ephesians 5:22 and other passages that the wife is called to be subject to her husband. The critics assure Christian wives that they are not to be in subjection to their husbands, but that there is equality of authority in marriage, so that, in fact, husbands are to be subject to their wives as truly and fully as wives are to be subject to their husbands. Mutuality does away with the headship of the husband.

This milder criticism of scripture within reputedly conservative Reformed churches does not call itself criticism, nor is it treated as such by the churches in which it appears. It calls itself, and is received as, "hermeneutics," that is, a new interpretation of the Bible. The name of the evil is part of its deception. The explanation of the days of Genesis 1 as millions of years is not, in fact, a new hermeneutic, but criticism of the Bible regarding its account of the origin of the heavens and the earth. To explain the appearance of the various creatures in terms of the descent of one from the other, including the descent of man from the beast, is not at all a new explanation of Genesis 1 and 2, but criticism of the scriptural account in the interests of adopting the unbelieving account of evolutionary theory. Rejection of the biblical law governing the relationships in marriage of husband and wife is not an interpretation of the biblical passages whatsoever, but the imposition upon the texts of contemporary, feminist thought.

The new hermeneutic in the nominally conservative Reformed and Presbyterian churches is *criticism* of the Bible. Behind this criticism, as behind every form of criticism, is opposition to, or doubt concerning, the authority of the Bible. All doubt concerning the authority of scripture betrays unbelief concerning the inspiration of scripture. Viewing the days of Genesis 1 as millions of years is concession to the contradiction of the biblical testimony in Genesis 1 by contemporary scientists. Not scripture but science is authoritative in the matter. Denial of the headship of the husband in marriage is concession to the loud insistence of contemporary culture that there must be perfect equality of husband and wife in marriage. Not scripture but the culture is authoritative. But scripture yields to the authority of science and culture in matters upon which scripture pronounces to the contrary of science and culture only if scripture is not inspired by God. Science and culture are inspired.

Inspired by God, or "God-breathed," scripture is infallible, or without error, in everything it teaches and, since teachings are made up of the words that express the teachings, the infallibility of scripture is an inerrancy extending to its words. Scripture is the word of God, and God neither lies nor makes mistakes.

As the various books of the Bible themselves make abundantly plain, the divine work of inspiration was organic. It was not mechanical. This means that for the inspiration of his word God used the various writers with their differing personal characters and abilities, their differing spiritual gifts and insights, and their differing styles of expressing the truths revealed to them. The four writers of the one gospel of the birth, ministry, death, and resurrection of Jesus display not only differing styles of writing, but also differing insights into the reality that is Jesus and his ministry, as well as differing concerns regarding that reality. Thus they do not contradict each other, but complement each other. Thus they present to the church the full revelation of Jesus and his ministry that God was pleased to give his church and that is necessary for the salvation of the church. The epistles of the logically reasoning Paul concerning the love of God in Jesus Christ differ in style from the epistles of John, whose message of the love of God in Jesus Christ is intuitive—a flash of insight, not an argument. The church, her theologians, and her members need, and respond to, both Paul and John.

The recognition of organic inspiration refutes the

charge against inspiration by the foes of scripture that the various writers with their differing styles and insights prove that the Bible is merely a human book, whose message is merely the religious insights of the various writers, and that these insights are often contradictory. God used the different writers with all their natural and spiritual differences to reveal his word in the rich fullness that was necessary for the salvation of the church. God prepared the writers for this work, not only calling them to the work and guiding them in the work, but also giving them the gifts, insights, and style of writing that would serve the full revelation of himself.

The ground of the Reformed church's and the believer's reception of scripture as the inspired word of God is stated in article 5 of the Confession. But already here should be noted the two outstanding passages of the Bible that teach the inspiration of scripture, 2 Timothy 3:16 and 2 Peter 1:20–21. Both passages, it must not be overlooked, are scripture's self-identification, as is fitting. It would not be appropriate that mere man gives the authoritative identification of the Bible as the word of God. Only God can and may identify his word as his very own. The Reformed believer does not receive the Bible as the inspired word of God because the Belgic Confession identifies the Bible as the word of God. But he receives it as the word of God because the Bible itself claims to be the word of God. Because the Bible itself claims to be the word of God, the Belgic Confession confesses it to be the word of God.

Second Timothy 3:16 identifies "all scripture" as the very word of God inasmuch as it is "given by inspiration of God." Literally, the Greek original of the word *theopneustos* that the Authorized Version translates as "given by inspiration of God" is "God-breathed." All scripture is breathed out by God. What is breathed out by God is the word of God. Since "God-breathedness" is ascribed to "all scripture," all scripture is the word of God.

The implications of this origin and nature of scripture are expressed by the second part of verse 16, as well as by verses 15 and 17. Scripture is a profitable book, as is no other. It is "profitable for doctrine, for reproof, for correction, for instruction in righteousness" (v. 16). Scripture has unique power: "[It is] able to make thee wise unto salvation through faith which is in Christ Jesus" (v. 15). The accomplishment of the God-breathed scripture is marvelous: "That the man of God may be perfect, throughly furnished unto all good works" (v. 17).

As for 2 Peter 1:19–21, this passage penetrates as deeply into the wonder of inspiration as even the sanctified mind of an apostle can go. At the same time, it is the strongest affirmation of the infallibility, authority, and therefore trustworthiness of scripture in all of the inspired book. This is the passage that article 3 quotes in part: "Holy men of God spake as they were moved by the Holy Ghost."

The passage is speaking of the written word of God, of what the Belgic Confession calls "holy and divine scriptures." Literally, verse 20 reads: "All of prophetic scripture," or "the whole of prophetic scripture." The reference is to all of scripture. All of it is prophetic, not only because all of it foretells the future, the Old Testament foretelling the first and second comings of Christ as one great event, and the New Testament prophesying the second coming of Christ. But all of scripture is prophetic in that it "forth-tells" the word of God. Prophecy is not only foretelling the future. It is also simply "speaking forth" the word of God.

Of the scripture, the passage describes its origin. It is not describing the right understanding and explanation of scripture, as the word "interpretation" in verse 20 might suggest. That the origin of scripture is the subject of the passage is evident from the explanation of verse 20 in verse 21. The reason scripture is not of private interpretation is that it did not come, or originate, by the will of man, but by the Holy Ghost. The origin of scripture is the grand subject of the passage. One may rightly read verse 20 as stating, "The entire prophetic scripture does not come into existence by private interpretation [on the part of the human writers]."

The meaning of verse 20 is that none of scripture, from Genesis 1 through Revelation 22, originated in the private interpretation of spiritual things, from the truth of creation to the truth of the new world, by the individuals who wrote the scriptures. The prophetic scripture is not their thinking about spiritual things. It is not their (religious) word, as, for example, the book of Mormon is merely the private interpretation of religious things by the man who wrote the book and the Koran is merely the private interpretation of religious things by Mohammed. These books were not inspired. They are of "private interpretation."

The reason the Bible does not have its origin in the private interpretation of humans, specifically the human writers of the Bible, is given in verse 21: "For the prophecy came not in old time by the will of man: but holy men of God spake as they were moved by the Holy Ghost." Although verse 21 speaks of "the prophecy" and of the speaking of the prophecy, the reference is to the prophetic scripture of verse 20. The holy men in view here, Moses, David, Isaiah, and the others who wrote scripture, wrote *what* they spoke, and they wrote *as* they spoke: "moved by the Holy Ghost."

The phrase "moved by the Holy Ghost" is the most profound account in all of scripture of the "God-breathedness," or inspiration, of the Bible. The writers of the Bible spoke and wrote *because* they were moved by the Holy Ghost. They spoke and wrote entirely *as* moved by the Holy Ghost. Nothing of their prophesying by either speaking or writing was due to their own will. All of their speaking and writing was the work, by means of them, of the Holy Ghost. So forceful is the testimony of scripture in 2 Peter 1 to its origin in God the Holy Ghost that the word translated "moved" in the Authorized Version can with right be rendered "carried along": "holy men of God spake as they were *carried along* by the Holy Ghost."

This was the nature of the inspiration of scripture: the Holy Ghost carried along the human writers, to write and in their writing. As a mighty wind carries along some small object whither the wind blows, so the Holy Ghost, the infinitely powerful breath, or wind, of God, carried the prophets and apostles in their writing of the scripture. In their writing, they were utterly under the control of the heavenly wind.

Equally astounding is the nature of scripture by virtue of its origin, according to verse 19: "[It is] a more sure word"—more sure than the voice of God that Peter heard from the excellent glory in the holy mount when he witnessed the transfiguration of Jesus, "This is my beloved Son, in whom I am well pleased" (vv. 17–18). If scripture is more sure than the word of God spoken in the holy mount, scripture must also be the word of God. A word of man cannot be more sure than the word of God. Only the word of

God can be more sure than the word of God. Scripture is "more sure" exactly because it is the *written* word of God. It is more sure in its permanency, in its sure, reliable, and certain availability to the church down the ages. The spoken word, sure in itself, can nevertheless unwittingly be changed or forgotten over the course of time: "Did God on the mount say this, or did he say that?" It can even be forgotten by later generations: "What *did* God say to the disciples on the mount?" But the written word has a permanency that the spoken word does not have. It is in this respect "more sure."

The benefit of scripture, therefore, is unique and great. According to 2 Peter 1:19 the benefit is that it is the light of salvation shining in the dark place of this world in which the church finds herself. This light illumines the way of the church and of each member of the church to the dawning of the day at the return of Jesus Christ. In the words of the Confession: "God, from a special care which he has for us and *our salvation*, commanded his servants, the Prophets and Apostles, to commit his revealed Word to writing."

If scripture has this benefit, according to the purpose of God who inspired it, the church and the individual member "do well that ye take heed" to scripture (2 Pet. 1:19). To refuse to take heed to scripture, whether by neglecting the preaching of it, or by failing to read and study it, or by challenging the inspiration of it, or by corrupting the message of it, is wickedly to despise its inspiration and foolishly to turn off for oneself the only light in this dark place, so that one wanders in the darkness, never to share in the coming dawning of the day.

The implications of article 3 of the Confession are clear. First, God is the author of the Bible, by inspiration—the sole author. Men did not produce any of the Bible: "This Word of God was not sent nor delivered by the will of man." We should not, therefore, refer to the human writers of the Bible as "secondary authors." They were not authors. They were merely writers.

Second, scripture is authoritative, trustworthy, and reliable. If it is "more sure" than the word that God spoke from heaven at the mount of transfiguration, scripture is "sure." Any doubt of the trustworthiness of its content, for example, its account of the origin of the universe and especially of the human race as this account appears in Genesis 1 and 2, is doubt of the word of God and therefore of God himself. All criticism of scripture, for example, its doctrine of marriage as the lifelong bond of one man (male) and one woman (female), is daring, damnable criticism of God himself.

A third implication of scripture's inspiration is that God has preserved scripture in the copies that have come down to us. The original documents are lost to us. But by his providence, God, who treasures his own word and who still has a "special care...for us and our salvation," has surely seen to it that the copies available to us are faithful copies of the originals. The Westminster Confession gives expression to this implication of inspiration: "The Old Testament in Hebrew...and the New Testament in Greek...being immediately inspired by God, *and by His singular care and providence kept pure in all ages*, are therefore authentical."[1]

Fourth, the implication of the inspiration of scripture regarding the translation of scripture is that there must be fidelity to the very words of scripture. This condemns

---

1 Westminster Confession of Faith 1.8, in Schaff, *Creeds of Christendom*, 3:604; emphasis added.

theories governing translation known as dynamic equivalence and paraphrase. The former renders the Hebrew and Greek text of scripture in words that, in the judgment of the translators, express to moderns the idea of the text in the words not of scripture, but of the moderns. The latter, even more loosely attached to the very words of scripture, allows the translators to put the thoughts expressed by the words of scripture into words that they consider (or desire) to express the general idea of the text. In neither case does the translation consist of the very words of scripture in the corresponding words of the language into which the original language of the Bible is translated. The reader can never be sure that his Bible in any part of it is, in fact, the word that God inspired.

The New International Version is an example of the first error of translation. The Living Bible is an instance of the second. Of both it is true, in the words of the Confession, that they were "sent [and] delivered by the will of man." A faithful, trustworthy, and still the best translation of the Bible into English is the Authorized, or King James, Version. It is the word of God that "holy men of God spake [and wrote] as they were moved by the Holy Ghost" in a sound, faithful English translation.

SCRIPTURE AS REVELATION (ARTICLES 2 AND 3)

As inspired by God the Holy Ghost, scripture is divine revelation.

Inspiration and revelation are not identical works of God. They can be distinguished, although they are closely related. Inspiration was the act of God that produced the Bible as his word. Revelation is the activity of God that makes himself known to humans.

The inspired scripture is revelation in two respects. First, it itself is the truth about God that God once made known, or revealed, to the writers of scripture—Moses, David, Amos, Luke, John, Paul, and the others. The content of scripture is not human ideas but the truth about God. The sacred writing is itself, apart from anyone's knowledge of it, revelation. It is, as the Confession declares in article 3, "his [God's] revealed Word." Being the revelation of God is scripture's dignity.

Second, scripture is revelation in that it is the means by which God makes himself known to his elect people. Although this aspect of revelation can be distinguished from the first, it is, in fact, implied by scripture's being God's revealed word in itself. For revelation has its purpose in God's making himself known to humans. Apart from God's revealing himself to people, there would be no purpose in his inspiring a book whose content is the knowledge of himself. Article 2 of the Confession expresses this second aspect of scripture's being revelation: "He makes himself more clearly and fully known to us by his holy and divine Word." Being the instrument of God's making himself known to (elect) humans is scripture's value and worth.

Scripture does not make God known apart from the Holy Ghost, who works faith in men's hearts—a faith that consists of the believing knowledge of God. But the Spirit uses scripture to give this saving knowledge, especially the preaching and teaching of scripture, but also, in connection with the preaching, the personal reading and study of scripture. Scripture has this value and worth, as it has its dignity, because it is the revealed word of God, and this word is about Jesus Christ. Indeed, this inspired word may be described as the "inscripturated" Christ.

Paul expresses the necessity that the scripture be the revelation of God *in Jesus Christ* in the passage that describes scripture as "given by inspiration of God": holy scripture makes one "wise unto salvation through faith which is in Christ Jesus" (2 Tim. 3:15–16). Because salvation is only through faith in Christ Jesus, and since scripture is the revelation that is saving, the revelation of scripture is, and must be, the making known of God in Jesus Christ. "Search the scriptures," said Jesus; "they are they which testify of me" (John 5:39).

The truth that all scripture is the revelation of God *in Jesus Christ* is the teaching of the Bible itself, and not only in the express testimony of Jesus himself in John 5:39. Everywhere, the New Testament witnesses to Jesus Christ, in the obedience of the apostles by the Holy Ghost to the command of Christ at his departure in the ascension: "Ye shall be witnesses unto me" in the whole world (Acts 1:8). The content of every epistle is that proclaimed in Romans 1:1, 3: "the gospel of God...concerning his Son Jesus Christ our Lord."

Also the book of Revelation, in the exposition of which Jesus often is buried in the mass of eschatological theory or argument concerning a rapture of the church, an antichrist who persecutes the Jews for three and half years, a restored Jewish kingdom, and an earthly millennial kingdom, is "The Revelation of Jesus Christ...and [the] record of the testimony of Jesus Christ" (Rev. 1:1–2). The central, dominant figure in the last book of the Bible is not the dragon, the beast out of the sea, or the beast from the earth, much less an earthly nation of Israel, but the Lamb who was slain and is now triumphant at the right hand of God. As the opening three chapters of the book make plain, the action that is on the foreground as the main theme of the entire book is not that of Satan, or of the antichrist, or of the false church, or of the Jews, but that of Jesus Christ, who judges, chastises, and saves his church in all the perils of the end time.

THE CANON OF SCRIPTURE (ARTICLE 4)

Article 4 of the Confession is the Reformed doctrine of the canonicity of scripture. Canonicity is an important aspect of the inspiration of scripture. Without a clear, definite doctrine of canonicity, the truth of inspiration is endangered.

The canon of scripture is a certain number of specific books that belong to the category of "holy and divine scriptures," because they were inspired by the Holy Ghost. These books are canonical because, as inspired, they are the standard of the right doctrine by which God reveals himself. The Greek word *kanoon* means standard, or rule. The idea of scripture's being a standard, or rule, governing faith and life is biblical. Galatians 6:16 blesses "as many as walk according to this rule, peace be on them, and mercy, and upon the Israel of God," where "rule" is the Greek word *kanoon*, that is, canon.

One thing a standard of the saving revelation of God must be is definite and fixed. About this standard, there may be no doubt or confusion. As article 5 of the Confession will observe about the function of the canonical books of scripture, they serve for nothing less than the "regulation, foundation, and confirmation of our faith." Accordingly, God, who inspired the scriptures, has infallibly led his church to recognize and receive all of the inspired writings, and only the inspired writings, as canonical. The Reformed church acknowledges and receives a certain, definite list of books as comprising the canon of scripture.

These are listed so that no one can be doubtful about the content of the canon. The canon consists of thirty-nine books of the Old Testament and twenty-seven books of the New Testament, for a total of sixty-six books.

Such is the importance of the canon, functioning as it does as the standard, or rule, of the gospel of Jesus Christ regarding both doctrine and practice, and because of the controversy over the canon, both in the early days of the church of the new dispensation and in contemporary times, that the article adds a solemn warning: "against which nothing can be alleged." In the early days of the church of the new dispensation, the heretic Marcion rejected the entire Old Testament as inspired and canonical. Even Martin Luther in the early stages of his ministry, under the extreme pressure of the appeal to a part of the book by his inveterate enemies, was inclined to question the canonicity of the New Testament book of James.

It is not likely that a Reformed theologian in the twenty-first century will forthrightly question, much less challenge, the canonicity of any of the books listed in article 4. Nevertheless, it is possible that he violates the spirit of the list by ignoring a book in the forming of his theology, or even contradicting a book in his theology. "Against which nothing can be alleged," then, is a necessary admonition to him, as much as to the modern disciple of Marcion.

Listing the canonical books, with the added warning that against them nothing can be alleged, serves the purpose that if a book does not square with our theology, rather than dismiss the book on behalf of our theology, we are to enrich our theology in harmony with this book. The rich and big gospel of Jesus Christ is made up of all sixty-six books of scripture.

Article 4 of the Confession is at pains, in identifying the canon, to distinguish the two large sections of the canon, namely, the "Old and New Testaments." There is more significance in the mention of this distinction—not division—of the scriptures than may be apparent at first glance. First, these two distinct sections of the Bible make up the one, unified holy scriptures. The oneness is not only formal: both are inspired. But the oneness of the two main sections of the scriptures is also material: there is one message, or gospel.

This one gospel is proclaimed in embryonic form in Genesis 3:15 against the background of the sin of the human race in Adam and is the determining background of the message of the entire scriptures. The one gospel set forth in Genesis 3:15 is the promise of Jesus Christ as savior from sin, death, and Satan: "I will put enmity between thee and the woman, and between thy seed and her seed; it shall bruise thy head, and thou shalt bruise his heel." This message of the savior from sin and conqueror of Satan is the one gospel of both Old Testament and New Testament. The Old Testament reveals the Savior and his salvation in type and shadow and promises his coming. The New Testament reveals the Savior and his salvation in reality and announces his presence, as well as promising his return.

The unity of the Old Testament and New Testament, as confessed by the Reformed faith, rejects an explanation of the Old Testament as the message of God's earthly promotion of the Jews as a carnal kingdom, virtually apart from Jesus Christ, whereas the New Testament is the message of God's spiritual salvation of a Gentile church by Jesus Christ. According to the Reformed confession, Old and New Testament are one in their message and gospel. The Reformed faith, therefore, rejects and condemns the popular heresy of premillennial dispensationalism. In its own way, this false doctrine denies the oneness of holy scripture, its claims to believe the inspiration of both Testaments to the contrary notwithstanding.

At the same time, without disturbing the oneness of the two testaments, the Reformed faith respects and does justice to the distinction of the two large sections of scripture. The first thirty-nine books have the old, typical form of the covenant, or testament, of God as their content. The last twenty-seven books are the revelation of the new, fulfilled form of the covenant of God in Christ with his church. One who knows the distinction between old and new does not read the old in the same way he reads the new. He reads the old in the light of the new. The reality shines its explanatory light upon the darker shadows of the Old Testament. The Reformed believer does not understand the symbolic, typical prophecies of Christ and his church in the Old Testament as forecasting literal, earthly vineyards and victories or a literal, earthly millennium of the reign of either Jews or triumphant Christians in the world. But the riches, victories, and power are, as the New Testament interprets the prophecies, spiritual and therefore significant for both believing Jew and believing Gentile.

There is one, great, unified book of holy scripture. All of the sixty-six components are so many chapters of this one book about Jesus Christ and his kingdom and people, the church.

Concerning the fixing of the canon of scripture, that is, official recognition of the books that make up the canon, what is important is that the church with some kind of sovereign decision did not determine for herself which books belong to the canon and which pretender books do not. Determining the canon does not lie either within the church's authority or within the church's competency. Determining the canon of God's word is solely his work, whose word it is. No human authority decides, or is needed to decide, that a word is the word of God. God's word is not dependent upon a word of man, including a synodical word of man, for its authentication. The word of God authenticates itself.

The church in history did not determine the canon. The church recognized the canon and pronounced her finding, which books belong to the list of inspired books and which spurious books do not.

By its own clear and strong manifestation of itself as inspired, scripture itself decided the canon for the church. The true church then was guided by the Holy Spirit infallibly to recognize the canon. This recognition of and pronouncement upon the canon took place in two stages. The canon of the Old Testament was "fixed" by the Jewish church some time before the birth of Christ. This Old Testament canon consisted of the same Old Testament books mentioned in article 4 of the Confession, although the Jews numbered them differently.

Regarding the New Testament canon, the fixing of the canon was not as clean and simple. Very soon after the death of the last apostle, the churches recognized the four gospels and most of the other books of the New Testament as the inspired word of God, although there was uncertainty concerning a few books. In AD 367, in a letter the church father Athanasius listed the twenty-seven books of the New Testament as canonical scripture, to the exclusion of all other books. In AD 397, the Synod of Carthage mentioned the twenty-seven books of the New Testament as canonical. The Protestant churches of the Reformation of 1517 accepted this recognition of the canon on the part of both the Jewish church and the early Christian church, as the list of the inspired books of both the Old Testament and the New Testament in article 4 of the Confession demonstrates.

The canon of scripture is closed. This is the assertion of the opening line of article 5 of the Confession: "We receive all these books [mentioned in article 4], *and these only*, as holy and canonical" (emphasis added). Not only does this assertion exclude non-canonical books that the Roman Catholic Church adds to the canon of scripture, which books are mentioned in article 6 of the Confession. It also precludes adding to the scripture of the sixty-six books mentioned in article 4 any other books that might be discovered and for which the claim might be made that they too are inspired. Other books than those included in the New Testament were written by the apostles, for example, Paul's lost letter to Laodicea (Col. 4:16). Even if this letter should be found, it would not be recognized as part of the canon of the New Testament.

God conceived and planned one, great, complete word, made up of the present sixty-six books of the Bible. These books are the full revelation of himself in Jesus Christ, necessary for the salvation of his church. The God of inspiration is also the God of providence, particularly the God of *special* providence, as it is called, with reference to the guiding of his church. If the lost letter to Laodicea was, in fact, part of the canon of scripture and necessary for the salvation of the church, God would not have permitted it to remain lost for two thousand years.

Now the question is, *why* do we receive these books as

canonical, that is, as inspired scripture? This question has two parts: why do we receive scripture as the very word of God, and why do we receive just these books that are listed in article 4 and no others?

To this twofold question, article 5 gives the answer.

Chapter Three

THE WITNESS OF THE HOLY GHOST

(ARTICLE 5)

ART. V. WHENCE DO THE HOLY SCRIPTURES DERIVE THEIR DIGNITY AND AUTHORITY.

We receive all these books, and these only, as holy and canonical, for the regulation, foundation, and confirmation of our faith; believing, without any doubt, all things contained in them, not so much because the Church receives and approves them as such, but more especially because the Holy Ghost witnesseth in our hearts that they are from God, whereof they carry the evidence in themselves. For the very blind are able to perceive that the things foretold in them are fulfilling.

INTRODUCTION

Article 5 of the Confession is obviously part of the Confession's lengthy and thorough doctrine of scripture. The Confession's treatment of holy scripture begins in the concluding paragraph of article 2 and extends through article 7. This is certainly the most extensive exposition and defense of the doctrine of scripture in all the three forms of unity and arguably the most thorough and important treatment of the doctrine of scripture in all the Reformed creeds.

As was noted previously, in the explanation of article 4 of the Confession, article 5 establishes, almost in passing, the Reformed faith's conviction that the canon of holy scripture is closed: "These books, and these only, [are] holy and canonical." In this aspect of its confession concerning scripture ("these only"), the Reformed faith condemns the addition by the Roman Catholic Church of a number of books to the list of canonical books mentioned in article 4 of the Confession. These non-canonical books are named in article 6.

In addition, the Confession here condemns the thinking of certain liberal Protestant theologians of modern times concerning the canon of scripture. Some suggest the possibility of finding inspired manuscripts in the sands of Palestine that rightfully belong in holy scripture. Others, even more radical, allow for the possibility that gifted theologians today may aspire to write books that belong in the canon of scripture.

The main aspects of the Reformed doctrine of scripture that article 5 contributes to the confession concerning scripture are, first, the authority and reliability of scripture and, second, the reason for, or explanation of, the high doctrine of scripture of the Reformed church and believer.

AUTHORITY AND RELIABILITY OF SCRIPTURE

According to the Reformed faith, as confessed by article 5 of the Confession, scripture has authority. Its authority is that it is "the regulation, foundation, and confirmation of our faith." In view of the functions of faith as the only means of one's salvation, as the source of the true worship and service of God, and as the power of a godly life, this authority of scripture is awesome. The thought of the Confession is that, since scripture is uniquely holy and canonical, because it is uniquely inspired, that is, inasmuch as it is the word of God, scripture is thus *uniquely* the regulation, foundation, and confirmation of our faith. Scripture *alone* governs, grounds, and maintains and strengthens our faith.

Why does the Reformed believer believe what he or she does, especially that Jesus Christ is the only savior by faith in him alone according to the grace of God alone? Upon what does his or her faith in Jesus Christ depend, especially in times of spiritual struggle and sore temptation? What strengthens his or her faith particularly when faith must confess Christ in fearful circumstances of life, or when faith is weak? The answer to these questions is: "Scripture!" "Scripture alone!"

If scripture is to exercise this authority in the lives of the Reformed believers, the Reformed church must preach and confess the authority of scripture by virtue of its inspiration of God. Where nominally Reformed churches no longer preach and confess the authority of scripture, because the preachers and theologians no longer believe this authority, the result will be that the faith of the members is unregulated, so that the members believe anything and everything, except that which the Bible teaches; the faith of the members is unfounded, so that it is unsure of even the most fundamental biblical truths; and the faith of the members, becoming weak as water, cannot be confident even of their own salvation. Where scripture loses its authority, usually by the wicked attack on its authority on the part of heretical theologians and ministers, there is the unbelief of the members of the churches.

The Reformed confession of article 5 is also that scripture is reliable: "believing, *without any doubt*, all things contained in them." "All things" include what to the mind of the theologian are central teachings and what are peripheral teachings, the doctrine of marriage as well as the doctrine of the deity of Jesus. Here again is an implied confession of infallibility, or inerrancy. One is bound to believe "all things" the Bible teaches because the Bible is infallibly inspired *in its entirety*. The Heidelberg Catechism expresses the same truth concerning scripture in question 21: in "true faith," the Reformed believer "hold[s] for truth *all* that God has revealed to us in his Word."[1]

This reliability of the scriptures is due to the fact that "they are from God," that is, they are the word of God, not the word of men. This, in turn, is due to the inspiration of the scriptures. The doctrine of the reliability of scripture in article 5 depends on the doctrine of inspiration that is confessed in article 3.

Recognition of this authority and reliability of scripture is reverence: scripture with all its teaching—all its full and rich gospel of Jesus Christ—is "holy." This confession concerning scripture is strong. Holiness belongs alone to God. Scripture therefore is holy, because it is the word of the holy God.

Such reverence for the written word of God is necessary: "To this man will I look, even to him that...trembleth at my word" (Isa. 66:2). All criticism and doubt of the scripture is sin. To the critic and doubter of holy scripture, God

---

1 Heidelberg Catechism Q 21, in ibid., 3:313; emphasis added.

will not look in favor. If he does not look to one in favor, he looks upon him in wrath.

One trembles at the word of God by believing that the world and its history began exactly as Genesis 1 and 2 describe; that there was a fall into sin on the part of the human race through a speaking serpent; that there was a universal flood; that Jonah was in the belly of a great fish, to emerge alive and chastened after three days; and that the eternal Son of God became a man by the virgin birth in order to redeem the elect of God in all nations.

One trembles at the word of God by believing that marriage is the intimate union of one man and one woman for life; that the husband is to love and treat his wife with the love that Christ has for his bride, the church; that the wife is to be in submission to her loving husband as the church is subject to Christ her head; that all remarriage after divorce while the original mate still lives is adultery; that sex is good, honorable, and right only within the bond of lawful marriage; and that sodomy and lesbianism are gross perversions.

One trembles at the word of God also by believing that God loves him or her who believes on his Son, even though he or she is a sinful, though penitent, human; that God governs every detail of his or her life with fatherly love and concern; that all that has befallen him or her—every disappointment, grief, pain, and evil—is for the good of the believer; and that at the end of history God will raise the believer in his or her body so that in the body the believer will live with God in a new world in unimaginable bliss and glory.

All of this is the word of God. There may be no doubt of the word. All doubt is unbelief, and unbelief is sin.

As authoritative and reliable, scripture has dignity. This is implied by what article 5 confesses about scripture. Such is the dignity of scripture that the true church makes the preaching of it the main element of the church's worship on the Lord's day and the teaching of it in catechism the church's rearing of the children of believers. Reformed believers read the scripture, study it, and teach it to their children. This teaching of the children includes that their instruction at school does not contradict the scripture, as is the case in the state schools, but is based on the scripture, as is the nature of the instruction in the Christian day school. The believer confesses the doctrine of scripture and obeys its precepts.

The question is, why? Why does scripture have this authority, reliability, and dignity? This is the second aspect of the doctrine of scripture in article 5 of the Confession.

EXPLANATION OF THE REFORMED FAITH'S HIGH DOCTRINE OF SCRIPTURE

The reason the Reformed church and the Reformed believer receive as holy and canonical the books listed in article 4 and the reason they believe all things contained in these books are "because the Holy Ghost witnesseth in our hearts that they are from God." This witness is the internal testimony of the Holy Ghost. This witness the Holy Ghost does not give apart from the content of scripture. Rather, the Holy Ghost witnesses to the church and in the hearts of believers by means of scripture: "whereof they [all the books that make up the scriptures] carry the evidence in themselves." One element of this evidence in scripture that it is "holy and canonical" is the fulfillment of biblical prophecy: "The very blind are able to perceive that the things foretold in them are fulfilling." Only the word of God accurately foretells the future.

The things foretold in the Old Testament were fulfilled or are being fulfilled at present. From Abraham came the "seed," or child, Jesus, in whom Abraham would be the father of many nations and in whom all nations would be blessed (see Gen. 17). In David's "seed," Jesus the Christ, God fulfilled his promise that he would establish David's seed forever and build up David's throne to all generations, in the amazing way of the humiliation of this seed (Ps. 89). Long before the event, Isaiah foretold that the Persian king, Cyrus, would release Judah from captivity and instruct the Jews to rebuild the temple and Jerusalem (Isa. 44:28; 45:1–13). Micah foretold the birthplace of God's Messiah, the king of Israel, as "Bethlehem Ephratah" (Micah 5:2).

Likewise, the prophecies of the New Testament "are fulfilling" as "the very blind are able to perceive." Old Zacharias and Elisabeth did have a child, even though both were too old to have a child and even though Elisabeth was barren. Their child did make ready a people prepared for the Lord (Luke 1:5–17). The virgin Mary did bear a child, who is the Messiah (Isa. 7:14; Luke 1:26–38). The gospel of Jesus Christ has gone out, and is going out, in the whole world for a witness unto all nations (Matt. 24:14; Acts 1:8). In these last days there is a falling away, or apostasy, of the churches from the truth of holy scripture, which will culminate in the appearance of the son of perdition, the antichrist (2 Thess. 2:3). So pronounced is this apostasy that even the spiritually blind can see it.

The explanation, then, of the believer's reception of all the books of scripture as "holy and canonical, for the regulation, foundation, and confirmation of our faith," as of his "believing, without any doubt, all things contained in them," is that the word itself convinces us. Scripture is made convincing to the believer by the same Spirit who inspired scripture.

The faith of the Reformed believer concerning scripture rests on the word itself, and on the word only. That is, scripture depends on itself, and on nothing outside itself, for belief concerning itself. This is necessary. God's word must not depend on something besides itself, even were that something the church. Were scripture to depend on something or someone other than itself for belief concerning its authority and reliability, God himself, whose word scripture is, would depend upon that something or someone. This would be the denial of the Godhead of God. God is independent.

According to the Reformed confession, in accordance with the fundamental acknowledgment of the Reformed faith that God is sovereign, scripture is "self-authenticating." It is a serious mistake, and futile, therefore, that Reformed apologists try to prove to an unbeliever that scripture is the inspired word of God from evidences outside and other than scripture itself.

The Reformed apologist simply confronts the unbeliever with the testimony of scripture itself that it is God-breathed (1 Tim. 3:16) in that "the prophecy came not in old time by the will of man: but holy men of God spake as they were moved by the Holy Ghost" (2 Pet. 1:21). He points out to the unbeliever that the scriptures accurately foretold, and still foretell, future events concerning Jesus the Messiah. If the unbeliever rejects this witness of scripture to itself, the believer must "shake off the dust of your feet" against the unbeliever as one who refuses to "hear your words" (Matt. 10:14).

The explanation of our receiving the scriptures as the

authoritative and reliable word of God is not the testimony of the church: "not so much because the Church receives and approves them as such." This is the confession of the Roman Catholic Church: scripture depends on the Roman Catholic Church in all respects. The church determines the canon of scripture. The explanation of the belief of all things contained in scripture by the members of the church is the reception and approval of the teachings of scripture by the church.

In Roman Catholic thinking, scripture depends on the Roman Catholic Church. The word of God depends on the human word of Rome. This arrogant usurping of the glory of God by the Roman Catholic Church is the fundamental sin of Rome in all aspects of her theology and practice.

Nevertheless, there is some relation between the believer's reception of scripture and the faithful confession of the true church concerning scripture: "*not so much* because the church receives and approves them as such, but *more especially* because the Holy Ghost witnesseth in our hearts." The relation is that the testimony of the church is a means, indeed the chief means, by which the Spirit instructs one so that he is convinced that scripture is the word of God. This gives to the true church her solemn calling: witness to the holy and canonical books of scripture as the "regulation, foundation, and confirmation of...faith," and call to belief of all things contained in them. The church that raises doubt concerning scripture and its contents shows itself a false church and makes itself responsible for the unbelief and damnation of its members.

The reason that a Reformed church and her members reject other books as non-canonical is that these books themselves show that they are not inspired. The Spirit does not testify that they are of God. Working through the canonical books, the Spirit exposes the non-canonical books as containing foolish, false, and heretical teachings.

This brings the Confession to an express listing of certain non-canonical books in article 6.

Chapter Four

THE APOCRYPHAL BOOKS
(ARTICLE 6)

*ART. VI. THE DIFFERENCE BETWEEN THE
CANONICAL AND APOCRYPHAL BOOKS.*

*We distinguish these sacred books from the apocryphal, viz.,
the third and fourth book of Esdras, the books of Tobias,
Judith, Wisdom, Jesus Syrach, Baruch, the appendix to the
book of Esther, the Song of the Three Children in the Fur-
nace, the History of Susannah, of Bell and the Dragon, the
Prayer of Manasses, and the two books of Maccabees. All
which the Church may read and take instruction from, so
far as they agree with the canonical books; but they are far
from having such power and efficacy as that we may from
their testimony confirm any point of faith or of the Christian religion; much less to detract from the authority of the
other sacred books.*

INTRODUCTION

The significance of article 6 of the Belgic Confession escapes
most Reformed churches today. Why the Confession should

devote an article to a list of unfamiliar books that do not belong to the canon of holy scripture is a mystery.

Fundamentally, the significance is that the Reformed faith has such a high regard for the word of God, holy scripture, that it is determined that that word not be corrupted by the intrusion into the canon of books that do not belong and that would corrupt the gospel revealed by the canonical books.

In addition, the article carries on the controversy of the Reformed faith with Roman Catholicism. This controversy concerns not only the message of scripture, the gospel of grace, but also the book that contains the message, scripture itself. A lively issue at the time of the Reformation, when the Belgic Confession was written, had to do with the content of scripture. This issue, article 6 of the Confession decides for the Reformed churches.

Besides, there was some struggle within the Reformed churches themselves, not whether the books mentioned in article 6 were legitimately part of the inspired scripture, but whether these books should be included in the Reformation Bibles as useful books for the instruction and piety of the Reformed believers. At the Synod of Dordt, for example, there was disagreement whether the books mentioned in article 6 of the Confession should be included in the official translation of the Bible into the Dutch language. Francis Gomarus (1563–1641), prominent champion of Reformed orthodoxy at the great synod, was one who argued against this inclusion. Nevertheless, the Synod of Dordt approved the inclusion of these books in the Dutch Bible, although with the express warning that the books are not part of the canon. In light of the popularity of the books among the Reformed people, stemming from the inclusion of the books in the printed versions of the Bible and in ecclesiastical literature prior to the Reformation, it was necessary for the Reformed Confession to list these books and expressly to declare that, regardless how they may be used in the life of the people, they are not part of the canon of holy scripture.

NAME AND HISTORY OF THE APOCRYPHA

Apocryphal books are certain books that the Roman Catholic Church claims are inspired of God and are rightly part of the canon of Old Testament scripture, and therefore authoritative for the faith and life of the people of God. Protestantism, however, and the Reformed churches in particular, reject these books as uninspired, as article 6 plainly states: "We distinguish those sacred books [listed in article 4 and confessed to be holy and canonical in article 5] from the apocryphal."

The word *apocryphal* literally means "hidden." The etymology of this term as the name of these books is complicated and controversial. All that a Protestant needs to know about the name is that it refers to books Rome includes in its Bible, but that are rejected as belonging to the canon of inspired scripture by Protestantism, and by Reformed churches in particular.

The brief history of these books is that they were never part of the Hebrew canon of inspired books of the Old Testament. They were, however, included in a Greek translation of the Old Testament, made before the birth of Christ during the time between the testaments, that is, between the prophet Malachi and the birth of Jesus. The name of this Greek translation of the Old Testament is *Septuagint*, that is, "seventy," because the translation was supposedly done by seventy-two Jewish scholars. The strongest argument on behalf of including the apocryphal books in the canon of scripture is that Jesus and the apostles likely used and quoted from the Septuagint translation of the Old Testament. This was because Greek was the universal language of the time. But Jesus and the apostles never quoted from the apocryphal books.

Some of the apocryphal books were included in the list of canonical books made by the church councils of Hippo and Carthage in the fourth century AD. This does not prove that the books are inspired. It only shows that the increasing spiritual darkness of the church extended to its confusion concerning the content itself of holy scripture.

The Reformation rejected these books, as article 6 of the Confession states: "They are far from having such power and efficacy" as belong to inspired scripture.

The Roman Catholic Church officially included the books in their scriptures at the Council of Trent (1543–63). The Fourth Session of the Canons and Decrees of the Council of Trent includes most of the books rejected in article 6 of the Belgic Confession as part of the Old Testament. Upon those who reject these apocryphal books as part of inspired scripture, that is, upon the Protestant churches, Rome passes its monotonous, impotent curse: "Let him be anathema."[1]

The fundamental reason why the Reformed churches reject the apocryphal books as non-canonical is that the books themselves plainly show that they are not inspired by the Holy Ghost. In the language of article 5 of the

---

[1] Canons and Decrees of the Council of Trent, Fourth Session, "Decree concerning the Canonical Scriptures," in Schaff, *Creeds of Christendom*, 2:79–82.

Confession, the Holy Ghost witnesses in our hearts that they are *not* from God, whereof they carry the evidence in themselves. The very blind are able to perceive that they contain false and foolish things. The apocryphal books teach heresy, including purgatory, prayers for the dead, meritorious good works, and free will. They teach foolish, false, and historically inaccurate things, including that Daniel killed a dragon by feeding it cakes that it could not digest and that Nebuchadnezzar was king of Nineveh.

The most important of the apocryphal books are First and Second Maccabees. These books give some of the dramatic and stirring history of the Jews in the time between the Old Testament and the New Testament. An important part of this history was the persecution of the Jews by the Syrian king Antiochus Epiphanes, a historical type of antichrist, prophesied in the book of Daniel. Reformed people could read these two books with profit.

It is likely that as ecumenical relationships with the Roman Catholic Church are increasingly promoted by Reformed churches, the Reformed believer will increasingly also hear of the worth, and even inspiration, of the apocrypha. Appeal will be made to the apocrypha in support of the heresies espoused by Rome. At the very least, the issue of the apocrypha will be dismissed as of no fundamental importance. Therefore, the testimony of article 6 of the Confession concerning the apocrypha will soon again have great practical importance to the Reformed Christian.

Chapter Five

THE PERFECTION
OF SCRIPTURE
(ARTICLE 7)

*ART. VII. THE SUFFICIENCY OF THE HOLY SCRIP-
TURES TO BE THE ONLY RULE OF FAITH.*

*We believe that these Holy Scriptures fully contain the will
of God, and that whatsoever man ought to believe unto salvation, is sufficiently taught therein. For since the whole
manner of worship which God requires of us is written in
them at large, it is unlawful for any one, though an Apostle, to teach otherwise than we are now taught in the Holy
Scriptures: nay, though it were an angel from heaven,
as the Apostle Paul saith. For since it is forbidden to add
unto or take away any thing from the Word of God, it doth
thereby evidently appear that the doctrine thereof is most
perfect and complete in all respects. Neither may we compare
any writings of men, though ever so holy, with those divine
Scriptures; nor ought we to compare custom, or the great
multitude, or antiquity, or succession of times or persons, or*

councils, decrees, or statutes, with the truth of God, for the truth is above all: for all men are of themselves liars, and more vain than vanity itself. Therefore we reject with all our hearts whatsoever doth not agree with this infallible rule, which the Apostles have taught us, saying, Try the spirits whether they are of God; likewise, If there come any unto you, and bring not this doctrine, receive him not into your house.

INTRODUCTION

Regardless of the heading above article 7 in the English translation, the subject of the article is the perfection of scripture. Sufficiency is one aspect of the perfection. There are other aspects taught or suggested in the article. The heading above the article in the Latin edition is correct: "*De Perfectione Sacrae Scripturae,*" that is, "The Perfection of Sacred Scripture."

Several terms or phrases in the article suggest the perfection of scripture: "Holy"; "the Word of God"; "divine"; "the truth of God"; "this infallible rule." The article expressly states scripture's perfection: "The doctrine thereof is most perfect and complete in all respects."

How vitally important is this confessional affirmation of scripture's perfection and the Reformed believer's submission to this confession in our day of relentless, bold denial of this perfection! From the rejection of the historicity of Genesis 1–11, which chapters clearly present themselves as history, to the rejection of scripture's prohibition of divorce and remarriage in 1 Corinthians 7 and of sodomy and lesbianism in Romans 1, scripture is openly judged, that is, criticized, as imperfect. This takes place even in the Reformed churches that have the Belgic Confession as their creed.

ABOVE ALL CRITICISM

As perfect, scripture is not to be criticized. All criticism implies imperfection. What the liberal scholars today are doing openly and what nominally conservative biblical scholars are doing shrewdly by other names, that is, engaging in a study of the word of God that takes the liberty to criticize it, is forbidden and condemned. All such criticism amounts to a rejection of scripture's perfection by imposing upon the text the ideas of modern, unbelieving scholars. All the scholars who engage in this criticism of the Bible come to scripture with the presupposition that the Bible is imperfect and therefore subject to such criticism. But if scripture is not perfect, it is not the word of God. Thus the scholars, whether liberal or conservative, deny the inspiration of holy scripture.

The calling of the scholar, as of the unscholarly believer, is simply to bow to, understand, believe, and confess the doctrine of scripture. Their presupposition of faith should be that scripture is as far above criticism as God, whose word it is, is above criticism.

Jesus forbade all criticism of scripture, thus acknowledging scripture's perfection, in John 10:35: "The scripture cannot be broken." "Broken" in the text is the Greek word *luoo* that literally means "loose." The thought in John 10:35 is that scripture cannot be annulled, deprived of authority, or rendered invalid. It may not be criticized. Jesus referred to the sinful criticism of scripture that takes the form of setting aside some teaching of the Bible, deliberately neglecting a doctrine, or in any way making some part of scripture of no effect in our thinking or behavior. Reasons for this criticism of scripture would include that the aspect of biblical teaching that is thus criticized does not harmonize with the apparent findings of contemporary science; or meet with the approval of society; or make life as easy as humans desire; or represent the opinion of most theologians; or facilitate ecumenicity.

Jesus' testimony to the perfection of scripture is extraordinarily powerful, because he was referring specifically to what we would consider an incidental, minor passage and teaching in Old Testament scripture. The specific passage of the Old Testament to which he referred was Psalm 82:6, where the psalmist called the civil and ecclesiastical rulers "gods." Such a text and such a teaching "cannot be broken," inasmuch as the whole of scripture "cannot be broken."

Scripture cannot be broken when it calls the rulers "gods." It cannot be broken, as Jesus immediately goes on to affirm, when it identifies Jesus as the "Son of God" (John 10:36). It cannot be broken when it ascribes the Pentateuch to Moses. It cannot be broken when it teaches creation, the fall, the flood, and Babel as historical events. It cannot be broken when it teaches justification by faith alone, apart from all works of the sinner. It cannot be broken when it teaches double predestination, election and reprobation. It cannot be broken when it forbids office in the church to women. It cannot be broken when it teaches marriage as the lifelong, unbreakable bond between one man and one woman. It cannot be broken when it condemns homosexual relations as shameful sin.

Every criticism of scripture is an attack on Jesus and the denial that he is the perfect Son of God. This is the case, first, because he regarded scripture as the perfect, unassailable word of God, as John 10:35 reveals. To criticize scripture is to criticize him in his estimation of scripture.

But, second, every criticism of scripture is inherently the "breaking" of Jesus, in the language of John 10:35, because scripture both in its entirety and in every part is the revelation of Jesus. The truth of this is shown by John 10:35 in its context. The seemingly obscure and minor text in Psalm 82 about the rulers serves the purpose of substantiating Jesus' claim to be the Son of God: "If he called them gods...and the scripture cannot be broken; say ye of him, whom the Father hath sanctified and sent into the world, Thou blasphemest; because I said, I am the Son of God?" (John 10:35–36). Because all of scripture, particularly the Old Testament, which is the part of the Bible that the critics especially love to devastate by their criticism, testifies of Jesus (5:39), to "break" scripture at any point and regarding any doctrine is to "break" Jesus.

SUFFICIENT

The leading element of scripture's perfection in this article of the Confession is its sufficiency: "These Holy Scriptures fully contain the will of God, and that whatsoever man ought to believe unto salvation is sufficiently taught therein...The doctrine thereof is most perfect and complete in all respects." Perfection is not only that the Bible is infallible, or without error, but also that it is full and complete. As he came forth from the hand of his Creator, Adam was imperfect, not because he was sinful, but because he lacked the woman who would complete his humanity.

Scripture is sufficient for the salvation of the people of God: "whatsoever man ought to believe unto salvation." Scripture contains every doctrine, all of the history, and every precept of the life of the redeemed that the church and her members must believe unto salvation. Nothing is missing that must be added from another source. This truth of the sufficiency of scripture is what the Reformation had in mind when it confessed *sola scriptura*, that is, "scripture alone."

This sufficiency of scripture for salvation does not imply that the preaching of scripture is unnecessary for salvation. Scripture itself reveals that the Spirit exercises the saving power of scripture by means of the sound, lively preaching of the Bible. "Preach the gospel [contained in scripture]" was the mandate of the risen Jesus to the church in Mark 16:15, which mandate was repeated at the ascension of the Lord: "Ye shall be witnesses unto me" (Acts 1:8). As questions 83 and 84 of the Heidelberg Catechism teach, the Reformed faith confesses the "preaching of the holy gospel" to be the main means by which God opens the kingdom of heaven to humans. But it is scripture and its doctrines that are to be preached. By the preaching of the scripture, men believe unto salvation.

An important element of scripture's sufficiency regarding salvation is its sufficiency regarding the worship of the church and of the individual believer: "The whole manner of worship which God requires of us, is written in them at large." The right worship of God is salvation's purpose. Only by the right worship of God does the instituted church realize salvation's purpose. Only in the way of the right worship of God does the believer enjoy his salvation and carry out the purpose of God in saving him, that is, salvation's goal. What constitutes this right worship of God is fully revealed in scripture.

This right worship of God is, first, the elements of the formal worship of God by the congregation on the Lord's day. That the article definitely has public worship in view is evident from what follows in the article concerning "custom...the great multitude" and what follows. Scripture governs the public worship of God by the instituted church. Not only may nothing be introduced into the worship of the church that conflicts with the biblical prescriptions for worship, for example, the lusty singing of lively Arminian hymns instead of the God-glorifying psalms. But nothing may be added to the elements of worship by imaginative worship committees, for example, band concerts and choir performances. Nor may the Reformed church omit from its worship of God at any service anything that scripture requires, for example, the lively preaching of the word.

This Reformed confession's rule of the church's worship by the Word of God is known as the "regulative principle of worship." Scripture governs the church's worship. It does so because it is sufficient to this end. The truth of the regulative principle of worship is the express topic of article 32 of the Confession. A more thorough explanation of the elements of right, public worship is reserved for the treatment of article 32.

It might seem unnecessary to state that this truth about the public worship of the church is binding upon the individual believer. He may not participate in any worship that "add[s] unto or take[s] away anything from the Word of God" concerning public worship, including preaching that either adds to or takes away from the "doctrine" of scripture. But the behavior of many confessing Reformed Christians demonstrates that the statement is necessary. Many enthusiastically engage in public worship that sins against the regulative principle of worship. They suppose that the manner of worship is merely a matter of their own discretion and decision. What they like or find moving governs their conduct in worship. With their church, they add to and subtract from what "God requires of us," as they please. They please themselves in their worship. They do not please God. All their fervor in this will-worship is fervent disobedience to God.

By "the whole manner of worship," the Confession also refers to the content of the faith and the substance of the entire, holy, Christian life of the Reformed believer. This too is the worship of God. All that the Christian must believe unto salvation and all that makes up the saved, Christian life are taught in scripture. To this, none may add. From this, none may take away. "Doctrine" in this article of the Confession ("the doctrine thereof is most perfect and complete in all respects") must be taken broadly in the sense of the teaching of scripture, whether of belief or of behavior.

ROMAN CATHOLIC TRADITION

As would have been unmistakably evident at the time of the writing of the Confession, and as is necessary for Reformed Christians to be reminded of in our ecumenical age, the emphasis of this article on the sufficiency of scripture and its warning against adding to or taking away from scripture are vigorous polemic against Roman Catholic error. Rome denies the sufficiency of scripture. Rome teaches that "tradition" is a necessary source of the knowledge of God that is necessary for salvation and for the right worship of God alongside, and in most cases in contradiction of, scripture.

Rome confessed tradition to be an authority with scripture for "faith [and]...morals" in its creed, "The Canons and Decrees of the Council of Trent." It declared that "saving truth...[is] contained in the written books [scripture], and the unwritten traditions." It added that the Roman Catholic Church "receives and venerates with an equal affection of piety and reverence, [scripture]...as also the said traditions, as well those appertaining to faith as to morals." It then passed its anathema upon those who "knowingly and deliberately contemn the traditions." With scripture, tradition is the "foundation of the Confession of faith [of Rome]...confirming dogmas, and...restoring morals in the Church."[1]

Tradition is the custom of the Roman Catholic Church regarding worship, often of long standing in the history of that church ("antiquity"), which, however, has no basis in scripture. Rome can often find support for its traditions in the "writings" of some of the church fathers, who undoubtedly were "ever so holy." A "great multitude" has embraced these traditions. The Roman, or Romanizing, church has confessed and practiced these traditions over a long "succession of times." The "persons" of notable church leaders have promoted these traditions. In addition, auspicious church "councils" have authoritatively enforced the traditions by their "decrees or statutes."

For all its impressive credentials, tradition lacks one thing, the one essential thing: basis in scripture. On the contrary, Rome's tradition contradicts the word of God. Scripture condemns Rome's tradition. With regard now to doctrine that it is necessary to believe unto salvation and to the behavior that is a necessary aspect of the Christian life, none of these things that make up and buttress tradition, nor all of them together, either overrule scripture

---

1 Canons and Decrees of the Council of Trent, Fourth Session, "Decree concerning the Canonical Scriptures," in ibid., 2:79–82.

or compare with it. The Confession declares that tradition does not "compare" with the scriptures in governing the Christian faith and its worship. The issue is not simply that tradition may not set aside the doctrine of scripture. But the issue is that tradition may not even establish necessary Christian doctrine and behavior, where scripture is silent.

Here we may find in the Confession, as an aspect of scripture's perfection, the teaching of scripture's incomparability. Tradition with all the impressive elements that contribute to it does not compare with scripture, because tradition is the word and work of man, and scripture is the "truth of God." The "truth is above all." In addition, for all its impressive appearance, in the end tradition is the word of men, and "all men are of themselves liars, and more vain than vanity itself."

The best of godly believers are depraved by nature and sinfully weak, so that even their best efforts in theology, concerning the worship of God in doctrine and life, are susceptible to error. Augustine taught justification by faith and works. Luther taught an erroneous doctrine of the sacraments. These were the holiest of men. The church may, and should, use the writings of such holy men in understanding the word of God. But the church may never elevate them to an authoritative position above or alongside the scriptures. Always the church must compare the teachings of her theologians and ministers with scripture, to determine that the teachings are the truth.

If there is any critical activity in the church regarding the teaching and understanding of scripture, it is that the believing congregation critically compares what she is taught with the scripture, to be confident that what she hears is the truth. For this, the saints in Berea are praised:

"These were more noble than those in Thessalonica, in that they...searched the scriptures daily, whether those things [taught by Paul and Silas] were so" (Acts 17:11). Nor may the church stifle this noble activity of the members. The theologians and ministers must understand their glorious task to be opening up the scriptures to the people of God.

By its tradition, the Roman Catholic Church both adds unto the word of God and takes away from the word of God, which is forbidden. The Creed here refers to, and partially quotes, Revelation 22:18–19. Upon those who commit such sacrilege—the Roman Catholic Church— the passage passes the effectual curse of God himself (in contrast to Rome's ineffectual "anathema"): "God shall add unto him the plagues that are written in this book...God shall take away his part out of the book of life, and out of the holy city, and from the things which are written in this book."

Rome adds to the word of God by its doctrine of the mediatorship of Mary, which includes that Mary was immaculately conceived, that she was assumed bodily into heaven at death, and that she must be prayed to and worshiped. Not a word of all this is found in scripture. In addition, the entire doctrine and practice of the papacy are addition to the word of God. None of this doctrine and practice, which are fundamental to the Roman Catholic Church, is revealed in scripture. All has its source in tradition, including the writings of theologians and the decrees of church councils.

Rome takes away from the word of God in virtually every one of its doctrines, denying as it does unconditional election; the sole mediatorship of Jesus; justification by faith alone, without good works; and the right, if not the calling, of the clergy to marry.

The error of adding to the scripture that the Confession could see only dimly in the sect of the Anabaptists characterizes the contemporary movement known as neo-Pentecostalism, or the charismatic movement. By its doctrine of continuing revelation of God's will in extraordinary, extra-scriptural operations of the Holy Ghost, the charismatic movement commits itself to doctrines and practices that "add unto...the Word of God."

The inescapable implication of the charismatic movement is that scripture is *not* "most perfect and complete in all respects." The spirit of the charismatic movement does not work *through* scripture and *on behalf of* scripture—scripture *alone*. Rather, the charismatic movement's spirit works independently of scripture, alongside of scripture, and above scripture. It is not the biblical Spirit. For this reason alone, ignoring the doctrinal heresies, the unregulated worship, the emotional frenzy, and the lack of discipline of the movement, the Reformed faith is not open to the charismatic movement but opposed to it. In obedience to the command of God in 1 John 4:1, which the Confession quotes, that the church try the spirits, whether they are of God, the Reformed believer has tried the spirit of the charismatic movement and has found that it is not "of God."

NECESSITY

Two fundamental elements of scripture's perfection are implied. One is the necessity of scripture. Scripture is necessary for salvation and for the right worship of God. Scripture is sufficient for all that man ought to believe unto salvation and for the whole manner of worship that God requires of us, because God has inspired scripture as the one, necessary means of salvation and of the right worship of God. When the rich man in Jesus' parable asked that Lazarus be sent to his family for their salvation, Abraham replied, "They have Moses and the prophets; let them hear them." When the rich man replied that the testimony of one who was raised from the dead would be more effective, Jesus had Abraham respond, "If they hear not Moses and the prophets [that is, scripture], neither will they be persuaded, though one rose from the dead" (Luke 16:27–31). This conviction of the necessity of scripture was a hallmark of the sixteenth-century Reformation of the church.

That this necessity of scripture is still the conviction of Reformed churches in the twenty-first century may be ascertained from the prominence of the preaching of scripture in their worship services. Where, in some nominally Reformed churches, the preaching of scripture is buried under or even replaced by a host of liturgical antics, there, regardless of a church's name, the Reformed insistence on the perfection and necessity of scripture has been subdued. There article 7 of the Reformed Belgic Confession is denied.

CLARITY

Still another aspect of the perfection of scripture that is implied in article 7 is its clarity. Believers are able to understand scripture and all its "doctrine," as well as its prescription of the "whole manner of worship." If scripture was not clear, clear to the *believer*, its sufficiency unto salvation and its necessity for doctrine and worship, that is, its perfection, would be of no use to the believer. If scripture was not clear, the believer certainly could not judge all teachings by comparison with scripture. The clarity of scripture is, first of all, the property, or perfection, of scripture itself as the divine writing. Scripture is God's letter to his people. God was at pains to write intelligibly. He willed, above all, to be understood. As a father who has an important message for his children will write in a manner that the children will grasp, so God wrote. It would be a reflection on God's fatherhood to allege that he wrote unintelligibly, or in such a dark manner that his children would be dependent upon the interpretation of a few scholars, who, as the Confession states, are "liars, and more vain than vanity itself."

Scripture is clear to the believer, in the second place, because the believer has the Holy Ghost, who inspired the scripture. The Holy Ghost, who ought to know the meaning of what he inspired, enables the believer to understand scripture. The spiritual man has the mind of Christ to enable him to know the things of the Spirit of God as taught in the apostolic words of scripture and to judge all things that have to do with doctrine and worship (1 Cor. 2:10–16). The believer has "an unction from the Holy One," so that he knows all things that scripture teaches. By means of scripture, this anointing teaches the believer all things that scripture contains (1 John 2:20–21, 27). Such is the clarity of the believer's knowledge of scripture that he is able to distinguish the true gospel from every form of the false gospel, and must do so (Gal. 1:8–9).

It is no insignificant aspect of Rome's spiritual enslavement of its millions that it strips the ability to know the scripture from the "laity" and attributes this ability to the clergy alone. Thus Rome denies the clarity of scripture. For Rome, scripture is imperfect, unintelligible to the vast majority of the members of the church. Thus regarding salvation itself and the right worship of God, members of the Roman Catholic Church are completely dependent upon the Roman clergy. Truth is not the doctrine of scripture, but whatever the priest, and ultimately the pope, declares truth to be. There is no slavery more wretched.

AUTHORITATIVE

A final aspect of the perfection of scripture is not so much implied as stated by the Confession: scripture's authority. Article 7 of the Confession calls scripture "this infallible rule." A rule is an authority. A rule that is "infallible" is a perfectly reliable authority. An infallible authority regarding doctrine concerning salvation, holy behavior, and the right worship of the one, true, and living God is an awesome authority. Such is scripture, according to the Reformed confession. No higher regard for scripture is conceivable.

Scripture is "this infallible rule." It is the only standard by which all doctrine and practice are judged: "We reject with all our hearts whatsoever doth not agree with this infallible rule." It determines the truth concerning what the Reformed church and Christian believe. It determines the soundness of the practice of the church and of the believer. Whatever conflicts with scripture, whether a belief or a way of life, is rejected because it conflicts with scripture.

This claim on behalf of scripture, awesome as it is, ought not to strike the Reformed Christian as strange. Scripture is the inspired word of God. As God is the sovereign ruler of his church and of his child, so is his word the authoritative rule of the worship of his church and of the belief and life of his child. Just as an earthly father's authority is acknowledged by his child's submission to the father's word, so God's authority is acknowledged by his child's recognition of and yielding to the authority of his word.

CONTROVERSY

The use of the word "infallible" to describe scripture is controversial today. Many Reformed theologians, whose doctrine of scripture is formed more by the critical, unbelieving scholarship of the day than by the Confession or by the witness of scripture itself to itself, attempt to explain away this confession of scripture's being "infallible." One explains the confessional infallibility as referring only to the main message of the Bible. Another explains it as describing only the outstanding doctrines of the Bible (which they, of course, will identify for the church). Yet another explains that infallibility merely means that the Bible will not fail of its saving purpose.

All deny, and intend to deny, that the scripture itself, in everything it teaches, is without error. All deny, and intend to deny, that the church and the believer can believe all the teachings of the Bible as true doctrine and that the church and the believer must obey all the precepts and prohibitions of the Bible as the truth for holiness of life. All affirm, and intend to affirm, that there are errors in scripture both of doctrine and of conduct. All insist, and intend to insist, that scripture is fallible. To these biblical scholars the creedal "infallible" means "fallible."

All, therefore, are guilty of unfaithfulness to their creed in the fundamental article of scripture's sufficiency (science, or cultural development, or contemporary scholarship, or modern religious opinion is necessary to correct scripture), scripture's clarity (passages judged to be erroneous are obviously not clear), and scripture's authority (some other authority overrules scripture). All are guilty of blatantly contradicting the Confession's declaration that scripture is "infallible." Thus they take issue with the

Confession's statement that "it is unlawful for any one, though an Apostle, to teach otherwise than we are now taught in the holy scriptures." Thus they deny the inspiration of scripture as the word of God. Surely, the inspired Word of God cannot be erroneous and fallible. Thus they cast the church and the believer adrift on the seas of uncertainty, regarding the origin of the world; the origin of humanity; the explanation of sin and death in the world— the historical reality of the fall of Adam; the universal flood; the miracles of the Old Testament; the history of Israel; the virgin birth of Jesus; the nature of the cross as satisfaction of the justice of God; the second coming; the unbreakable bond of marriage; the nature of marriage as the union of a male and a female; and indeed, whatever in scripture offends the scholar or does not meet with the approval of contemporary, godless society.

Whatever else this unbelief concerning scripture as the word of God may be, for a Reformed man it is the rejection of his own confession of faith: "infallible rule." The Belgic Confession describes scripture—not some vague message or some undefined purpose of the book, but scripture itself, in its entirety—as this "infallible rule."

Regarding the content of scripture in its entirety—"the doctrine thereof"—it "is most perfect and complete in all respects." The scriptures in their entirety are "divine," not human, "the truth of God," not at all the lies or errors of men.

Bound by the Confession, the Reformed man rejects with all his heart "whatsoever doth not agree with this infallible rule." He does not reject the "infallible rule" wherever it does not agree with contemporary science, or with the thinking and practice of modern, unbelieving culture, or with the opinion of apostate theologians and churches.

SELF-TESTIMONY

One feature of article 7 on scripture might be overlooked. Woven throughout the article, explicitly but also implicitly, is the witness of scripture to itself. The article is not simply the confession of the Reformed church and believer to the perfection of scripture, but it is scripture's testimony to itself. That it is unlawful for an apostle to teach otherwise than we are taught in scripture is the warning of Galatians 1:8–9. The prohibition against adding to or taking away from scripture is scripture's own warning in Revelation 22:18–19. The praise of the truth "above all" is a theme that resounds throughout scripture. The exhortation to "try the spirits" is the quotation of 1 John 4:1. The Confession appeals to 2 John 10 in support of its demand that the church test all doctrines by scripture.

The article therefore is not, at bottom, the Reformed faith's confession of scripture. It is scripture's testimony to itself. Since scripture is the word of God, the article is God's own testimony concerning his written word. Therefore, whoever opposes article 7's confession of scripture's perfection is, in actual fact, opposing God's own word concerning his word.

Reformed theologians and churches that engage in this rebellion by denying, or even casting doubt on, the perfection of scripture do well to remember that the fall of the human race into sin and death under the severe judgment of God was occasioned by the question, "Yea, hath God said?" (Gen. 3:1).

The one raising the question was the serpent.

Chapter Six

THE TRINITY

(ARTICLES 8 AND 9)

ART. VIII. GOD IS ONE IN ESSENCE, YET DISTINGUISHED IN THREE PERSONS.

According to this truth and this Word of God, we believe in one only God, who is one single essence, in which are three persons, really, truly, and eternally distinct, according to their incommunicable properties; namely, the Father, and the Son, and the Holy Ghost. The Father is the cause, origin, and beginning of all things, visible and invisible; the Son is the Word, Wisdom, and Image of the Father; the Holy Ghost is the eternal Power and Might, proceeding from the Father and the Son. Nevertheless God is not by this distinction divided into three, since the Holy Scriptures teach us that the Father, and the Son, and the Holy Ghost have each his personality, distinguished by their properties; but in such wise that these three persons are but one only God. Hence, then, it is evident that the Father is not the Son, nor the Son the Father, and likewise the Holy Ghost is neither the Father nor the Son. Nevertheless these persons thus distinguished are not divided nor intermixed; for the Father hath not assumed the flesh, nor hath the Holy Ghost, but the Son only. The Father hath never been without his Son, or without his Holy Ghost. For they are all three co-eternal and co-essential. There is neither first nor last; for they are all three one, in truth, in power, in goodness, and in mercy.

ART. IX. THE PROOF OF THE FOREGOING ARTICLE OF THE TRINITY OF PERSONS IN ONE GOD.

All this we know, as well from the testimonies of Holy Writ as from their operations, and chiefly by those we feel in ourselves. The testimonies of the Holy Scriptures, that teach us to believe this Holy Trinity, are written in many places of the Old Testament, which are not so necessary to enumerate as to choose them out with discretion and judgment. In Genesis i. 26, 27, God saith: Let us make man in our image, after our likeness, etc. So God created man in his own image, male and female created he them. And Gen. iii. 22: Behold, the man has become as one of us. From this saying, Let us make man in our image, it appears that there are more persons than one in the Godhead; and when he saith God created, this signifies the unity. It is true he doth not say how many persons there are, but that which appears to us somewhat obscure in the Old Testament is very plain in the New.

For when our Lord was baptized in Jordan, the voice of the Father was heard, saying, This is my beloved Son: the Son was seen in the water; and the Holy Ghost appeared in the shape of a dove. This form is also instituted by Christ in the baptism of all believers. Baptize all nations, in the name of the Father and of the Son, and of the Holy Ghost. In the Gospel of Luke the angel Gabriel thus addressed Mary, the mother of our Lord: The Holy Ghost shall come upon thee, and the power of the Highest shall overshadow thee, therefore also that holy thing which shall be born of thee shall be called the Son of God. Likewise, The grace of our Lord Jesus Christ, and the love of God, and the communion of the Holy Ghost be with you. And There are three that bear record in heaven, the Father, the Word, and the Holy Ghost, and these three are one. In all which places we are fully taught that there are three persons in one only divine essence. And although this doctrine far surpasses all human understanding, nevertheless we now believe it by means of the Word of God, but expect hereafter to enjoy the perfect knowledge and benefit thereof in heaven.

INTRODUCTION

An explanation of the Belgic Confession's treatment of the doctrine of the Trinity may well begin by correcting common mistakes concerning the truth of the Trinity. Many contemporary, nominal Christians suppose that the doctrine of the Trinity is insignificant, so that it is of little or no importance that one is ignorant of it and fails to confess it, or even that a church ignores it or denies it.

In reality, the doctrine of the Trinity is an essential doctrine in the Bible. Upon this truth all other doctrines depend. To lose the doctrine of the Trinity would be to lose Christianity. To deny the doctrine of the Trinity is to reveal oneself as an unbeliever.

A second mistake is the supposition that, even though it may be a biblical truth, the doctrine of the Trinity has no practical importance, no effect upon or benefit to the everyday life of the Christian. On the contrary, the doctrine of the Trinity is intensely practical and full of benefit, not only for our enjoyment, experience, and practice of salvation, but also for our everyday, earthly life as human creatures.

A third mistake is the notion that the doctrine of the Trinity is not prominently revealed in the Bible, but that there are, here and there, merely some faint indications of the doctrine, from which clever theologians constructed the doctrine. The truth about scripture's revelation of the Trinity is that scripture is full of the doctrine. Rightly, the Belgic Confession declares the abundant revelation of the doctrine in the Old Testament, in which the Trinity is less obvious than in the New Testament: "The testimonies of the Holy Scriptures that teach us to believe this Holy Trinity are written in many places of the Old Testament, which are not so necessary to enumerate, as to choose them out with discretion and judgment" (art. 9).

A fourth mistake is common among believers. This is the conviction that it is impossible to understand the doctrine of the Trinity, at least for those who do not have a formal theological education or for those with only an average intelligence. This conviction must be shattered. It is possible for every Christian of normal, but sanctified, intelligence to understand the doctrine of the Trinity. Understanding the doctrine is necessary. It is a fundamental truth of the knowledge of saving faith. In article 9, the Belgic Confession acknowledges that "this doctrine far surpasses all human understanding," but the meaning is that the believer cannot *comprehend* the doctrine, not that he cannot understand it, and understand it rightly and well. In what immediately follows in article 9, the Confession holds before the believer the prospect that he will "enjoy the perfect knowledge" of the doctrine "hereafter...in Heaven." In this life, he has knowledge of the doctrine—sound, right knowledge; in heaven, he will have "perfect knowledge."

The Athanasian Creed, to which reference is made at the end of article 9, concludes its explanation of the doctrine of the Trinity thus: "He therefore that will be saved, must thus *think* of the Trinity."[1] Thinking implies understanding. And understanding the Trinity is an essential element of salvation: "He therefore that will be saved..."

What then must we think of the Trinity?

THREE IN ONE

In the one being (or substance, or essence) who is God are three different and distinct persons. As to his being, God is one: "[the] one only God, who is one single essence" (art. 8). By God's being is meant everything that makes up his Godhead, or deity, and in which he exists, just as the being of a human is everything that makes him who and what he is, everything in which he exists. God's being is his "Godness," just as the being of a human is his humanness.

The being of God is one. This does not mean only that there is no other divine being, no other god, although it does mean this. Again and again in the Old Testament, the one, true God who is confessed in articles 8 and 9 of the Belgic Confession declares that he is God and that there is no other. The oneness of the being of God exposes the worship of other supposed gods as idolatry.

But the oneness of the being of God means also that this being is not divided into parts. This perfection of God

---

1 Athanasian Creed, in Schaff, *Creeds of Christendom*, 2:68.

is called his simplicity (see art. 1 of the Confession). If the being of God were divisible, the possibility would exist of there being two or more gods, as many gods as there were parts of the divine being. This oneness of God warns against any understanding of the threeness of God as the division of the being of God into three, equal parts. The threeness of the Trinity does not divide the one being: "God is not by this distinction [of three persons] divided into three" (art. 8).

So repeated and prominent in scripture is the testimony that God is one, and so uncontroversial is the truth of the oneness of God, that the Confession scarcely takes the trouble to prove it with biblical quotations. The sole biblical reference is Genesis 1:27: "God created man in his own image." According to the Confession, when the text says "*God created*, this signifies the unity [of being of the Godhead]."

Nevertheless, there are in scripture explicit, strong affirmations that God is one in being. Deuteronomy 6:4 exhorts, "Hear, O Israel: The LORD our God is one LORD." Likewise, the New Testament proclaims the oneness of God with special application to the exposure of the idols as nothings: "We know that an idol is nothing in the world, and that there is none other God but one. For though there be that are called gods, whether in heaven or in earth, (as there be gods many, and lords many,) But to us there is but one God, the Father, of whom are all things and we in him" (1 Cor. 8:4–6). Even though the emphasis in these passages may be on the truth that there is one God, not many gods, basic to this truth is that the being of God is one and indivisible, for if the being of God is divided into parts, there is not one Lord and God, but as many as there are parts of the divine being.

The jealous defense everywhere in scripture of the oneness of God makes it most remarkable that this same scripture, without any criticism, records the claim by Jesus to be God. God himself, who is jealous of his exclusive Godhead, not only does not condemn Jesus for claiming to be God, but also honors Jesus as his beloved Son. Evidently, Jesus is God with the Father without dividing the Godhead.

As to his persons, God is three. By person is meant an individual; a thinking, willing subject; someone who says "I" in relationship to another who is a "thou" to this "I." In the one God are three individuals; three thinking, willing Subjects; three who say "I" in relationship to the other two "thous."

These three persons are distinct from each other. They are different personalities. They are not one and the same person. The Confession is as clear and strong on the threeness as it is on the oneness: "three persons, really, truly, and eternally distinct"; "The Father is not the Son, nor the Son the Father, and likewise the Holy Ghost is neither the Father nor the Son. These persons thus distinguished are not...intermixed; for the Father hath not assumed the flesh, nor hath the Holy Ghost, but the Son only" (art. 8).

The real difference of the persons from each other, their distinction, is expressed by their names, and their names make known their unique personal properties within the Godhead. The Confession locates the real distinction of the three persons in their "incommunicable properties" (art. 8). The property of the Father, which is expressed by his name, is that he is the eternal origin of the other two persons. The Father begets the Son and breathes forth the Holy Ghost. The property of the Son, which is expressed by his name, is that he is begotten of the Father. Thus he is the image of the Father. The property of the Holy Ghost, which is expressed by his name, is that he is breathed forth from the Father to the Son and from the Son to the Father.

Regarding the Holy Ghost, or Spirit, both "Ghost" and "Spirit" mean "Breath." The Holy Ghost is the Holy Breath of the Father proceeding to the Son and proceeding from the Son to the Father. Jesus identified the property of the Holy Ghost as his procession in the sense of being breathed forth as the divine Breath in John 15:26: "But when the Comforter is come, whom I will send unto you from the Father, even the Spirit of truth, which proceedeth from the Father, he shall testify of me." As the Breath of God, the Holy Ghost is the "eternal Power and Might" of the God-head. Fittingly, the sign of the outpouring of the Spirit on Pentecost was the sound "as of a rushing mighty wind" (Acts 2:2). The Breath of God is a tornadic wind.

John 15:26 instructs us to view Pentecost, to which the Lord refers when he speaks of his sending of the Holy Ghost to the church, as Jesus' breathing forth the Spirit to the church. There is a breathing of the Holy Ghost by God upon Jesus so that Jesus can breathe the Holy Ghost upon the church. The preview of the Pentecostal breathing forth of the Spirit upon the church was the incident recorded in John 20:22: "He [the risen Jesus] breathed on them, and saith unto them, Receive ye the Holy Ghost."

Whether the breathing of the Spirit from the Father to the Son and from the Son to the Father in the eternal trinitarian economy, or the breathing of the Spirit from the one God upon Jesus at his baptism, or the breathing of the Spirit from Jesus upon his church at Pentecost, always the proceeding, or breathing, of the Spirit is the breathing of ardent love. As the love of the Father for the Son and of the

Son for the Father does the Holy Ghost proceed from the one to the other in the eternal being of God. As the love of God for the man Jesus did the Holy Ghost proceed from God upon Jesus at his baptism. As the love of Jesus for the church did the Holy Ghost proceed from the risen Jesus upon the church at Pentecost.

Concerning the property of the Holy Ghost, the Confession describes it as his "proceeding from the Father *and the Son*" (art. 8). The phrase "and the Son" is controversial. It occasioned the first great schism in the church of the new dispensation. In AD 1054 the church split over the issue whether the Holy Ghost proceeds from the Father and from the Son or only from the Father. The controversy came to be known as the *filioque* controversy, the word being Latin for "and the Son," with reference to the procession of the Holy Ghost. That faction of the church that denied, and still today denies, that the Spirit proceeds from the Son as well as from the Father is the Orthodox Church. As article 8 of the Belgic Confession makes plain, the Reformed churches maintain the confession of the church that in 1054 affirmed that the Spirit proceeds also from the Son.

Admittedly, there is no explicit teaching in scripture that the Spirit proceeds also from the Son in the being of God. The biblical evidence of the procession from the Son is the teaching that on Pentecost it was Jesus who sent the Spirit upon the church by breathing him forth (see John 15:26; 20:22). The convincing argument is that the historical breathing, or procession, of the Spirit from the Son must have its source in the eternal procession of the Spirit from the Son to the Father.

Nor is the controversy of the Reformed church with

Orthodoxy without its practical implications. In its worship and preaching, Orthodoxy separates the Spirit and his work from Jesus the Son and his salvation. Orthodoxy is mystical. It does not do justice to the truth of the Spirit expressed by Jesus: "When the Comforter is come...even the Spirit of truth...he shall *testify of me*" (15:26; emphasis added). Denying as it does that the Holy Ghost eternally proceeds from the Son in the being of God, Orthodoxy does not identify the Spirit of Pentecost as the Spirit of Christ, the Son of God. Proceeding as he does from the Son, the mission of the Spirit of Pentecost is strictly to reveal Jesus the Son and to apply his salvation to his people.

"Holy" in the name of the Holy Ghost expresses that in the Godhead, eternally, the Holy Ghost is the Fellowship between the Father and the Son, uniting them in the familial bond of love. In the Holy Ghost, the Son "is in the bosom of the Father" (1:18). "Holy" in the name of the Holy Ghost has the sense of "consecrating," which is the basic meaning of "holy" and "holiness" in scripture. The Holy Ghost is the consecration of the Father to the Son and of the Son to the Father, such a consecration of the one to the other as to be their intimate communion in love. Accordingly, the Pentecostal Spirit accomplishes the fellowship of God with his elect people and of them with God. Indeed, the Holy Ghost *is* this communion in love.

Important to note is that the begetting of the Son and the procession of the Holy Ghost in the being of God are eternal so that the Father is never without the Son and the Father and Son are never without the Holy Ghost.

Nevertheless, begetting and proceeding imply a certain order among the divine persons. The order is not temporal. Neither is it an order of rank. The Belgic Confession warns against these misunderstandings: "They are all three co-eternal and co-essential. There is neither first nor last; for they are all three one, in truth, in power, in goodness, and in mercy" (art. 8). One could add here what the Confession declares earlier in the article: all three persons are one in "essence," or being: "one single essence, in which are three persons."

But the order is the unique order of trinitarian life: first eternal, divine person; second eternal, divine person; third eternal, divine person. The order derives from the personal properties. The first person is the one begetting the second person and effecting procession of the third person; the second person is the one begotten of the first person and effecting the procession of the third person; the third is the one proceeding from the first person and from the second person.

In a family, there must be order. God, who is the original, heavenly Family, is a God of order.

Since each of the three persons shares and possesses the full, undivided being of God, each is God, the one, true God. The Father is God, the Son is God, and the Holy Ghost is God. "These three persons are but one only God" (art. 8). Since the perfections of God belong to the divine being, all three persons possess the perfections of the Godhead. All are eternal; all are immutable; and so on. It is therefore sin against the Trinity himself, as well as sin against the gospel of grace, that some teach that, whereas the Father is almighty, the Son powerlessly fails to accomplish the salvation of all for whom he died and that the Spirit cannot effectually preserve to the end all in whom he commences the work of salvation.

The Trinity, then, in summary, is this: "three persons in one only divine essence" (art. 9).

How does the church know this? Why has the Christian church always confessed this? On what basis does the Reformed church confess this doctrine in article 8 of her Belgic Confession?

THE BIBLICAL REVELATION

The sole source and basis of belief and confession of the truth of the Trinity is scripture. That scripture is the basis of the belief of the Trinity as described in articles 8 and 9 is the confession of the opening words of article 8: "According to this truth and this Word of God, we believe in one only God, who is one single essence, in which are three persons." This is also the testimony of article 9, which provides the proof of the doctrine of the Trinity from scripture: "All this we know...from the testimonies of Holy Writ...The testimonies of the holy scriptures, that teach us to believe this holy Trinity, are written in many places of the Old Testament...We now believe it [the doctrine of the Trinity] by means of the Word of God."

The basis of the Reformed believer's belief of the Trinity is not evidence in creation, for example, various sets of three, admittedly striking as these are. Even the way in which the believer perceives and experiences the Trinity is biblically based and informed. To this experience of the Trinity, the Confession refers in article 9: "their operations, and chiefly by those we feel in ourselves...We must observe the particular offices and operations of these three persons towards us."

The central, compelling revelation of the Trinity in scripture is Jesus the Christ. The doctrine of the Trinity is decided by the answer that the Bible requires us to make to the question, "Who is Jesus?" In Jesus, we are confronted by one who is both personally distinct from God the Father and himself the true God. Both the oneness of Jesus and the Father (in being) and the personal distinction of Jesus from the Father, Jesus himself taught in John 10:30: "I and my Father are one." There is personal distinction: "I and my Father are." There is oneness of being: "are one."

It is significant that the New Testament church arrived at its settled, developed doctrine of the Trinity exactly in the way of confronting the question, "Who is Jesus?" This was true of the confession of the Trinity by the Council of Nicea (AD 325). The Nicene Creed is one of three early confessions that Reformed churches "willingly receive" in the "point" of the Trinity, according to article 9 of the Belgic Confession.

The fundamental element of the ecumenical creed is its description of Jesus as "the same essence (substance or being) with the Father (Greek: *homoousios*)." By this word, which confesses that Jesus is God, the Council of Nicea established the truth concerning Jesus and the Trinity over against the heretic Arius, who taught that Jesus merely was *like* God (Greek: *homoiousios*), and therefore not God, but a mere creature. The difference between truth and heresy, orthodoxy and heterodoxy, the gospel of salvation and the false gospel shutting all humans up to damnation was the little, Greek letter "*i*." Nicea taught the deity of Jesus and thus the doctrine of the Trinity also by the pregnant phrases, "only-begotten Son of God, begotten of the Father before all worlds"; "very God of very God"; "begotten, not made"; "by whom all things were made"; "came down from heaven, and was incarnate by the Holy Ghost...and was made man."[2]

---

2 Nicene Creed, in Schaff, *Creeds of Christendom*, 2:58–59.

Similar to the Arian heresy in our day is the message of the cult of the Jehovah's (False) Witnesses. Although this cult is not mentioned by the Confession in its list of heretics who deny the Trinity, nor could be since it arose after the writing of the Confession, the heresy of the Witnesses is essentially the same as those that are referred to by the Confession. The heretical message of this sect is that Jesus was merely a "god" (with a small *g*), by which is meant that Jesus was merely a man, although the highest and best, who very much resembled God. Accordingly, God is one person. Denying that Jesus is God, the cult denies the doctrine of the Trinity. For the Reformed believer who is confronted by a member of the cult, it is the part of wisdom to ignore the memorized lines by which the cultist is taught cleverly to approach his intended victim and to strike bluntly to the heart of the Witness's gospel-denying, false doctrine: "You deny that Jesus is God and therefore are outside the Christian church, testifying a false gospel, and under the wrath of God. In obedience to the command of 2 John 10, I do not receive you into my house."

Fleshing out the revelation of the Trinity in Jesus Christ are a number of passages of scripture, in article 9 of the Confession, that clearly make known God as one being and a number of persons. Among "many places of the Old Testament," article 9 chooses two that teach that God is "unity" (of being) and "more persons than one." They are Genesis 1:26–27 and Genesis 3:22. Both passages teach the oneness of God's being in that it is the one God who speaks: "God [singular] said." Both passages also indicate that this one God is also a plurality (of persons): "our [plural] image," "our likeness," and "one of us [plural]."

The New Testament teaches the same with the difference

that the New Testament makes plain that the plurality of persons is three in number: "that, which appears to us somewhat obscure in the Old Testament [concerning the number of persons] is very plain in the New" (art. 9). Three persons in the Godhead are present at the baptism of Jesus in Matthew 3:16–17. The Son is baptized; the Father says about Jesus, "This is my beloved Son"; and the Holy Ghost appears as a dove. One being in three persons is the clear revelation of the baptism formula: one is baptized into the one name of the three whose name it is: Father, Son, and Holy Ghost (28:19). Three divine persons are present in the wonder of the incarnation, according to the annunciation in Luke 1:35: the "Highest"; the "Son of God"; and the "Holy Ghost." Likewise, the benediction of 2 Corinthians 13:14, surely the blessing that comes from the one, true God, identifies him as three and attributes distinctive blessings to the three: "The grace of our Lord Jesus Christ, and the love of God, and the communion of the Holy Ghost be with you all. Amen."

The last New Testament passage adduced by the Confession in support of the Trinity is also the most complete and clear and therefore the most conclusive: "There are three that bear record in heaven, the Father, the Word, and the Holy Ghost, and these three are one" (1 John 5:7). Contemporary ministers and theologians are hesitant to appeal to this text, because its authenticity is challenged by scholars of the text of the New Testament. Whatever one may judge concerning the textual issue, the text certainly fits in the immediate context. If the text is omitted from the chapter, the doctrine of the Trinity is clearly taught in the rest of the chapter. There is repeated mention of the Son of God, which implies God the Father. Verses 6 and 8 speak of the Spirit as the one who bears witness to Jesus as the Son of

God and eternal life in him. Inasmuch as the deity of Jesus decides the truth of the Trinity, verse 20, which declares of Jesus Christ that he is "the true God, and eternal life," is yet conclusive revelation of the Trinity, regardless of the questioning of verse 7.

In all these passages, especially of the New Testament, "we are fully taught, that there are three persons in one only divine essence" (art. 9).

Intriguing is article 9's appeal in evidence of the Trinity to the believer's experience of the three persons: "All this we know, as well from the testimonies of holy writ *as from their operations, and chiefly by those we feel in ourselves.*" To these operations that are experienced by the believer, the Confession returns toward the end of article 9: "We must observe the particular offices and operations of these three persons towards us." The thought is not that the believer's experience of the works of the three persons is a proof of the Trinity with the testimony of scripture. But the testimony of scripture to the three persons of the one God is borne out by the believer's experience.

Salvation is the work of the one God. The one God accomplishes this salvation in such a way that, although all the work is the accomplishment of the one God, each person has his own characteristic role. The Father creates, which includes election of the sinner, by his power, which includes authority. The Son redeems by his blood. The Holy Ghost sanctifies by his dwelling in our hearts. Thus the reality of the three persons is verified by the divine works, or operations, of God.

Therefore, so far is it from being true that the doctrine of the Trinity is virtually unknowable to the believer and that the truth of it is of no practical value to him that, in reality, it is a matter of the believer's daily experience. The knowledge of the doctrine of the Trinity is experiential.

"This doctrine of the Holy Trinity hath always been defended and maintained by the true Church, since the times of the Apostles to this very day" (art. 9). That the apostolic church confessed the doctrine of the Trinity has been demonstrated from the texts of New Testament scripture adduced by the Confession. That the church after the apostles always confessed the Trinity is proved by three post-apostolic, ecumenical creeds: Nicene (AD 325); Apostles' (c. AD 500); and Athanasian (c. AD 800). The "ancient fathers" whose doctrine concerning the Trinity is approved by article 9 of the Confession include especially Tertullian, Athanasius, and Augustine.

By the favorable mention of these early creeds and church fathers, the Reformed faith shows its oneness with the church of the past, indeed, that the Reformed churches are the continuation of the early post-apostolic church. The church of the present time is one with the church of the past, not by a succession of officebearers, or even of organization, but by a succession of sound doctrine, a succession of the truth. Genuine, Christian tradition is the handing over from the past to the present and from the present to the future of sound doctrine, of the truth of the gospel.

It is a mark of the Reformed faith that, like the Christian faith of which it is the pure exponent, it not only confesses the truth, but also exposes and condemns the lie that is opposed to the truth. This is highly unpopular with nominally Reformed churches at the present time. But it is part of the authoritative confessions of all Reformed churches. Such is true of the Belgic Confession's treatment of the doctrine of the Trinity. After it has finished explaining the doctrine positively, it names and condemns religions and individuals who deny the Trinity.

In contrast with and opposition to the "true Church," that defends and maintains the Trinity, are two false religions: the "Jews [and] Mohammedans." Denying that Jesus is God, both deny the Trinity. For the Jews, or Judaism, God is one person, Jehovah or Yahweh. Inasmuch as their Yahweh is not the eternal Father of Jesus Christ, so that Jesus is not the eternal Son come in the flesh, the god of the Jews is an idol. It is not the Jehovah of the Old Testament. The Jews' religion, therefore, is a false religion and hostile to the Christian religion. The hostility of the Jews toward Christianity is evident throughout the New Testament, especially in the book of Acts. Paul wrote of this hostility: "the Jews, who both killed the Lord Jesus, and their own prophets, and have persecuted us; and they please not God, and are contrary to all men: forbidding us to speak to the Gentiles that they might be saved, to fill up their sins always: for the wrath is come upon them to the uttermost" (1 Thess. 2:14–16).

The Mohammedans, or the religion of Islam, also deny that Jesus is God. Therefore, they also deny the Trinity. The idol-god of the Mohammedans is also a god of one person, Allah. The hatred of Islam for Christianity is writ large on the pages of church history. The hordes of Islam swept through especially North Africa, where the early Christian church was flourishing, killing the members of the church who would not convert to Mohammedanism and thus zealously exterminating the church as a company of infidels. In doing so, they carried out the commands of Allah as found in Islam's holy book, the Koran. That the attitude of that false religion toward Christianity has not changed in our day is evident from the holy war that Islam is carrying out against what it regards as the "Christian West." Western civilization needs a contemporary Charles Martel.[3]

The Confession also names and condemns "some false Christians and heretics." Marcion (second century) taught that there are two gods, one of the Old Testament, the other of the New Testament. Jesus was supposed to have been the appearance of the New Testament god, who is one in person.

Manes, or Mani (216–c. 276), was the father of Manichaeism, which posited such a dualism between God and the devil as amounted to polytheism, that is, the doctrine of two gods, a good god and an evil god. Nevertheless, the good god of Manes was one person.

Praxeas (flourished c. 200), who was born late in the second century AD, taught that God is one person, the Father. Jesus was this Father in human form. Therefore, this heresy came to be known as "Patripassianism," that is, the suffering (including the death) of the Father.

Sabellius (flourished in the early third century) was a heretical teacher in the early church who taught that God is one person. Father, Son, and Holy Ghost are three modes in which this one person appears at various times for different works. Therefore, the teaching of this heretic came to be known as "modalism." This false doctrine seriously troubled the church for some time. The Belgic Confession guards against the error of this doctrine when it confesses that the

---

3 Charles Martel (the "Hammer") was the Frankish ruler who defeated the invading army of Islam in AD 732 in the Battle of Tours. Thus he saved not only France, but also all of Europe from not only the rule, but also the false religion of Islam. The historian Edward Gibbon called Martel the savior of Christendom.

three persons are "really, truly and eternally distinct, according to their incommunicable properties" (art. 8).

Samosatenus (third century), bishop of Antioch from AD 260 to 272, and therefore occupying a strategic position in the early church, taught that the Word and the Spirit of the New Testament are impersonal powers. Therefore, God is one person. The man Jesus, however, became divine by being increasingly filled with God. Thus the heretic grudgingly bowed in his own heretical way to the powerful testimony of the New Testament that Jesus is God.

Arius (256–c. 336) was the arch-heretic refuted and condemned by the Council of Nicea (AD 325). Arius taught that Jesus was only a creature, who nevertheless by his matchless qualities was like God (*homoiousios*, rather than *homoousios*). For Arius too God is one person.

What all these false religions and heretics have in common is their denial of the truth that is fundamental to the doctrine of the Trinity, as it is also fundamental to the gospel of salvation, namely, the truth that Jesus is God.

By its condemnation of the anti-trinitarian heretics and heresies, the Reformed faith shows itself to be one with the early, post-apostolic, Christian church. At the beginning of its confession of the doctrine of the Trinity, the Athanasian Creed, one of the three creeds appealed to by article 9 of the Belgic Confession, utters this warning against those who deny the Christian faith concerning the Trinity: "Which Faith except every one do keep whole and undefiled: without doubt he shall perish everlasting." At the conclusion of its treatment of the Trinity, the same creed admonishes: "He therefore that will be saved, must thus think of the Trinity." Lest anyone yet has failed to hear and heed the warnings, the ecumenical creed ends its confession of the

Trinity and of the incarnation, which is fundamental to the truth of the Trinity, thus: "This is the Catholic Faith: which except a man believe faithfully, he can not be saved."[4] All who deny the Trinity, invariably by denying that Jesus is the eternal Son of God in human flesh, are damned.

The Confession's condemnation of the false religions of Judaism and Mohammedanism and of the anti-trinitarian heretics applies to all the modern forms of denial of the Trinity. These include all the cults, of which the Jehovah's (False) Witnesses are only one example. Such is the development of apostasy in our day that Unitarianism, that is, the denial of the Trinity, is widespread in many nominally Protestant churches both in the United States and in Europe. Every sizable city has its prominent representative of this liberal, usually culturally prominent ecclesiastical institution. In Grand Rapids, Michigan, it is Fountain Street Church. Upon the members of these false churches falls the condemnation of the Athanasian Creed: "He can not be saved."

The significance of the doctrine of the Trinity is huge. Some of this significance articles 8 and 9 state. Some of this significance the articles hint at. Some of this significance has become clear to the Reformed churches of later times.

First, the doctrine of the Trinity distinguishes the true God from all other gods. Article 8 of the Confession picks up the confession of God in article 1 and fills out this confession: the one, only God of article 1 is the "one single essence, in which are three persons." The confession of the Trinity therefore safeguards the true church from syncretism and from false ecumenicity. The test by which all idols

---

4 Athanasian Creed, in Schaff, *Creeds of Christendom*, 2:66–70.

and all false churches can be detected is the question: "Is Jesus God?" (1 John 4:1–3).

Second, the doctrine of the Trinity is the foundation of salvation. Only if God is triune is Jesus God, and only if Jesus is God can he redeem. No mere creature could sustain the wrath of God against sin and offer the acceptable sacrifice that atoned for sin. Only if God is triune is the Holy Ghost God, and only if the Holy Ghost is God can he regenerate, sanctify, and raise from the dead those whom the Father elected and whom Jesus redeemed. Zeal on behalf of the Nicene Creed's confession of the deity of Jesus must not overlook the Creed's confession also of the deity of the Holy Ghost: "the Lord and Giver of Life; who proceedeth from the Father and the Son; who with the Father and the Son together is worshiped and glorified."[5]

In sum, the awesome significance of the Trinity is that if God is not Trinity, there is no salvation of sinners from sin, death, and hell and unto holiness, eternal life, and heaven.

Third, the truth of the Trinity is the explanation of the creation and of earthly life, especially of the earthly life of humans. It is notable that the Trinity of God is revealed first in the account of creation in Genesis 1:16: "Let *us* make man in *our* image" (emphasis added). As triune, the eternal God is the God of fellowship within himself. His life is fellowship: Father and Son love each other, speak to each other (the Son is the Word of the Father, John 1:1–18), and enjoy each other's friendship in the Holy Ghost. God is the holy, divine Family. The personal Wisdom of God is always by God the Father, "as one brought up with him: and...was daily his delight, rejoicing always before him" (Prov. 8:30).

---

5 Nicene Creed, in Schaff, *Creeds of Christendom*, 2:59.

The Son who became flesh in Jesus is everlastingly "in the bosom of the Father" (John 1:18). Such is the intimacy of the fellowship of the Father and the Son, who is Jesus, personally, that the Father is in the Son and the Son is in the Father in the Love who is the Holy Ghost. This fellowship of love was "before the foundation of the world," that is, eternally (17:13–26). God is not the lonely, unloved, and unloving individual of all non-trinitarian religions and heresies.

God did not create the world, therefore, so that he could have fellowship. But he created the world so that he could reveal his own fellowship and share it, in a manner appropriate to creatures, with beings other than himself. Only because God is triune is there a creation. A god of one person could not have thought of a creation in distinction from himself. If a god of one person did conceive of a world alongside himself, and will it, the reason would have been the relief of his loneliness. Such a need would have been the contradiction of his self-sufficiency and independency, that is, of Godhead.

Basic to all earthly life is fellowship. This applies even to the animal world. Adam became aware of his unsatisfactory aloneness by observing that the animals were paired up (Gen. 2:20). But the necessity of fellowship for earthly life applies especially to humans. The rule is the fellowship of marriage (1:26–27; 2:18–25). The fundamental institution for human life is the family. Friendship and association are not only important for humans, but necessary. There are cities and nations; societies and leagues; even gangs. Human experience verifies that it is "not good that the man should be alone" (2:18).

Fellowship is fundamental to human life because God

created it so. And God created it so because he himself is the God of fellowship—the triune God.

A fourth aspect of the significance of the Trinity is that the Trinity is the divine source of the covenant of grace between God and his people in Jesus Christ. The covenant of grace, so prominent and important in scripture, is fellowship—rich, delightful, lively, and life-giving fellowship between God and the elect. The covenant formula makes this plain: I will be your God, and you shall be my people (Gen. 17:7; Jer. 31:33; Heb. 8:10). The earthly symbols or pictures of the covenant are relationships of love: parent/child and marriage.

The origin of the covenant is the very life of God himself, not his decree but his divine life as triune. In the covenant, he opens up his life to us, to share it, as though a Reformed family would take into their blissful life a miserable, lonely, doomed waif. The Holy Ghost who binds Father and Son eternally now binds the elect, believing sinner to God in Jesus Christ.

The significance of the Trinity for the elect church is the most blessed and blissful life: communion with God in the covenant of grace. This too "we feel in ourselves."

Chapter Seven

THE GODHEAD OF THE SON AND OF THE HOLY GHOST

(ARTICLES 10 AND 11)

ART. X. JESUS CHRIST IS TRUE AND ETERNAL GOD.

We believe that Jesus Christ, according to his divine nature, is the only begotten Son of God, begotten from eternity, not made nor created (for then he would be a creature), but co-essential and co-eternal with the Father, the express image of his person, and the brightness of his glory, equal unto him in all things. Who is the Son of God, not only from the time that he assumed our nature, but from all eternity, as these testimonies, when compared together, teach us. Moses saith that God created the world; and John saith that all things were made by that Word, which he calleth God; and the Apostle saith that God made the worlds by his Son; likewise, that God created all things by Jesus Christ. Therefore it must needs follow that he—who is called God, the Word, the Son, and Jesus Christ—did exist at that time when all things were created by him. Therefore the Prophet

*Micah saith: His goings forth have been from of old, from
everlasting. And the Apostle: He hath neither beginning of
days nor end of life. He therefore is that true, eternal, and
almighty God, whom we invoke, worship, and serve.*

ART. XI. THE HOLY GHOST IS TRUE AND ETERNAL GOD.

*We believe and confess also that the Holy Ghost from eter-
nity proceeds from the Father and Son; and therefore is
neither made, created, nor begotten, but only proceedeth
from both; who in order is the third person of the Holy Trinity; of one and the same essence, majesty, and glory with
the Father and the Son; and therefore is the true and eternal God, as the Holy Scripture teaches us.*

INTRODUCTION

Obviously, articles 10 and 11 of the Confession are related
to the preceding articles on the Trinity. Article 10 confesses
the Godhead of Jesus Christ. Article 11 confesses the Godhead of the Holy Ghost. The relation is that what came up
in articles 8 and 9 only as aspects of the truth of the Trinity now receive distinct, separate attention. The truth of
the Trinity implies that the Son is God and that the Spirit
is God. Indeed, the truth of the Trinity is arrived at by dis-
covering in the Bible that Jesus Christ is God and that the
Holy Ghost is God. In articles 10 and 11, the implications of
the Trinity are expressed regarding the Son and the Spirit.
Therefore, the articles examine more closely the personal
properties in God of the Son ("begotten") and of the Holy
Ghost ("proceeds").

There is no separate article on, or examination of the
property of, the Father. What was said earlier about the

Father is deemed sufficient. In addition, there is no controversy about the Father's being God.

Articles 10 and 11 are related to the preceding articles in yet another way. Articles 10 and 11 treat of the Trinity of revelation, or economic Trinity, whereas the preceding articles had in view the ontological Trinity. What is meant by this theological distinction is that the ontological Trinity is the triune God as he is in himself in eternity: Father, Son, and Holy Ghost. The Trinity of revelation is not a different Trinity, but the Trinity as God reveals himself to us in time, specifically, in the work of salvation: the Father, Jesus Christ, and the Spirit of Jesus Christ. Article 8 speaks only of Son and Holy Ghost, referring to the being of God as God is in himself in eternity. Article 10, in contrast, begins, "We believe that Jesus Christ, according to his divine nature, is the only begotten Son of God." These words introduce the Trinity of revelation. Likewise, the Holy Ghost of article 11 must be understood not simply as the Holy Ghost as he is eternally in God, but as the Holy Ghost who is given to the exalted Jesus Christ, who is given by Jesus Christ to the church on Pentecost, and who dwells in the church and in each living member of the church.

ARTICLE 10 ON THE GODHEAD, OR DEITY, OF JESUS CHRIST

What is so prominent in article 10's confession of the Godhead of Jesus that it can easily be overlooked is that the article is filled with biblical proof of this truth. Indeed, the article closely approximates being one extended quotation and paraphrase of scriptural testimony to the truth that Jesus is God. Leaving aside here the identification of Jesus as the "only begotten Son," found in John's gospel and epistles, one does well to take note of this extensive and significant biblical basis of the confession by the Reformed faith of the Godhead of Jesus and therefore of the doctrine of the Trinity.

That Jesus is "the express image of his [God's] person, and the brightness of his glory" is a quotation of Hebrews 1:3. Even though Luther's translation of the phrase "the express image of his person" can be criticized, as Calvin did indeed criticize it in his commentary on the passage, Luther caught the meaning of the text, as he invariably did. Luther's Bible renders the phrase in German as "*dass Eben-bild seines Wesens.*" The translation is: "the express image of his *being*" (or *essence*, emphasis added). Calvin criticized the translation of the word that the Authorized Version renders "person" as "being" or "essence": "for it would be strange to say that the essence of God is impressed on Christ, as the essence of both is simply the same." Nevertheless, Luther captured the profound sense of the phrase: Jesus Christ the Son shares the very being of God the Father. For all his criticism of the translation, Calvin himself comments on the phrase, "The Apostle indeed says...that the substance of the Father is in a manner engraven on the Son."[1] "Substance," or being, not "person."

"Equal with God [the Father]" quotes John 5:18. Naming Jesus "the Son of God," which, the Confession affirms, describes Jesus "not only from the time that he assumed our nature, but from all eternity," is done by scripture in Mark 1:1; Romans 1:3–4; and many other passages.

The gospel of John states in John 1:1–3 that all things were made by that Word whom John identifies as Jesus and "which

---

1 John Calvin, *Commentaries on the Epistle to the Hebrews,* trans. John Owen (Grand Rapids, MI: Eerdmans, 1949), 36–37.

he calleth God." The revelation of the Godhead of Jesus in this passage is especially clear and powerful. First, the Word who became flesh as Jesus Christ is called God: "the Word was God" (v. 1). Second, whereas Moses in Genesis 1 teaches that *God* created the world, John teaches that the Word, who is Jesus, made all things (v. 3). Jesus therefore is God. Third, because only God *can* create—creation being exclusively a divine act—if Jesus created all things in the beginning, as John says he did, Jesus must be the Creator-God.

The truth that he who is Jesus created all things is reiterated in Hebrews 1:2 by the statement that God made the worlds by his Son and in Colossians 1:16 by the doctrine that God created all things by Jesus Christ.

The implication of the truth that all things were made by him who is Jesus Christ is that Jesus existed prior to his birth as a human, that is, he is, as to his person, the eternal God. This implication, the Confession makes explicit when it continues its thoroughly biblical proclamation of the Godhead of Jesus: "Therefore it must needs follow that he—who is called God, the Word, the Son, and Jesus Christ—did exist at that time when all things were created by him." Micah 5:2 declares the eternity of him who comes forth to God from Bethlehem Ephratah to be ruler of God's people, that is, Jesus the Messiah: "[His] goings forth have been from of old, from everlasting." In Hebrews 7:3, the apostle finds in Jesus the reality of what was only typically true of the priest Melchizedek, namely, that "[He] hath neither beginning of days nor end of life."

Upon all of this abundant and perfectly clear revelation of holy scripture rest the belief and confession of the Godhead of Jesus by the Reformed church and believer, with the consequent worship and service: "He [Jesus] therefore is that true, eternal, and almighty God, whom we invoke, worship, and serve."

ON THE GODHEAD OF THE HOLY GHOST

The Confession does not offer similar biblical proof for the Godhead of the Holy Ghost. It merely asserts at the conclusion of its affirmation of the eternality, procession, and divine being of the Holy Ghost that he "is the true and eternal God, as the Holy Scripture teaches us." No doubt, the failure of the Confession to mention or quote specific biblical texts that teach the deity of the Holy Ghost, as it did regarding Jesus, is explained by the decisive nature of the Godhead of Jesus also regarding the Godhead of the Holy Ghost. Even the adversaries of the Godhead of the Holy Ghost grant that if Jesus is God, according to holy scripture, the Holy Ghost is also God. The controversy concerning the Godhead of the second and third persons of the holy Trinity centers on the Godhead of the Son, Jesus. Nevertheless, it is true as article 11 of the Confession states, that "Holy Scripture teaches us [the Godhead of the Holy Ghost]," so that the belief and confession of the Reformed church and believer in article 11 concerning the Holy Ghost are biblically based.

The Spirit was involved in the divine work of creation in the beginning, according to Genesis 1:2: "And the Spirit of God moved upon the face of the waters." Inasmuch as the Spirit is the personal Breath of God, Genesis 2:7 ascribes to the Spirit the creation of man: "The LORD God...breathed into his [Adam's] nostrils the breath of life; and man became a living soul." Accordingly, Psalm 33:6 ascribes the creation of the heavens and their starry hosts to the Spirit: "By the word of the LORD were the heavens made; and all the host of them by the breath of his mouth."

To the Spirit, as the Spirit of Jesus Christ, is ascribed the divine work of salvation. "When he, the Spirit of truth, is come, he will guide you into all truth…and he will shew you things to come" (John 16:13). This is the Spirit about whom Jesus has said in verse 7, "I will send him unto you." The reference therefore is to the Holy Spirit as the one whom the Father has given to the exalted Jesus Christ and whom Jesus pours out upon his church. Noteworthy in John 16:13 is that the Spirit is revealed to be a person. He is not an impersonal power, for the Lord refers to the Spirit whom he will send to the church by a personal pronoun: "He," or "This one." "*He*, the Spirit of truth," and so on. The Spirit does what only a person can do: he guides; he speaks; he hears; he shows people things.

Just as is the case with Jesus, the Spirit is explicitly called God in the Bible. In lying to the apostles about his gift on behalf of the poor in the church, Ananias lied "to the Holy Ghost" in that the apostles were the officebearers and representatives of the Holy Ghost. In lying to the Holy Ghost, he was lying "unto God" (Acts 5:1–4), because the Holy Ghost is God, the Holy Ghost. First Corinthians 3:16 teaches that the indwelling of the "Spirit of God" makes those who are so indwelt "the temple of God." This identifies the Spirit as God himself. "Therefore," that is, on the basis of clear, compelling scripture, the Reformed church confesses that the Holy Ghost is "the true and eternal God."

FURTHER ON THE GODHEAD OF JESUS CHRIST, THE SON OF GOD

Concerning Jesus Christ, article 10 confesses: "He…is that true, eternal, and almighty God." He is not merely "a god" or a godlike creature.

Jesus is God, the Confession states, "according to his

divine nature." Inasmuch as Jesus is a real man, he has also a human nature. More will be said about the two natures of Jesus and their union in the one, divine person in article 19 of the Confession. Article 10 concerns itself with the divine nature of Jesus, with his being "very God," in the language of the Nicene Creed, or "true God," in the language of article 10 of the Belgic Confession.

Jesus has his divine nature and is God by virtue of being "the only begotten Son of God." This description of Jesus, which is fundamental to confession of his Godhead, as it is also fundamental to the doctrine of the Trinity, is found in the gospel and first epistle of John. "The Word was made flesh, and dwelt among us, (and we beheld his glory, the glory as of the only begotten of the Father,) full of grace and truth" (John 1:14). "For God so loved the world, that he gave his only begotten Son, that whosoever believeth in him should not perish, but have everlasting life" (3:16). "In this was manifested the love of God toward us, because that God sent his only begotten Son into the world, that we might live through him" (1 John 4:9).

The meaning of "only begotten" is that, regarding his divine nature, Jesus Christ has his being from the being of the Father, so that, although he is a distinct person, he shares the very being of God the Father. Begetting is a father's act of love to produce another, distinct from himself, who shares his own being. This is what begetting is in earthly relationships. The earthly father begets a son who is like the father, often amazingly so, in that he shares his father's nature. First of all, this is the earthly father's *human* nature. An earthly father does not beget a dog or a cabbage. Then the son shares the national characteristics of the begetting father—the certain characteristics of the

Dutch race, if the father (and mother, in the case of earthly sons) is Dutch. Finally, the son often remarkably shows the personal characteristics of the father, both psychological and physical. All of this in the purely earthly realm is an imperfect sign of the sharing of the very being of God by the Son whom God has begotten.

"Only begotten," which is one word in the Greek language of the New Testament, is the single most important word in theology, as in the Bible itself, for the Godhead of Jesus and for the Trinity. Often theologians make this claim for the important Greek word in the Nicene Creed, *homoousios*, that is translated "of one substance" (or essence) with the Father. But the underlying reason for Nicea's confession of Jesus' being "of one substance," or essence, with the Father is Jesus' being the "only begotten" of the Father. Behind the "one substance" is the "only begotten."

As the only begotten of the Father, Jesus shares the being of the Father who begets him. If he were not the only begotten, neither could he be of one substance. Sharing the (entire, infinite) being of God—"co-essential...with the Father" is the language of the Confession—as he does by virtue of being begotten of the Father, Jesus is God the Son. When the Council of Nicea adopted "of one substance" concerning Jesus, it had its eye fixedly on John's "only begotten." Arius, the Jehovah's (False) Witnesses, and all other heretics and cultists who deny the Godhead of Jesus are refuted and condemned by "only begotten."

Although this is sometimes overlooked in the explanation of scripture's identification of Jesus as the "only begotten of the Father," this identification of the Son clearly implies the distinction of the person of the Son from the person of the Father. One does not beget himself.

One begets Another, who is personally distinct from himself. As begotten of the Father, Jesus is the second person of the Godhead, God the (begotten) Son in distinction from God the (begetting) Father.

The begetting of the Son by the Father is an eternal activity. "Begotten from eternity," declares the Confession, so that Jesus is "co-eternal with the Father," according to his divine nature. The begetting had no beginning. Jesus did not become the Son of God "only from the time that he assumed our nature." But he is the Son of God "from all eternity." Eternally the Father begot the Son. Never was the Father without the Son.

That Jesus according to his divine nature is the "only begotten," indeed, the only begotten "from eternity," means that he is "not made nor created (for then he would be a creature)."

As the only begotten of the Father, Jesus is the "express image" of the Father. He images the Father to the Father himself. In the Son, the Father sees himself in all the brightness of his glory, in the language of Hebrews 1:3. Thus God glorifies himself. This is the eternal reality of the work of the man Jesus in time, to glorify the Father who sent him. Within the being of God, the eternal Son is the revelation of his Father to the Father. In the Son, as the personal revelation of himself in all his glory and majesty, the Father eternally takes delight. In keeping with who and what he is in the Godhead, Jesus is the revelation of God to his people, so that God may be glorified by the church. In this church, which begins to radiate the brightness of the glory of God in Jesus Christ, by the Spirit of Jesus Christ, who sanctifies this church, God takes delight in time and history.

The eternal begetting of the Son by the Father establishes the intimate family fellowship between the Father and the Son. Between the two persons—*Father* and *Son*—is the most intimate communion of love in the Holy Ghost. This communion of love is the blissful life of the Trinity eternally. God does not merely exist, as a God of one person might exist, but he lives, and his life is bliss, the bliss of the love of one for the other, in the bond who is the Holy Ghost.

Speaking in his capacity as the personal Wisdom of God, the Son exults in this communion of love: "Then I was by him, as one brought up with him: and I was daily his delight, rejoicing always before him" (Prov. 8:30). Of the love of the Father for him as the Son, "before the foundation of the world," Jesus speaks in John 17:23–24: "Thou hast loved me. Father, I will that they also, whom thou hast given me, be with me where I am; that they may behold my glory, which thou hast given me: for thou lovedst me before the foundation of the world." Such is the intimacy of the love of the eternal Father and the eternal Son that the Father is in the Son: "thou in me" (v. 23). This mysterious "inness" of the fellowship of the Father and the Son is, in reality, the Holy Ghost.

The most arresting and moving revelation in scripture of the family fellowship of love of the Father and the Son is John 1:18, one of the passages, significantly, that describe the Son as the "only begotten": "the only begotten Son, *which is in the bosom of the Father*" (emphasis added). As a precious, dearly beloved child lies close to the heart of an earthly parent, in the parent's bosom, so the only begotten Son eternally lies close to the heart of his divine Father, in the Father's heavenly bosom.

In view of the fundamental importance of the description of Jesus as the "only begotten," regarding both the Godhead of Jesus and the doctrine of the holy Trinity, it is nothing less than an assault on the Christian faith, to say nothing of an inexcusable mistranslation of the Greek word, that modern translations of the Bible translate the word "only begotten" in the gospel and epistle of John as "only [Son]." This is the sin of the translation of the New International Version. In John 1:14 and 18, in John 3:16, and in other passages, this Bible translates *monogenees* ("only begotten") as "only": "only Son." This translation, which is not so much translation of as imposition upon the text, ignores the second part of the Greek word translated as "begotten." Thus it knowingly fails to do justice to the basic thought of the word, namely, that Jesus is the Son of God in a way that no one else is. In fact, the translation is simply false on its very face: Jesus is not the "only" Son of God. All elect believers are also sons and daughters of God. Jesus alone and uniquely is the only *begotten* Son of God.

Similarly erroneous, reprehensible, and doctrinally dangerous is the change in the Apostles' Creed in some churches of "only begotten Son" to "only Son." Fundamentally, this change amounts to a refusal to confess the Son of God and a failure to confess the Trinity.

Because Jesus is the only begotten Son of God, he "is our Saviour and Redeemer by his blood," as the Reformed church confesses in article 9 of the Belgic Confession. As the only begotten Son of God, he is invoked, worshiped, and served, in the language of article 10. The deacon and evangelist Stephen invoked Jesus: "Lord Jesus, receive my spirit" (Acts 7:59). The twenty-four elders worship Jesus: "The four beasts and four and twenty elders fell down before the Lamb" (Rev. 5:8). Every believer serves Jesus: "Servants, be obedient to them that are your masters... as unto Christ...as the servants of Christ...with good will doing service, as to the Lord" (Eph. 6:5–7).

FURTHER ON THE GODHEAD OF THE HOLY GHOST

In article 11 the Reformed churches and believers confess the Godhead of the Holy Ghost as explicitly as they confess the Godhead of the Son: "of one and the same essence, majesty, and glory with the Father and the Son; and therefore...the true and eternal God." The Holy Ghost has his Godhead by his procession from the Father and Son. This procession is eternal: "from eternity proceeds." Since the procession is eternal, the Holy Ghost has no beginning. There was never a moment in eternity when the Holy Ghost was not. The Father and the Son were never without their Holy Ghost.

The significance of the procession of the Spirit is that he has his being from the being of the Father and Son. By procession, he shares this being fully. He is of "one and the same essence...with the Father and the Son." Sharing fully the one, divine essence, he is God. Inasmuch as he does not beget and cause to proceed, he is not the Father. Inasmuch as he is not begotten, he is not the Son. Inasmuch as his distinct, personal property is that he proceeds from Father and Son, he is Spirit.

As proceeding, the Spirit is neither "made" nor "created." As little as the Son is he a creature.

The relationship of the Spirit to the Father and the Son in the being of God is procession, not begetting. It is similar to begetting in that it is the divine manner in which the Holy Ghost has his being, which is the one being of

God. But the Spirit is not begotten. If he were begotten, he would be a second Son, not the Holy Ghost. Procession is on the order of divine breathing forth, more specifically the breathing forth of love, the breathing forth of the love of the Father to the Son and the breathing forth of the love of the Son to the Father. It would not be amiss to call the Holy Ghost, and think of him as, "the Holy Breath [of love]." The biblical basis for conceiving of him as the Breath of the Father and the Son is John 20:22. Jesus breathed on the disciples and said to them in explanation, "Receive ye the Holy Ghost."

As was explained and defended in the commentary on article 8 of the Confession, concerning the Trinity, the procession of the Holy Ghost is double: "from the Father and Son." The Confession repeats this in article 11. As was indicated in the explanation of article 8, the procession of the Spirit from the Son is more implied in scripture than explicitly stated. If Jesus, the Son in human nature, breathes forth the Spirit upon the disciples, as John 20:22 teaches, and on Pentecost sends forth the Spirit, as chapter 15:26 teaches, this unique relationship of the Son and the Spirit must have its archetype in the relationship of the Son and the Spirit in the being of God. Just as the Father gives conception and birth to the baby Jesus according to the Father's eternal begetting of the Son in the being of God, so the Spirit is sent to the church by the Son according to the Spirit's eternal procession from the Son in the being of God.

The significance of the Godhead of the Holy Ghost for salvation is essential. As God, the Holy Ghost can save from sin and death, unto holiness and life eternal. He can regenerate dead sinners; can sanctify sinners who are totally depraved by nature and who all their lives retain a totally depraved nature that is inclined to hate God and the neighbor; can gather a godly church out of a world of humanity that is ungodly and preserve that church and every member of it despite the assaults upon it of Satan and the allurements of the wicked world; can raise the dead on the last day; and will be able to re-create the universe on the world's last day, as he also created the present world in the beginning.

Only God can perform these wonders. God can perform these wonders of salvation only in the "particular office and operation" of the Holy Ghost, in the language and thought of article 9 of the Confession. The Father elects; he does not sanctify. The Son redeems; he does not regenerate. The Holy Ghost can do all this saving work, from regeneration and sanctification to resurrection, because he is the Power of God. He is the Power of God exactly as the divine Breath, which Breath is infinitely powerful—a tornadic Breath, or Wind, only beneficent, not destructive. So Ezekiel 37:1–14 prophesies the saving work of the Holy Ghost. The very dry bones come to life by the breath, or wind, of God: "Come from the four winds, O breath, and breathe upon these slain, that they may live…and the breath came into them, and they lived" (vv. 9–10). The explanation is that God "shall put my spirit in you, and you shall live" (v. 14).

Nor may it be overlooked that Jesus himself was miraculously conceived by the operation of the Holy Ghost as the infinite power of God and that Jesus performed all his redemptive work in the power of the Holy Ghost. The angel announced to the virgin Mary that "the Holy Ghost shall come upon thee, and the power of the Highest shall overshadow thee: Therefore also that holy thing which shall be born of thee shall be called the Son of God" (Luke

THE BELGIC CONFESSION: A COMMENTARY

1:35). The incarnation was the infinitely powerful work of the Holy Ghost in the womb of the virgin, where only the Breath of God could operate and doing what only the infinitely powerful Breath of God could effect.

At the beginning of his earthly ministry, Jesus received the Holy Ghost to enable him to carry out the ministry that God had sent him to do (Luke 3:21–22). This Spirit, Jesus received in all the infinite, divine fullness of the Spirit, something that was necessary for the great work that Jesus must perform and something that could be true only for one who is more than a mere man. Only one who is God can receive the Spirit without measure. "God giveth not the Spirit by measure unto him" (John 3:34). Only one who is God can empower God in the flesh to accomplish the grand work of salvation.

The significance of the Holy Ghost regarding salvation also bears on the nature of this salvation. As the personal fellowship in the Godhead of the Father and the Son, the Holy Ghost, as the Spirit of Jesus Christ, is the fellowship of the elect believer with God. This fellowship, which is the covenant of grace, is the essence of salvation. The believer experiences this salvation as communion with God: "I will be their God, and they shall be my people." As the Breath of love from the Father to the Son and from the Son to the Father, the Holy Ghost is the sweet communion of the Father and the Son in the Godhead. Because he is this communion in God, he can be the communion of the church with God and the communion of the members of the church with each other (1 Cor. 12:13; 2 Cor. 12:13).

Has the church neglected the Holy Ghost in the past?

This is the charge of the charismatic movement. This is not necessarily true. It is certainly not true on the ground that the charismatic movement adduces in proof of its charge, namely, its purported restoration of the extraordinary works of the Spirit, especially speaking in tongues.

An important truth about the Spirit is that he prefers to be incognito. When he is present and at work, he reveals and calls attention to the Son and through the Son to the Father. In all the work of salvation, the Spirit fulfills his office not independently, but as the Spirit of Christ Jesus. In this work, according to Jesus, "He shall glorify me" (John 16:14). The Spirit of truth does not call attention to himself, as does the spurious spirit of the charismatic movement, but he calls attention to Jesus, the Son, and to the Father who sent the Son. The apostle was determined in his proclamation of the gospel to know nothing "save Jesus Christ, and him crucified" (1 Cor. 2:2) as the agent and spokesman of the Holy Ghost. Through the apostle, the Holy Ghost directed all attention upon Jesus, the Son in human flesh.

Every spirit that cries out in the ministry of its advocates, "Look at me! Look at me," as is the clamor of the spirit of the charismatic movement, is thereby exposed as a false spirit.

This characteristic office of the economic Spirit, that is, the Holy Ghost in the work of salvation, has its pattern and source in the ontological Spirit, that is, the Holy Ghost in the eternal being of God. There, the Holy Ghost reveals the Son to the Father and the Father to the Son. He gives the Father pleasure in the Son and the Son delight in the Father. In the triune being of God, his personal perfection is that he does not call attention to himself, but to the others.

The saving work of the Spirit, therefore, will be that he causes the elect child of God to believe in Jesus Christ and in this faith to live unto God. In the power of the Holy Ghost, the church will confess Jesus Christ. Rather than emphasizing extraordinary, spectacular gifts and deeds, the salvation worked by the Holy Ghost will consist of holiness of life. His outstanding work is sanctification, as the Reformed church has always preached. This sanctification will not take form in men and women shouting, "Look at me! Look at me! Stand in wonderment at me and my supernatural abilities!" But the saved sinner who is indwelt by the Holy Spirit will point away from himself to Jesus Christ and, through him, to God. He will love God and the neighbor. His bliss, his life, his salvation will be communion with God in the covenant of grace.

As for the extraordinary gifts of apostolic times, especially the gift of tongues, of which the charismatic movement makes much, they were only for the apostolic age. Their purpose was the confirmation of the gospel of the apostles. When this purpose had been accomplished, the extraordinary gifts passed away with the apostles themselves, with whose ministry they were connected. "Truly the signs of an apostle were wrought among you in all patience, in signs, and wonders, and mighty deeds" (2 Cor. 12:12; see also Heb. 2:3–4). The only ministry today that still needs extraordinary gifts, including tongues, is a ministry that is not apostolic.

That the Spirit in the Reformed church is true and eternal God, present and working his wonderful salvation, is not proved by extraordinary gifts, particularly tongues. Rather, he "is the true and eternal God, *as the Holy Scripture teaches us.*"

Chapter Eight

THE CREATION
(ARTICLE 12)

ART. XII. OF THE CREATION.

We believe that the Father, by the Word—that is, by his Son—created of nothing the heaven, the earth, and all creatures, as it seemed good unto him, giving unto every creature its being, shape, form, and several offices to serve its Creator; that he doth also still uphold and govern them by his eternal providence and infinite power for the service of mankind, to the end that man may serve his God. He also created the angels good, to be his messengers and to serve his elect: some of whom are fallen from that excellency, in which God created them, into everlasting perdition; and the others have, by the grace of God, remained steadfast, and continued in their primitive state. The devils and evil spirits are so depraved that they are enemies of God and every good thing to the utmost of their power, as murderers watching to ruin the Church and every member thereof, and by their wicked stratagems to destroy all; and are therefore, by their own wickedness, adjudged to eternal

damnation, daily expecting their horrible torments. There-
fore we reject and abhor the error of the Sadducees, who
deny the existence of spirits and angels; and also that of
the Manichees, who assert that the devils have their origin
of themselves, and that they are wicked of their own nature,
without having been corrupted.

INTRODUCTION

Having confessed the one, true God as the Trinity, the creed proceeds to the confession of the first of God's works outside himself: the creation of the world.

In its confession of creation, the Reformed faith's confession concerning scripture in articles 3–7 is put to the test. Scripture teaches the creation of the world, plainly and in detail, especially in Genesis 1 and 2. The Reformed faith confesses about scripture that it is inspired (art. 3) and authoritative so that the Reformed man, or woman, or young person believes "without any doubt, all things contained in them" (art. 5) and so that Reformed believers "reject with all our hearts whatsoever doth not agree with this infallible rule" (art. 7).

Modern science criticizes the Genesis account of creation. Therefore, much of the Christian church, including the Reformed churches, abandons the biblical account of creation for the evolutionary theory of the origin of the world. This raises a question, a question that divides members of Reformed churches into the categories of those who are truthful in their confession concerning scripture and those who lie. The question is, do they truly believe what they have confessed about scripture?

Article 12 of the Confession is closely related to the following article. Both have creation as their content. Article

12 confesses God's work of bringing the universe into existence, as taught especially in Genesis 1 and 2. Article 13 treats of God's care of the world after he brought it into existence, the divine work known as providence. In fact, such is the close relationship between creation and providence that article 12, on the creation, cannot omit a brief reference to providence: "He doth also still uphold and govern them [all creatures] by his eternal providence and infinite power."

Article 12's treatment of creation is very brief. It consists of a part of one sentence: "We believe that the Father, by the Word—that is, by his Son—created of nothing the heaven, the earth, and all creatures, as it seemed good unto him, giving unto every creature its being, shape, form, and several offices to serve its Creator." This part of a sentence is completed by the assertion that God continues to be related to the world he made by his work of providence. Surprisingly, the article concludes with a lengthy section on the creation of angels and the fall of some of them, which accounts for the existence of devils and their war against the church and its members.

Brief as the treatment of creation is, the main elements of the biblical doctrine concerning this great and fundamental work of God are all included. It should be noted that the Confession treats of the creation of man in article 14, in connection with his fall into sin.

WHAT CREATION WAS

Creation was the work of the triune God in the beginning (which beginning of time was also a creature of God) of giving existence to the universe and every part of it, as well as forming each creature to occupy its own place and to perform its own function in the (originally unified) whole of the creation.

According to Genesis 1, there were two distinct phases of the creative work of God. The first was the instantaneous bringing into existence of the entire universe as an unformed, chaotic mass of material. With this phase of the work of creation, Genesis 1 begins, in verse 1: "In the beginning God created the heaven and the earth." Verse 2 describes this phase of creation as the bringing into existence of an earth that was "without form, and void."

The second phase was the forming of the chaotic mass into an orderly, harmonious universe over the period of six days. This, the Creator did by bringing into being the distinct creatures: light, firmament, and the rest.

According to the Reformed Confession, the universe was created "of nothing." There was no pre-existing matter, for example, a huge mass of gas, with which God worked and from which the present universe developed. That God made the universe "of nothing" is not only the obvious implication of the account of creation in Genesis 1 but is also the explicit testimony of Hebrews 11:3: "[The] things which are seen were not made of things which do appear." Matter is not eternal; only God is eternal. The universe had a beginning, as Genesis 1:1 teaches: "*In the beginning* God created" (emphasis added).

The origin of the present world is not in some eternal matter, but in the mind and counsel of God, who conceived and decreed a world alongside himself and who then carried out his decree by creating. The Confession traces the world to the divine counsel when it says, "The Father…created…as it seemed good unto him."

Creation is a work that only God is able to perform.

Man cannot create, bringing something into existence out of nothing. The world cannot bring itself into existence out of nonexistence. Only God, who is almighty, can create. Creation is a work of infinite, astounding power. It is also the work of amazing wisdom, as not only creation in its entirety, but also each individual creature abundantly testifies. One who has been delivered from the blindness and ignorance of unbelief stands amazed at the power, wisdom, and artistry of God the creator revealed in the heaven and the earth, but also in a blade of grass.

In the work of creation, all three persons of the holy Trinity were involved, in the proper trinitarian order: out of the Father, by the Son, and in (the power of) the Holy Ghost. Appropriately, the Confession recognizes the Father as the source of the work of creation: "The Father...created." But the Father performed the work "by his Son." As is evident from the Confession's calling the Son "the Word," the Confession depends here especially upon John 1:1–18. God created everything by his efficacious Word (as Genesis 1 teaches by its "God said"), and this creative Word is personal—the second person of the Trinity. This is the Word who became flesh in Jesus Christ. Therefore, in Colossians 1:16, the apostle attributes creation to God's "dear Son: in whom we have redemption through his blood" (vv. 13–14).

Scripture also teaches that the Holy Ghost was active in creating. He was the power who realized the counsel of the Father as expressed by the Word. Genesis 1:2 has the "Spirit of God" moving upon the chaotic waters, powerfully to effect the creative Word that is spoken by the Father.

Inasmuch as creation is the work of the Father of the Word, who is Jesus Christ, it is the work of the Father of the believer. The material creation, therefore, is not a world in which the believer must live as an intruder and alien. On the contrary, the creation belongs to the believer. It is now, and will everlastingly be, his rightful home. What is yet a more important implication of the truth that the world was made by God is that the believer is jealous of the honor that is rightfully God's as the creator.

The Reformed believer, who means what he says when he confesses article 12, rejects with indignation and condemns with vigor the theory of evolution as a lie. The gravity of this lie is not so much that it is a grossly false explanation of the origin of the world, although it is this, but that it is robbery of God of the glory that is due him on account of one of his greatest and grandest works. Evolution teaches that matter is eternal, thus failing, in fact, on its own terms, to explain the origin of the universe. To evolutionary theory as an explanation of the universe, the question is put, "What explains the existence of the original mass of matter from which our present world evolved?" Evolution has no answer. For the evolutionist, an eternal God is absurdity. But eternal matter is wisdom. From absurdity, evolutionary theory advances to idiocy: the present world with all its complexity and inter-relatedness developed from the chaos of the original mass of matter by sheer chance over a vast period of time, as though the marvel of one living human could develop from a mass of inanimate gas over an eternity of time.

To this intellectual monument of folly, the multitudes bow unquestioning today. Especially the educated in the Western world embrace this foolishness with the fervor of the unbelief that is determined to deny God. The evolutionary fool has said in his heart, "No God!" (see Ps. 14:1). If the explanation of the universe, including the human race, is creation, God the creator is reality. If God lives, he must be worshiped and obeyed, particularly in the matter of chastity. Against this, the evolutionary theorists, including Darwin, rebelled in unbelief.

That the explanation of evolutionary theory is unbelief is implied by the Confession. Article 12 finds the source of the confession of creation in faith. The opening words are, "We believe." Faith confesses creation. Denial of creation, therefore, is unbelief, not intellectual difficulty but spiritual unbelief.

But even the unbelief of the masters and disciples of evolutionary theory as the explanation of origins fails fully to account for the foolish doctrine. Seeing clearly the invisible things of God from the creation of the world, as every human does, including Darwin and his disciples, so that they knew God, they glorified him not as God. Rather, they denied the Creator, who is blessed forever. God therefore gave them over to the folly of evolution with the licentious behavior that accompanies the theory of evolution, culminating in the reprobate mind that approves and practices sodomy and lesbianism (see Rom. 1:18–32).

The truth of creation demands good Christian schools for the children of believers. The one great subject in a school is creation. Whether the world has its origin in the work of God, as taught in Genesis 1 and 2 and as confessed in article 12 of the Belgic Confession, or in evolution as taught in the state schools, affects every subject in the curriculum. It affects every subject decisively. The natural effect of the evolutionary theory of the state schools is immorality of life, sheer unbelief, and the kingdom of antichrist. The power of the education of covenantal children in the good Christian school is obedience of life to the creator God, the protection and promotion of faith, and the advance of the kingdom of Christ. On the foundation of the good Christian school is engraved, "We believe that the Father, by the Word—that is, by his Son—created of nothing the heaven, the earth, and all creatures," that is, article 12 of the Belgic Confession.

The work of creation had a definite purpose. According to the Confession, this purpose was twofold: that every creature might "serve its Creator" and "for the service of mankind, to the end that man may serve his God." The latter is expressly the purpose of providence, but the relationship of providence and creation is such that the purpose of providence is also the purpose of creation.

First and foremost, the purpose of creation is the service of God. But creation serves God by serving man. It is true, as the Confession goes on to say, that the ultimate purpose of creation is God himself: "to the end that man may serve his God." Man serves his God with the creation by acknowledging the creation as the handiwork of the Creator, something that the evolutionist refuses to do, thus dishonoring God, and by living in the creation according to the law of God, something that the unbeliever fails to do. The end of creation as also the end of salvation is the glory of God. Here the characteristic note of the Reformed faith is sounded by the Confession. That the creation should end in God is only right. He is the creator of it; it is his.

But the creation has its end in God in the way of its serving man: "for the service of mankind." The service of man is not a second, independent purpose of God with the creation. It is a purpose that is closely related to the ultimate purpose of man's serving his God: "the service of mankind, *to the end that man may serve his God.*" If men and women do not use and enjoy the creation in the service of God, they sin against the purpose of God with his creation. The creation and all creatures then do not serve the blessing and good of that man or woman, but the curse and condemnation.

Nevertheless, God is not self-centered with his creation and stingy, as though man must serve God with it in such a way that man himself is deprived of the use and enjoyment of the creation and its various creatures. On the contrary, God intended the blessed welfare of man with the creation. He made the world with all its creatures for the benefit of man. With the creation, God was good to man. He expressed this generosity to man at the conclusion of his creative work at the end of the sixth day: "Behold, I have given you every herb bearing seed...and every tree...to you it shall be for meat" (Gen. 1:29). God's goodness to man by creating all things in the service of man is the implication of man's kingship over all creation: "have dominion" (v. 28). If man was king, all the creation served him. That God saw that everything was "very good" (v. 31) means not only that the creation glorified its maker, but also that all served man. All glorified God by serving man, creation's king under God.

The question is, who is the "mankind" for the service of whom God made all things? The quick, unthinking answer of many who read the Confession is probably, "all humans without exception." But this answer implies that the purpose of God with creation failed, for much of the human race does not serve God with the creation and its creatures. Others may answer, "Adam." But this answer also fails for neither did Adam "serve his God" by his kingship over the earthly creation. On the contrary, he failed to serve God in the matter of the forbidden tree and plunged the entire race that descended from him into the inglorious slavery to Satan.

The answer to the question, who is the "mankind" for the service of whom God made all things and the "mankind" that does, in fact, serve God with the creation, is provided by scripture in Colossians 1:12–29. It is not the old human race of whom the first Adam (see 1 Cor. 15:45–58) was the head, but the new human race of the elect out of all nations, of whom the second Adam, Jesus Christ, is the head. As Colossians 1:16 explicitly states, "All things were created by him, and for him." God did not create all things in the beginning for all humans without exception. He did not even create all things for the first Adam. But he created all things for Jesus Christ. He created all things for Jesus Christ as the head of the new human race, made up of the elect out of all nations. The creation exists for Jesus Christ and, in him, believers and their children, who, by the grace of Christ Jesus, do serve the Creator with their own lives and with whatever in the creation they use and enjoy.

Nor is this reference to the elect missing from article 12 of the Confession. Regarding the creation of the angels sometime during the six days of the week of creation, the Confession states that God "created the angels good...to serve his elect." First Timothy 4:3 teaches that God "created [meats] to be received with thanksgiving of them which believe and know the truth." The Timothy passage makes explicit what the truth of the doctrine of creation taught in article 12 of the Belgic Confession implies: "Every creature of God is good, and nothing to be refused, if it be received with thanksgiving: for it is sanctified by the word of God and prayer" (1 Tim. 4:4–5). The material creation is not an evil, to be avoided as much as possible. It is good, and good for the human, "if it be received with thanksgiving."

The Confession binds upon the Reformed church and believer the truth of the *manner* of God's work of creation in the beginning. This is not an insignificant aspect of the truth of creation, as is widely supposed. First, both the creed and the Bible emphasize the way in which God created. Second, denial of the biblical manner of creating opens the door to errors that corrupt the truth of creation itself. Third, the manner of God's creating was part of the work of creation, so that rejection of the biblical manner is a rejection of creation itself.

The manner of God's creating was "by the Word." Thus the Confession: "The Father, by the Word—that is, by his Son—created." This is the teaching of Genesis 1: "God *said*: Let there be." It was this Word of God that brought each creature into being, instantly: "and it was so." Reformed theology sums up this manner of creation as fiat creation, that is, literally, "let there be" creation, implying instantaneous coming into existence by the Word of God.

Therefore, the creation and each creature individually unmistakably make known the power and Godhead of God the creator. "The invisible things of him [God the creator] from the creation of the world are clearly seen, being understood by the things that are made, even his eternal power and Godhead" (Rom. 1:20). All things make God known, not only because they are his workmanship, his artistry, his handiwork, but also because the creation is a word of God, indeed a most elegant book of many words, all declaring their maker's might, wisdom, and awesome deity. "The heavens declare the glory of God; and the firmament sheweth his handywork" (Ps. 19:1).

It belongs to the manner of God's creative work in the beginning that he made everything in six days, each of which consisted of one evening and one morning, according to the inspired revelation in Genesis 1. Such is the blatant apostasy of churches and theologians in our day that one is required to state about the days of creation that they were normal, twenty-four-hour days. In order to indicate the folly of the exegetical and doctrinal error rampant in evangelical and even Reformed churches in the twenty-first century concerning the days, one is tempted to assert that the days of creation were "day" days. Cravenly and wickedly yielding to the philosophy of evolution, which proposes that the world is millions or billions of years in age, much of Christendom makes biblical revelation do obeisance to evolutionary theory by explaining the days of Genesis 1 as millions, or even billions, of years.

The defense by the advocates of the "long days" of Genesis 1, that nothing fundamental to the Christian religion is compromised, to the contrary notwithstanding, the doctrines of creation, of the fall, and of redemption are at stake. Defending the Reformed doctrine of creation as taught in article 12 of the Confession requires, therefore, the rejection and condemnation of the theory of periods instead of days in Genesis 1.

First, the theory is guilty of deliberate exegetical outrage, which is, implicitly or explicitly, the rejection of the inspiration and authority of scripture. A day that is limited and made up by one evening and one morning is not a million years of days. No believing Jew in Moses' time would have thought so. It is the familiar day into which God himself has divided time. When the fourth commandment of the law in Exodus 20, basing the week of work and rest upon the week of Genesis 1, calls believers to work six days and to rest one day, no one understands the commandment to call the believer to work six billion years and to rest one billion years. The cause of the teaching that the days of Genesis 1 were billions of years is not faithful interpretation of scripture, but evolutionary theory. This theory is allowed to corrupt and subvert the teaching of scripture.

Second, the exegetical outrage necessarily wreaks havoc with the entire biblical account of creation, the fall, and the first promise of the gospel, out of which, as a fountain, flows all the biblical message of the coming of Jesus Christ. The theory of billions of years, instead of biblical days, implies, if it is not a purpose, the evolution of species. The evolution of species directly contradicts the repeated testimony of Genesis 1 that each species reproduces "after his kind." This evolution of species includes that humans evolved from animals, with all that this implies regarding the image of God. Evolution's, including so-called theistic evolution's, explanation of the origin of man contradicts what article 14 of the Confession teaches concerning this origin. Also, a world of billions of years necessarily is a world in which death is prior to any fall by a human. Thus the account of Genesis 3 is denied. In addition, if death is natural to animal and human death, God is to blame for the dreadful reality of death, not man himself.

On the concession to evolution of a world of billions of years, during which humans developed from animals, there is no place for the creation of the woman out of the rib of the man and for the man as his wife. Rather, coincidentally, a female happened to evolve from an animal about the same time that a male came out of the ur-slime, and in the vicinity. What this implies for Christian marriage and the covenantal family is evident to all.

If the sixth day of the biblical creation week was

millions of years, there never were a historical Adam and a historical Eve. This does away with the fall of the human race into sin, as recorded in Genesis 3 and as confessed in article 14 of the Confession. Neither does a sixth day of millions of years allow for a historical Adam and Eve in whose presence God proclaimed the original, mother promise of the gospel of a coming Jesus Christ: "I will put enmity between thee and the woman, and between thy seed and her seed; it shall bruise thy head, and thou shalt bruise his heel" (Gen. 3:15). So serious is the loss of the "day" day of Genesis 1 that with this loss is lost Jesus Christ, the seed of the woman.

The New Testament posits such a relationship between the first Adam and God's covenant with him, on the one hand, and the second Adam and God's covenant with him, on the other hand, that to jeopardize the reality of the first is to call into question the second (see Rom. 5 and 1 Cor. 15).

The Christian religion itself is at stake in the concessions made to evolutionary theory by the churches today. In light of the importance of creation in the Bible and in Christian theology, this should surprise no one. Therefore, even though article 12 of the Belgic Confession does not expose what is called today "theistic evolution," nor could it be expected to do so since the theory is of recent vintage, a Reformed explanation and defense of the doctrine of creation taught in article 12 would be derelict if it neglected to take note of and to criticize this contemporary attack on the doctrine. It would be irresponsible, if not cowardice, loudly to profess the doctrine of creation as found in article 12 of the Confession, while overlooking or silently acquiescing in a heresy that gutted the doctrine.

KNOWLEDGE OF CREATION

Knowledge of creation is not absurd. It is not nonsense. It is not irrational. On the contrary, evolution, whether atheistic or in its guise as theistic, is absurd. Simply as an intellectual theory, it is absurd. It is the great hoax. The marvelous creature man does not accidentally develop from a frog. The inanimate cannot become life, regardless of the multiplication of aeons in order to impress the doubter. Only because it is the folly of the rebellion of fallen, sinful mankind against the Creator does evolution pass for wisdom in the world.

Believers know creation. They know the doctrine by faith, which faith receives God's revelation of how the world, including mankind, came into existence. The creed begins its confession of creation with the words, "We believe." Faith always has the testimony of scripture as its content. Scripture speaks: "God created." Faith listens. Knowledge of creation is not a matter of science, modernity, and intellectual ability. It is the spiritual matter of faith that receives scripture as the word of God.

Neither is the source of the knowledge of creation modern, scientific theory, deceptively disguised as general revelation. It is popular in Christian circles effectively to set aside the biblical explanation of creation in the name of general revelation. There is a making known of himself as the creator by God through the creation and its creatures. This is a revelation of himself and his creative work to all humans without exception. This revelation of himself by God is distinguished from his particular or special revelation of himself, which is by the gospel and to the elect only. Romans 1:18–32 teaches that God makes known himself in his eternal power and Godhead to all humans and that he does this by means of the world that he has created. But the passage also teaches that the effect of this revelation of himself to the unbeliever is that he immediately holds the truth of God in unrighteousness. He changes the glory of God into something shameful.

There is no saving effect of this general revelation. Indeed, there is no positive effect whatever. Nor is this the purpose of God in making of himself known by creation. On the contrary, God's purpose with general revelation to the unbelievers is that they are "without excuse." General revelation will never move the unbelieving scientist to confess God as the creator of the universe. It cannot. Only the revelation of the gospel of scripture will do this and can do this.

Also the believer knows God by general revelation. That is, the creation will declare to him that God is the creator of the universe and that this God is God of almighty power and great wisdom. To the believer, general revelation is subservient to the revelation of scripture. It will never contradict the revelation of scripture. As article 2 of the Belgic Confession states, "[God] makes himself more clearly and fully known to us by his holy and divine Word," that is, more clearly and fully than he makes himself known, even to the believer, in creation. It is a mistake, indeed a slight of scripture, to set the revelation of scripture aside in the interests of general revelation. But general revelation must be seen in the light of scripture.

Not the findings of alleged scientific investigations determine for the Reformed Christian the manner of creation, but only the clear testimony of holy scripture. Besides, scientific investigation, masquerading as general revelation, cannot speak to the manner of creation in any case. The manner of creation was a wonder. It is therefore inaccessible to scientific investigation. How can science with all its instruments, experiments, and analyses get hold of the wonder of, "And God said, Let there be light: and there was light" (Gen.1:3)?

It is with the manner of creation as it was with the incarnation and virgin birth of Jesus. No medical doctor, with all his superb training, scientific expertise, and natural theory of conception and birth, examining Jesus immediately after his birth could have determined the manner of his conception and birth. Nor could he have disproved scientifically that the Child was virgin conceived and born. The conception of Jesus belongs to the category of the wonder. General revelation does not reach to the wonder. Only faith that hears the word of God—special revelation—can know the wonder. So it is with the manner of creation.

God alone can, and does, explain his great deeds. He does so by his word. The word accompanies the deed. Faith receives the word, and thus faith, and faith alone, knows the wonderful works of God. "We believe."

THE SIGNIFICANCE OF CREATION

The significance of creation is tremendous. First, it was one of the greatest of the works of God and, as a work of God, of daily, practical importance for the thoughtful life of every human. It is the answer to the most fundamental questions that humans can, and sometimes do, ask. Where did the world and we humans come from? Whose world is the world in which we live? Are we accidental offspring of animals or the handiwork of a creator? Is the brief life that each lives all there is, so that human life with its accomplishments and enjoyments, as well as its disappointments and sufferings, is vain and hopeless, ending in the grave, or is there judgment to come and an eternal life and an eternal death after this earthly life? Are humans independent lords of our own lives, or do we belong to, are we subject to, and are we dependent upon the creator?

Regarding our normal, earthly, daily life, what about maleness and femaleness? Do we decide ourselves? Or does our Creator decide? And what about marriage and family? Are they merely human inventions? Or are they divine institutions for the human race? If the latter, what are the regulations of marriage and family as laid down by the Creator?

Above all, is the meaning of life, the *ultimate* meaning of life, with consequences for time and eternity, that man glorify God his creator, or that man strive for his own glory?

The doctrine of creation answers these fundamental questions and more.

Second, creation is the foundation upon which is built the Christian doctrines of the fall and of redemption. If there was no creation by God, neither was there a fall of mankind, and neither was there redemption. If there was no Adam the first, who plunged all mankind into sin and death, there was no last Adam, who delivered elect humanity from sin and death (Rom. 5:12–21; 1 Cor. 15:45–58).

Third, in the doctrine of creation, Jesus Christ is at stake. He is at stake directly. Jesus Christ created all things, as the second person of the Godhead who would become the man Jesus (John 1:1–18). In addition, the triune God made all things *for* the incarnate Son, Jesus the Christ (Col. 1:13–29). As if this were not enough to demonstrate that the denial of creation is, by virtue of this fact, direct assault on Jesus Christ, the denial of the historicity of the account of creation in Genesis 1 and 2 inevitably and necessarily involves the denial of the fall as recorded in Genesis 3. At stake, finally, is the promise of the gospel in verse 15. But from the promise of the gospel in Genesis 3:15, as from its fountain, flows the entire history of redemption culminating in the coming and work of Jesus Christ, who is the seed of the woman who crushed the head of the serpent.

CREATION OF THE SPIRIT WORLD

Striking is the attention paid in article 12 concerning creation to the creation of the world of spirits—the angels—and to the fall of many of them—the devils. More than half the article is devoted to these subjects. The Reformed faith recognizes a spirit world and its influence upon the church and the believing member of the church. Thus the Reformed faith distinguishes itself from the materialistic Sadducees and their contemporary disciples, "who deny the existence of spirits and angels" (see Acts 23:8).

Angels are personal, spiritual beings whose function is "to serve his [God's] elect." Angels appear as servants of the elect throughout the Bible. When the prophet of God was in seemingly dire straits, surrounded by the hosts of the Syrians, who were bent on killing him and thus putting an end to the word of God that defended the people of God, God enabled the servant of Elisha to see that the prophet was protected by a host of heavenly horses and chariots that outnumbered the Syrian army (2 Kings 7:8–23). When Peter attempted to defend Jesus in Gethsemane with a sword, more than twelve legions of angels stood ready to deliver Jesus from his foes, had Jesus called upon his Father for them (Matt. 26:53). Hebrews 1:14 describes the angels as "ministering spirits sent forth to minister for them who shall be heirs of salvation."

Devils are personal, spiritual beings who oppose God by assault on the church and on every confessing Christian. According to the Confession, the devils and evil spirits are "enemies of God and every good thing to the utmost of their power, as murderers watching to ruin the Church and every member thereof, and by their wicked stratagems to destroy all." It was a devil, indeed the prince of the demonic host, who tempted Adam by the serpent and thus accomplished the fall into sin of the human race and, apart from grace, its destruction. In his temptation by Peter, to detour around the cross to his glory, Jesus saw Satan himself present and at work and rebuked him: "Get thee behind me, Satan" (Matt. 16:21–23). Many of Jesus' miracles consisted of casting devils out of the demon possessed (see Luke 8:26–36). The apostle warns the New Testament church that ultimately her warfare is not with "flesh and blood," but against the devils (Eph. 6:12). The entire book of Revelation describes the enemies of the church in the last days as hordes of demons.

That the foes of the church, as of each member of the church individually, are clever, powerful, supernatural, spiritual, personal powers does not terrify the people of God, for Christ has already defeated Satan and his demonic army (Col. 2:14–15). But this does put the church and her members on their guard. The first rule of warfare, whether physical or spiritual, is: "Know the enemy!"

By the inclusion of the spirit world in its treatment of creation, the Confession emphasizes that the spirits are creatures. This is true particularly of the devils. They are not eternal, evil beings alongside the good being, God. The doctrine of the eternality of Satan and his demons is dualism. This was the teaching of the Manichees, a third-century cult with some influence upon some elements of the Christian church. As the Confession describes their doctrine, the Manichees taught "that the devils have their origin of themselves, and that they are wicked of their own nature, without having been corrupted." The Christian religion finding sound expression in the Confession declares concerning the devils that they "are fallen from that excellency, in which God created them, into everlasting perdition."

The truth is that the spirits that now are devils were created as part of the heavenly host of angels, with heaven as their proper abode. Originally they were good, although capable of revolt against God and becoming evil, just as was true of Adam and Eve. Many of the angels rebelled against God and fell from their original state of goodness. Genesis does not record the creation of the angels. Neither does it give information concerning the event itself of the fall of some of them, nor concerning the time of the angelic revolt, except that it took place after the sixth day of creation, since on the seventh day God saw that all that he had made was good.

Scattered throughout scripture, which is not so much interested in Satan and the demons as in Jesus Christ and the church, is revelation that makes known that the instigator of the revolt of angels in heaven against God was an angel named Lucifer, whose original sin was pride (Isa. 14:4–23; Ezek. 28:1–19; 1 Tim. 3:6). He likely was at the head of the heavenly host of angels. He took with him in his revolt against God a third of the angels (Rev. 12:3–4). It was Satan who used the serpent to tempt Eve and Adam in the garden in order thus to accomplish the fall of the human race (Gen. 3; John 8:44; Rev. 12:9). Therefore, Satan is represented in the book of Revelation as a great "dragon," a dragon being an enlarged serpent in symbolic and fearsome form.

The revolt and fall of what are now devils were decisive and final. There is no grace of repentance to them and no hope of salvation. As Jude 6 states concerning them, from the moment of their revolt they are "reserved in everlasting chains under darkness unto the judgment of the great day." This is due to God's reprobation of them. It is in accordance with the extraordinary wickedness of their sin. Created good, in heaven, they were privy to the beholding of the glory of God and the enjoyment of the unutterably blessed condition of heaven, if only for a short time. As was the greatness of their privilege, such was the enormity of their sin. And such is the dreadfulness of their punishment.

In characteristically Reformed fashion, the Confession attributes the faithfulness of the angels who refused to engage in the satanic revolution in heaven to the grace of God, rather than to their own will and power: "The others have, by the grace of God, remained steadfast, and continued in their primitive state." Wherever and among whomever there is salvation of any kind, whether the deliverance of humans or the steadfastness of angels, the explanation is the grace of God. In attributing the faithfulness of some angels to the grace of God, the Confession is biblical. First Timothy 5:21 calls those angels who resisted Satan's call to revolution "elect angels." According to God's election of them, they stood. They stood because God graced them with power to stand. The implication is that otherwise they too would have yielded to the satanic call to revolt. The implication clearly is also that Satan and the angels who fell did so according to God's non-election, or reprobation, of them.

Since the whole of God's election is the choice of some unto salvation in Jesus Christ, it is God's election that unites angels and humans in Jesus Christ. The desire of the angels to look into the things of the salvation accomplished by Jesus Christ and that are preached in the gospel, therefore, is not due to mere curiosity (1 Pet. 1:12). The angels also have a stake in that salvation. If Jesus' death did not redeem them from sin, they having never sinned, it was the basis for their not sinning in the "Heavenly Revolt." If they could have been the beneficiaries of the grace of God without having sinned, as the Confession says they were, they could also be the recipients of the benefit of the cross of Christ without having sinned.

The present time sees a resurgence of great interest in angels and devils, especially devils. For the most part, this interest is unhealthy. A nominally Christian people, who are bored by the gospel of grace and almost totally uninterested in the government of human life by a sovereign God, dabble in the world of spirits. This explains the fascination with the popular novels by Frank Peretti, among which are *This Present Darkness* and *Piercing the Darkness*. A war in the spirit world detracts from the real war of the church with an apostate church and an ungodly world. Angels replace God and Christ as governing and defeating evil. There is a virtually dualistic view of good and evil spirits.

Nevertheless, the true church and believer are to be aware of and on guard against demons, whom the Confession describes as "murderers watching to ruin the Church and every member thereof." In the wrath of a member of the church against another that is allowed to fester overnight is a devil working to destroy both the member himself and the congregation (Eph. 4:26–27). In the bottle of liquor from which a member of the church drinks excessively is a demon bent on destroying the drinker. The young people's use of drugs opens wide the entrance of their souls to devils. In the unclean embrace of two who date, a demon entices the two to sexual sin. False doctrines, though proclaimed by a minister who is never so friendly, are in reality doctrines of devils (1 Tim. 4:1; 1 John 4:1–3).

If the existence and operations of devils are a salutary warning to the Reformed believer, it is some consolation to him that the host of angels is on his side, fighting for him in the great, spiritual warfare that is the Christian life. This was the encouragement of Elisha's servant at Dothan and, indeed, of the prophet himself (2 Kings 6:15–17). Michael's help of the pre-incarnate Messiah in the battle against the kingdom of darkness was an important aspect of the warfare of the kingdom of God and the kingdom of Satan and encouraging to the prophet Daniel (Dan. 10).

As the angels were the servants of the Christ on behalf of his church throughout history, largely unseen, so they will serve as his mighty, and then visible, army on the world's last day: "When the Lord Jesus shall be revealed from heaven with his mighty angels, in flaming fire taking vengeance on them that know not God, and that obey not the gospel of our Lord Jesus Christ" (2 Thess. 1:7–8).

Chapter Nine

PROVIDENCE

(ARTICLE 13)

ART. XIII. OF DIVINE PROVIDENCE.

We believe that the same God, after he had created all things, did not forsake them, or give them up to fortune or chance, but that he rules and governs them, according to his holy will, so that nothing happens in this world without his appointment; nevertheless, God neither is the author of, nor can be charged with, the sins which are committed. For his power and goodness are so great and incomprehensible, that he orders and executes his work in the most excellent and just manner even when the devil and wicked men act unjustly. And as to what he doth surpassing human understanding we will not curiously inquire into it further than our capacity will admit of; but with the greatest humility and reverence adore the righteous judgments of God which are hid from us, contenting ourselves that we are disciples of Christ, to learn only those things which he has revealed to us in his Word without transgressing these limits.

This doctrine affords us unspeakable consolation, since we are taught thereby that nothing can befall us by chance, but by the direction of our most gracious and heavenly Father, who watches over us with a paternal care, keeping all creatures so under his power that not a hair of our head (for they are all numbered), nor a sparrow, can fall to the ground, without the will of our Father, in whom we do entirely trust; being persuaded that he so restrains the devil and all our enemies that, without his will and permission, they can not hurt us. And therefore we reject that damnable error of the Epicureans, who say that God regards nothing, but leaves all things to chance.

INTRODUCTION

Inseparably related to creation is providence, because providence is God's interest in and relationship to the world and its history after he made it. If the world's origin is, indeed, creation, as article 12 of the Confession has declared, it follows that the Creator will continue to take an interest in his handiwork and supervise its history. The fact is that the world cannot even continue to exist apart from the Creator. In addition, God has a purpose with the creation that he is determined to realize.

Deism is an error that the Reformed, Christian religion rejects. It rejects deism by its doctrine of providence, as confessed in article 13 of the Belgic Confession. Deism is the teaching that, having made the world, God withdraws from his creation, to allow it to exist and develop on its own, by its own inherent powers. Deism regards the creator as a divine watchmaker. Having made the world, God stepped back from his creation and allowed it to "run" on its own inherent powers. Apart from all the other erroneous aspects of the philosophical theory of deism, it does not, in the language of the Confession, afford anyone the "unspeakable consolation" that all that befalls him takes place "by the direction of our most gracious and heavenly Father." Deism falls silent at the bedside of the young mother dying of cancer. It is dumb in the presence of the martyr being burned at the stake. Deism's divine watchmaker is not the Reformed faith's God of creation and providence.

Denial of creation necessarily implies the denial also of providence. Atheistic evolutionary theory has no personal God, much less a gracious, heavenly Father, in control of the world and its history. The world of evolution is a world of pure chance or of cold determinism. The practical effect of evolutionary theory is despair. This was freely acknowledged by one of the outstanding philosophers who embraced and promoted the theory of atheistic evolution, Bertrand Russell. In his article "A Free Man's Worship," Russell wrote:

> That Man is the product of causes which had no prevision of the end they were achieving; that his origin, his growth, his hopes and fears, his loves and his beliefs are but the outcome of accidental collocations of atoms; that no fire, no heroism, no intensity of thought and feeling, can preserve an individual life beyond the grave; that all the labors of the ages, all the devotion, all the inspiration, all the noonday brightness of human genius, are destined to extinction in the vast death of the solar system, and that the whole temple of man's achievement must inevitably be buried beneath the debris of a universe in ruins—all these things, if not quite beyond dispute,

are yet nearly so certain that no philosophy which rejects them can hope to stand. Only within the scaffolding of these truths, only on the firm foundation of unyielding despair, can the soul's habitation henceforth be safely built...Brief and powerless is man's life; on him and all his race the slow, sure doom falls pitiless and dark. Blind to good and evil, reckless of destruction, omnipotent matter rolls on its relentless way; for man, condemned to-day to lose his dearest, to-morrow himself to pass through the gate of darkness, it remains only to cherish, ere yet the blow falls, the lofty thoughts that ennoble his little day...proudly defiant of the irresistible forces that tolerate, for a moment, his knowledge and his condemnation, to sustain alone, a weary but unyielding Atlas, the world that his own ideals have fashioned despite the trampling march of unconscious power.[1]

This is not so much philosophy as a wail of despair. It does frankly acknowledge the inescapable implication of evolutionary theory for human life: utter hopelessness! This hopelessness may then take form in profound philosophical theories such as existentialism, or in the crude thinking of "eat, drink, and be merry, for tomorrow we die," or in not thinking of the meaninglessness of life at all, so that one simply plunges himself into the activities of human life as a beast also engages in its beastly activities. But the truth is that, under the influence of evolutionary theory, humans

---

1 Bertrand Russell, "A Free Man's Worship," in *Mysticism and Logic* (London, Longmans, Green, and Co., 1918). The quotation is taken from the first U.S. edition (New York, NY: W.W. Norton, 1929), 56–57.

live without any sense of the meaning of life, without any comfort in the sorrows of life, and without any hope in the face of death.

Theistic evolution, which is the superficial (and illicit) baptism of atheistic evolution with a few drops of holy water, also fatally weakens the truth of biblical providence. Its proponents openly question whether God is in control of the evils in history, including the evils that afflict the lives of the children of God. The effects of this questioning of an important aspect of providence are that believers are fearful concerning the future and deprived of consolation regarding their troubles. Also theistic evolution robs the believer of the "unspeakable consolation" that providence affords him.

The Confession establishes the relationship between God's work of creation and his subsequent work of providence. It did this already in article 12, concerning creation. Into its confession of creation, it inserted, in one and the same line, the confession of providence: "that he doth also still uphold and govern them [his creatures] by his eternal providence and infinite power." The justification for the insertion of the statement concerning providence in a confession of creation is that God's act of creating had a purpose, namely, that all creatures serve their creator. If now this purpose is to be realized, God must see to it by his providence. The God of creation must also be the God of providence.

Also article 13 of the Confession indicates the necessary relationship of creation and providence. It does so in its opening sentence: "The same God, after he had created all things, did not forsake them, or give them up to fortune or chance, but...rules and governs them, according to his holy will." The idea is that it is incredible that God would perform the awesome work of creation only to abandon this world and its history to fortune or chance. Creation necessarily implies providence.

WHAT PROVIDENCE IS

Providence is the power of the triune God keeping all things in existence and governing all things according to God's eternal plan for all things. Providence is the plan of God, or counsel of God, eternally determining the history of the world and the place in that history of every creature with the movement of every creature. Providence is first the counsel of God regarding the creation.

When article 12 referred to providence, it spoke of "*eternal* providence." Eternal providence is the plan or counsel of God regarding the upholding and governing of all the creatures. Similarly, article 13 explains providence as God's ruling and governing all things "according to his holy will," adding that nothing happens in this world "without his appointment." God's holy will and appointment are his counsel of providence.

Again and again, scripture teaches that the will of God governs the direction of history and the happening of all events in history. "Our God is in the heavens: he hath done whatsoever he hath pleased" (Ps. 115:3). God's pleasure is his counsel, which governs what God does in history. Isaiah 46:10 has God "declaring the end from the beginning, and from ancient times the things that are not yet done, saying, My counsel shall stand, and I will do all my pleasure." The unfolding of history is the sovereign work of God. Governing this doing that is history is the good pleasure of the counsel of God. This grand reality—the governing counsel of providence—reveals that God is God and that he is God alone. At issue, therefore, in the confession or denial of the doctrine of providence is the confession or denial of the Godhead of God.

Acts 2:23 confesses the counsel of providence regarding the most wicked deed that sinful humans have committed. Regarding the wicked seizure, unjust condemnation, and evil crucifixion of the Son of God, the text explains: "Him, being delivered by the determinate counsel and foreknowledge of God, ye have taken, and by wicked hands have crucified and slain." Behind the crucifixion of Jesus, as the wicked deed of sinful men, stands the eternal counsel of God, foreknowing and fore-determining the crucifixion in all its evil details.

Acts 4:23–31 confesses the same about the suffering and death of Jesus Christ in still more detail and even more strongly. The raging of the heathen, the vain imagining of the people, the standing up of the kings of the earth, the gathering together of the rulers, and the wickedness of Herod, of Pilate, of the Gentiles, and of the people of Israel against the Lord God by their crucifixion of his Son, the holy child Jesus—all was the doing "whatsoever thy hand and thy counsel determined before to be done" (v. 28). God's counsel determined all this history and every event in it. This is the counsel of providence.

Providence is not only God's counsel. It is also his power that realizes his counsel regarding the universe, specifically the history that unfolds on earth from day to day and from moment to moment. Acts 4:28 speaks not only of God's counsel, planning all that befell Jesus Christ. But it speaks also of God's "hand," referring to the divine agency that executes the counsel.

The power of God that, with the counsel, is his providence is twofold. First, it is the power of giving continual existence to everything. The creation and each creature are dependent upon their maker for their very existence, not only originally but also continually. Did God by his providential power not keep the creation in existence every moment, the world would disappear into the nothingness whence it came by creation. Article 12 spoke of this providential power of God as his "upholding" all things. Article 13 alludes to this aspect of providence when it assures the believer that God keeps "all creatures so under his power that not a hair of our head...can fall to the ground without the will of our Father."

The apostle proclaimed this aspect of God's providence in Acts 17:25, 28: "He giveth to all life, and breath, and all things...For in him we live, and move, and have our being." Several aspects of this plain, powerful statement of God's providence as his power upholding everything are contextually noteworthy. First, it is this truth that reveals the sole and incomparable Godhead of God, thus distinguishing him from the gods of the heathen, including the superstitious Athenians. Second, this providential power is closely related to God's creation of all things. Verse 24, immediately preceding the confession of providence in verse 25, declares: "God that made the world and all things therein." Creation and providence are inseparably related.

Third, by virtue of his providence, God is not far off from humanity and their earthly lives, but very close—as close as humanity's everyday life and work in the world. Therefore, such unbelievers and idolaters as the Athenians are without excuse. Verse 27, again in the context of the declaration of the power of providence, affirms the responsibility of all humans to confess the God who is not far from them by his providence: "That they should seek the Lord, if haply they might feel after him, and find him, though he be not far from every one of us." Although providence is not sufficient for faith and salvation—only the gospel is the power of God unto salvation—it does render every human culpable for unbelief.

A fourth, noteworthy aspect of the apostle's proclamation of providence in Acts 17 is that, according to verse 18, among the Greeks to whom Paul spoke were Epicurean philosophers. To these and their error, the Confession refers explicitly at the end of article 14: "We reject that damnable error of the Epicureans, who say that God regards nothing, but leaves all things to chance." To these arrogant philosophers, who denied any relationship of God to the world, its history, and human life, if God even exists in their philosophy, Paul deliberately preached both that God created the world and that the world and its every creature depend upon God for their very existence.

In addition to the doctrine that was preached, this passage demonstrates regarding sound, biblical mission-method that a man sent by Christ does not tiptoe gingerly around errors known to be held by his audience, nor soften, if not omit, the doctrines that are opposed by the errors. Rather, he exposes the errors and sounds the truths that the errors gainsay. He does so bluntly. He does not wait years to do so.

But this incidentally.

Providence is the power of keeping the world in existence, or the power of upholding the world. It is also the power of governing all things. Creation is dependent upon its maker *as its Lord*. That God governs the world and every creature as creation's Lord, by his power, is the teaching of scripture everywhere and regarding every kind of creature.

God governs the movement of the heavenly bodies, so that on one occasion he made the sun to stand still for a day, with all that that entailed for all the bodies in the galaxy (Josh. 10:12–14). In the realm of nations, God raises up nations and destroys nations—huge happenings in history involving nothing less than upheavals in all of the lives of millions of humans (Daniel). In history, regarding human behavior, God governs the evil as well as the good. God governed the crucifixion of Jesus (Acts 4:28). In the personal life of every human, God so controls each human that not a hair falls from the head of anyone without the will of God (Matt. 10:29–30).

Article 13 of the Confession quotes Matthew 10, concerning God's government of the falling of hairs from one's head, in support of its contention that the providence of God is absolutely all encompassing, including the least significant elements of human life: "All creatures [are] so under his power that not a hair of our head (for they are all numbered), nor a sparrow, can fall to the ground, without the will of our Father." The logical thought of the creed, as of the Bible, is that, controlling the least of events, God certainly governs the greater.

As both counsel and power, providence is based on and testifies to the immanence of God. Immanence is God's presence to and in the world. God is present to the world and in the world everywhere with all his being. It is this basic aspect of providence that Paul affirmed in Acts 17. He is "not far from every one of us" (v. 27). So present is he, so closely present, that "he giveth to all life, and breath, and all things" (v. 25). "In him we live, and move, and have our being" (v. 28). The God who is immanent in the world is the God whose counsel planned the world. He is the God who upholds the world by his very presence to and in the world. If he is immanent, he is present as *God*, that is, as the governor of the world.

In addition to the explanation of providence that the Confession gives, scripture warrants fuller description of this important truth of the Reformed, Christian religion, especially in view of the attacks upon the doctrine by heresies and philosophies. First, providence is God's care of his world. He waters the fields, feeds the brute creatures, and clothes the lilies (Ps. 104; Matt. 6:26–34). In his care for his creation, God will in the end deliver the earthly creation from the vanity into which it was plunged because of man's disobedience. He will renew it so that it too shares in the liberty of the glory of the children of God (Rom. 8:19–22). God is father to the creation.

Second, there is an order and regularity about God's government that makes life and scientific investigation of the creation possible. Science calls this regularity "laws of nature." The Reformed Christian regards this regularity as the order of God's providential government of his world. This order causes the Christian all the more to adore the marvelous God of providence: he is the God of order.

But God is not bound by this orderly government, by "laws of nature." For his own greater glory in the salvation of his church, he can and does work differently in creation than is usual. This different working is the miracles. Miracles are God's extraordinary workings in creation and history. Ordinarily, as to human perception the sun moves around the earth once every twenty-four hours. When it pleased the God of creation and providence, for the salvation of his people, on one occasion "the sun stood still in the midst of heaven, and hasted not to go down about a whole day" (Josh. 10:12–14). Ordinarily, a woman conceives by sexual relations with a man. Science and popular opinion regard this ordinary working of God as an ironclad law of nature. To accomplish the wonder of salvation of the incarnation of the eternal Son of God, God worked so that a virgin conceived and gave birth to the child Jesus (Matt.1:18–25; Luke 1:26–38). The ministry of the apostles, recorded in the book of Acts, was filled with the performance of signs and wonders on behalf of the gospel that they preached.

Ordinarily, God upholds and maintains the heavens and the earth, so that they continue to exist. Comes the universe's last day, when the will of God for the revelation of the glory of Jesus Christ and the realization of the full salvation of his church is otherwise for the present creation. "[Then] shall the sun be darkened, and the moon shall not give her light, and the stars shall fall from heaven, and the power of the heavens shall be shaken" (Matt. 24:29).

Third, after Jesus' ascension into heaven, it is Jesus Christ who exercises providence on behalf of the triune God. Jesus now upholds and governs the world. This power was worked into the man Jesus in God's raising of him from the dead. This glory was bestowed upon him when God seated him at his right hand in heaven. The risen Jesus himself claimed this power in Matthew 28:18: "All power is given unto me in heaven and in earth." Jesus' exercise of providential government over all things is the clear implication of the confession of Jesus' being seated "on the right hand of the Majesty on high," in Hebrews 1:3.

When Revelation 5 teaches that the Lamb who was slain, who is at the right hand of God, takes the book from God and opens its seals, the meaning is that the exalted Jesus

Christ governs all that occurs in the last days, that is, all that is foretold in the book of Revelation. He himself personally carries out the counsel of God concerning the conflict of his kingdom and the kingdom of the beast throughout the history of the end time, beginning with the apostolic era and concluding with his return on the cloud of glory on the world's last day. That Jesus now upholds and governs all things, that is, that the man Jesus is executor of the providential counsel and power of God, is entirely appropriate in that as the second person of the Trinity he was also the creator of all things in the beginning (see John 1:1–18).

Fourth, the goal of providence, as of creation with which providence is closely connected, is the glorification of Jesus Christ with his elect church at the second coming of Jesus, and of God in Jesus Christ. All of the creation and its history serve this end, or goal. The one purpose of God with "all things" is "that in the dispensation of the fulness of times he might gather together in one all things in Christ, both which are in heaven, and which are on earth; even in him" (Eph. 1:10).

Colossians 1:13–20 is clear testimony that the entirety of providence is Christological, that is, based upon, accomplished by, and purposing Jesus Christ. For Jesus Christ were all things created; it pleased the Father that in Jesus Christ all the fullness of creation should dwell, being reconciled to him by the blood of Jesus' cross. All things were created "for him." By the one who would become the man Jesus were all things created. Thus Jesus is the creator as well as the one who upholds and governs in providence. Jesus is the one who upholds and governs all things: "By him all things consist."

Therefore, when article 12 confesses that God made every

creature "to serve its Creator" and that God's purpose with his providence is that "man may serve his God," the meaning is that God made the world to serve him in Jesus Christ and that the new human race of the elect in Jesus Christ would serve their God. All things were created for Jesus Christ. The purpose of God with creation and providence is that all things be reconciled to him by the blood of Jesus Christ.

The controversial question concerning providence, both at the time of the writing of the Belgic Confession and today, is: How extensive is providence? That is, does Christ Jesus on behalf of God his Father uphold and govern *all things, or only some things?* More specifically, does providence extend to the evils in human life, or only to the good events? More specifically still, does providence extend to sin, or only to good deeds of humans?

The answer of the Confession to these questions is emphatically that providence extends to "all things." "He rules and governs them [all things], according to his holy will." "Nothing happens in this world without his appointment."

Great things and small things are included in providence: the fall of the great empires of Assyria and Babylon, but also the fall of one sparrow to the ground. Evils as well as good events are governed by God's providence: not only the salvation of Noah and his family in the ark, but also the destruction of the wicked and their world in the flood.

In the latter is raised the problem of providence for the unbeliever, as also, obviously, for many who profess to be Christians. This is the problem of God's providential government of the evils that befall humans. There are, first of all, the evils that distress and destroy the ungodly. Biblically, these evils include the flood; the fiery destruction of Sodom and Gomorrah; the sickness and death of King Herod; and, as the ultimate evil, everlasting hell. In contemporary history, these evils are sickness, for example, AIDS; social turmoil, for example, that caused by poverty or by man's "inhumanity to man"; and war with its devastations.

These evils are not a problem to the believer—a grief, but not a problem. Upon the ungodly, these evils are God's awful, but just, judgments. Scripture does not hesitate to ascribe these evils to God's government. "Shall there be evil in a city, and the LORD hath not done it?" (Amos 3:6). "I form the light, and create darkness: I make peace and create evil: I the LORD do all these things" (Isa. 45:7). All these evils upon the reprobate, ungodly wicked are expressions of the realization of the word of God to Adam, as head of the human race, "In the day that thou eatest thereof [of the tree of the knowledge of good and evil] thou shalt surely die" (Gen. 2:17). The great and fundamental evil for the human race is death in all its forms and aspects, and death is inflicted upon guilty mankind by the just God.

But providence also governs the evils in the lives of his elect, believing, beloved children. Biblically, these evils include the selling of Joseph by his brothers (Gen. 50:20); the cursing of David by Shimei (2 Sam. 16:10); and the miseries of Job (Job 1:21–22). In every case, scripture teaches not only that God governed these evils, but also that the afflicted believer knew and confessed that God governed the evils that troubled him greatly. Noteworthy about these evils is that all of them were also sins on the part of those who inflicted the evils upon the children of God.

Likewise, all the evils in the lives of God's children throughout history originate ultimately in the counsel of providence and take place by the governing power of providence: sickness; poverty; bitter disappointments; loneliness; bereavement; pain; and "untimely" death. The apostle's "thorn in the flesh" may serve as the outstanding instance of the truth of the government of these evils in the lives of God's dear children by the providence of God (2 Cor. 12:7–10). The evil was extremely painful and distressing for the apostle. Only this explains that that extraordinarily strong man of God would pray three times for the removal of the thorn. It was inflicted upon Paul, whether in the body or in the soul, by God himself, even though Satan had a malignant role in the matter. It was "given" him; it had a good and saving purpose—lest he should be exalted above measure. God's sovereignty over the thorn is evident from the fact that God might have removed the thorn if it pleased him.

In its confession that God governs the evils that befall his people, the Reformed faith of the Belgic Confession distinguishes itself sharply from other alleged forms of the Christian religion. The explanation is that the other purported forms of Christianity deny the sovereignty of God over the evils in human lives. Their god is not the God of holy scripture, but a god of their own imagination. A glaring example of the outright denial of God's government of the evils in human life because of his lack of sovereignty over the evils is the booklet *Looking Up...While Lying Down*. This is a religious pamphlet that advertises itself as comfort for those suffering such evils as sickness, pain, and hospitalization. The author raises the question whether Romans 8:28 ("all things work together for good to them that love God") "means that we should look upon illness, tragedies, disappointments, and difficulties as being good for us." He notes that "some would say that God purposely sends misfortune our way, perhaps to keep us humble or to strengthen our character."[2]

The author repudiates this confession of God's sovereignty over the evils in our lives: "This I do not believe!" He then gives his own answer to the question he raised:

> Rather, I believe that God desires for us what we would characterize as a good life—bodily health, security, a long life of happiness ending in a natural death—all of which is meant by the single Hebrew word Shalom. That life is not always "Shalom" results not from God's intentional will but from circumstances over which God, like us on so many occasions, has no control. God's power was limited when God chose to create us with free wills and to create an evolving universe with natural laws not subject to arbitrary changes.[3]

The Reformed, Christian faith enables the believer to receive the evils in his life as sent by God and under his control because the believer knows that God is sovereign and almighty and because he knows that the universe is not enslaved to evolution with "natural laws." God is in control of the evils, which come to the believer, not according to "natural laws," but according to the will of the Father of Jesus Christ.

Such evils in the lives of God's believing people are never punishments in wrath, but chastisements, discipline, a filling up of the measure of the (non-atoning) sufferings

---

2 John E. Biegert, "Looking Up...While Lying Down" (New York, NY: The Pilgrim Press, 6th ed. 1981), 4.

3 Ibid.

of Christ in his body the church, and ways in which God glorifies himself in his suffering, but patient, people.

Believers are not to suppose that they can, already in this life, comprehend the reasons for the evils in their lives, much less in the lives of others. Sometimes, they know well that certain evils are direct chastisements for specific sins. David knew that the reason for his suffering the rebellion against him by his own son, his flight from Jerusalem and overthrow as king, the violation of his concubines, the death of his infant son, and the indignity of being cursed by the wretched descendent of Saul were divine chastisement because of his adultery with Bathsheba and murder of her husband (see 2 Sam. 12:9–14). God accomplished these evils according to his counsel and by his power of providence. But no sin on his part was the explanation of the intense and manifold suffering of Job, suffering that Job himself attributed to the providential power of God (Job 1:20–21; 2:10). Nor did God ever explain to Job the reason for his suffering.

The Confession acknowledges that there is mystery about the providence of God. Although the reference of the Confession is particularly the providential government of sin, this mystery extends also to the painful evils that God brings upon his children. Is there any believer who does not struggle with the question, "Why does God afflict me, or my fellow Christian, with this sore and painful 'evil'?" This was the spiritual struggle of the man of God in Psalm 73. His "feet were almost gone"; his "steps had well nigh slipped" (v. 2). The reason was his experience that "all the day long have I been plagued, and chastened every morning" (v. 14). In contrast to himself, the wicked prospered, in the providence of God (vv. 2–12).

In such circumstances of suffering and of struggle with doubt, the believer takes to heart the mystery of providence: "And as to what he doth surpassing human understanding we will not curiously inquire into it further than our capacity will admit of; but with the greatest humility and reverence adore the righteous judgments of God which are hid from us." As the Confession declares, the providence of God is "incomprehensible."

The incomprehensibility of providence applies above all to the extension of providence to sin. It is a distinguishing feature of the Reformed faith that it confesses that the providence of God, both counsel and power, extends to the sinful acts of devils and humans. The Belgic Confession is clear: "all things" are ruled and governed according to his holy will; his power is so great that "he orders and executes his work in the most excellent and just manner even when the devil and wicked men act unjustly." When the Confession inserts in this context, "Nevertheless, God neither is the author of, nor can be charged with, the sins which are committed," it is beyond question that it has sin in view. Nor by these words does the Confession deny that God planned and governs sin, but only that he is by this reality the "author" of sin.

In addition, the Confession goes on to teach that the "hurt" that the devil and the enemies of the church do to the church is subject to the "will and permission" of God. This "hurt" is persecution, one of the greatest sins committed by wicked humans in history. The student of the Confession should remember that at the time of its writing the Reformed churches in the Lowlands were suffering one of the most severe persecutions, if not the most severe persecution, in all the history of the church of Christ. What

Psalm 105:25 says about Egypt's persecution of Israel holds true of all the sinful persecution of the church throughout history: "He [God] turned their heart to hate his people, to deal subtilly with his servants."

The confession that God governs sin, although rare in Reformed churches and even rejected by Reformed theologians at the present time, is creedal for all Reformed churches and theologians. No Reformed person may deny this truth, much less a Reformed officebearer. Denial of God's providential government of sin for a Reformed preacher of theology is violation of his oath at his installation into office that he will "diligently...teach and faithfully...defend the aforesaid doctrine [which includes God's providential government of evil, as taught in article 13 of the Belgic Confession]."[4] Denial of God's providential government of evil subjects the preacher rightly to church discipline.

Scripture is clear and emphatic concerning God's government of evils. This is the implied doctrine in all the innumerable passages that teach that God is sovereign and omnipotent. Isaiah 13:6 describes all the sinful deeds performed upon Babylon, including the killing of the men, the raping of the women, and the dashing to pieces of the children as "a destruction from the Almighty."

If there are deeds that are outside the counsel and government of God, he is not *Almighty*, but *Partly*-mighty.

There are explicit passages in scripture that affirm God's sovereignty regarding sin. Such is the bluntness and forcefulness of these passages that when a Reformed theologian or preacher uses such language today, the enemies

---

4   Formula of Subscription, in *Confessions and Church Order*, 326.

of God's sovereignty over sin are quick to charge that the theologian or preacher makes God the "author of sin." Regarding reprobate Shimei's enormous wickedness of cursing David, the Lord's anointed, David confessed that "the LORD hath said unto him, Curse David" (2 Sam. 16:10). Since God had not exhorted Shimei, with an audible command, to curse David, the meaning is that God decreed this sin in his counsel of providence and realized his counsel by the government of his providential power. By his power, not his grace, God worked upon Shimei's depraved and hateful heart to purpose the cursing and moved his sinful lips to utter the dreadful curse. Thus with a providential command, which Shimei could not hear, God "said" to that totally depraved wretch, "Curse David."

Noteworthy is the salutary practical benefit for David of his knowledge of God's sovereignty over Shimei's sin. Knowledge of God's providential control of sin is not an abstract theological doctrine. This knowledge caused David to submit himself to the humiliation of Shimei's cursing. The cursing effected the salutary spiritual benefit upon David that God intended with the cursing: David's chastisement for the sin with Bathsheba and Uriah, and thus his growth in holiness of life. Shimei's gross sin was the promotion of David's salvation.

God's sovereignty over sins, even the worst of them, is put beyond all doubt by the church's confession of God's government of the crucifixion of Jesus by his counsel and hand. Concerning the supreme evil of the crucifixion of Jesus with all the wickedness leading up to the crucifixion and all the wickedness involved in it, the church confessed that all the sinful humans, and by implication the devils, did "whatsoever thy hand and thy counsel determined before to be done" (Acts 4:28). The divine counsel determined all that evil. The divine hand was the controlling power in the doing of all that evil.

Especially regarding the providential government of the crucifixion is the practical, saving benefit of the knowledge of this government evident. First, only as God's work by means of all the wicked does the cross have redeeming value. The cross was not ultimately the evil work of sinful men and devils. But God "spared not his own Son, but delivered him up for us all" (Rom. 8:32). Also, the benefit of the knowledge of God's government of sin is that which is on the foreground in the context of Acts 4:28. All the hostility against the church by the false church and the wicked world and all their persecution of the church are under God's control. The church that lives in the consciousness of the government of sin by God, as confessed in Acts 4:28, can pray the petitions of verse 29: "And now, Lord, behold their threatenings: and grant unto thy servants, that with all boldness they may speak thy word."

Concerning this reality of the sovereignty of God with respect to sin, the relationship between the divine sovereignty and the committing of sin is not that God is the author of the sin committed, that is, the one who commits the sin, so that he is blamable for the sin. Neither is the relationship such that God forces the sinner to commit the wicked deed against the sinner's own will. This is vitally important, for otherwise God is the "author" of sin, that is, the actual performer of the sinful deed, and chargeable with the guilt of the sin, something that the Belgic Confession denies: "God neither is the author of, nor can be charged with, the sins which are committed." The explanation why God is not the author of sin, even though he

governs the committing of sin, is, according to the Confession, "that he orders and executes his work in the most
excellent and just manner even when the devil and wicked
men act unjustly."

Two truths are important in this regard. First, the sinner always performs the sin freely and willingly, not because
God forces him to sin, contrary to the sinner's own will.
Thus the author, that is, guilty performer, of the sinful deed
is the wicked human himself.

Second, God has a good purpose in view with the sin
that the human commits, whereas the wicked human has
an evil purpose with the same sinful deed. This was stated
by Joseph concerning his brothers' selling him into Egypt:
"Ye thought evil against me; but God meant it unto good,
to bring to pass, as it is this day, to save much people alive"
(Gen. 50:20). That God's purpose with his sovereign government of the sinful deeds of wicked men is good, in
contrast to the evil purposes of the human authors of the
sinful deeds, is conclusively evident in the crucifixion of
Jesus. All the depraved human agents in the death of Jesus
had wicked motives and purposes. God's purpose with the
same death was the salvation of the church and the glorifying of his own name.

Another important truth concerning the relationship of
God's sovereignty to sin is that the relationship is not merely
permission. One may speak of permission in order to stress
that the devil or the wicked man willingly performs the evil
deed or speaks the sinful word, but permission does not
do justice to the reality of the providential government of
sin. God did not merely permit wicked men to torture and
kill Jesus. But God decreed the crucifixion by his counsel
and realized it by his hand (Acts 4:28). God did not permit

wicked men and sickness to afflict Job, but, as Job himself acknowledged, "the LORD hath taken away" (Job 1:21).

The Belgic Confession speaks of "permission" when it confesses God's government of the sin of the persecution of Christians by their enemies under the instigation of the devil. But it speaks of permission in close connection with the "will" of God, and it mentions the will of God first: "his will and permission."

In his government of sin and sinful creatures, God "restrains" the devil and the wicked, according to the Confession: "He so restrains the devil and all our enemies that, without his will and permission, they can not hurt us." The meaning, especially clearly in a chapter on providence, is that God controls the devil and the wicked world by his decree and power, so that their opposition to God's church, fierce as it may be, is completely subject to his decree and power. The wicked never slip the leash of divine providence. Caesar Nero was thus under God's restraint when, for his amusement, he made living torches of Christians in his gardens. When in the Netherlands in the late sixteenth and early seventeenth centuries, the duke of Alva brutally murdered more than a hundred thousand Reformed men, women, and children, he was restrained by God. So also were the pope and the Roman Catholic Church restrained, under whose auspices Alva conducted this bloody persecution. Antichrist will be subject to divine restraint in the future when he inflicts upon the church the great tribulation.

God's restraint of his and the church's enemies is not an internal, gracious work that keeps the enemies from being totally depraved, unless the devil is not totally depraved but partially good, and unless the enemies display some goodness when they are hurting God's people. But the restraint is that of providential power controlling the wicked so that in their wickedness, especially in the persecution of the church, they go so far and no further, and so that in their persecution of the church they serve God's purposes.

All of this having been said about the relation of divine sovereignty and sin, as only the Reformed faith confesses this relation, the truth is that the believer, including the believing Reformed theologian, cannot fully understand that God is sovereign over sin while the sinner himself is fully and solely responsible for his sin. The Reformed creed freely confesses the incomprehensibility of God's providential decree and power regarding sin. Indeed, it warns the Reformed believer, including the theologian, against illicit and dangerous speculation concerning this matter:

> And as to what he [God] doth surpassing human understanding we will not curiously inquire into it further than our capacity will admit of; but with the greatest humility and reverence adore the righteous judgments of God which are hid from us, contenting ourselves that we are disciples of Christ, to learn only those things which he has revealed to us in his Word without transgressing these limits.

Inability to comprehend the government of sin by providence does not, however, imply the denial of this government, as article 13 of the Confession makes perfectly plain.

The practical benefit for the Reformed Christian of the knowledge of providence, in its full extent, is plainly a leading purpose of the Confession with its doctrine of providence: "This doctrine affords us unspeakable consolation."

The consolation from providence for the believer is nothing less than the certainty that everything that happens to him, whether success or failure, riches or poverty, fame or shame, health or sickness, life or death, comes to him in the love of God his gracious Father for him and for his good.

"All things work together for good to them that love God...He that spared not his own Son, but delivered him up for us all, how shall he not with him also freely give us all things" (Rom. 8:28, 32)? The passage not only speaks of the favorable attitude of God toward the elect believer, but also implies the providential power of God that effectually realizes the good that God purposes toward him. All things "work" the good of the believer, because God purposed the good in his counsel of providence and effectuates the good by his power of providence.

In this life this comfort of providence is a matter of faith, and of faith only. The experience of the salvation of providence, like justification, is by faith only. Twice in article 13 the Confession makes the comfort of providence a matter of faith. The article opens with the words, "We believe [the truth of providence with its comfort]." Applying providence to the consolation of the believer, article 13 declares concerning the Father of the Reformed Christian, "in whom we do entirely trust." Trust is an element of faith.

The believer does not yet figure out—understand comprehendingly—the providential goodness of God to him in the events of his life, especially the calamities and griefs of his life. Like old Jacob, he sometimes feels, and says, "All these things are against me" (Gen. 42:36). But he believes the word of promise, sealed in the gift of the Son of God for his redemption.

The poet, who himself knew sorrow, expressed in lovely

verse the comfort of providence for the believer in circumstances of distress and trouble.

God moves in a mysterious way
His wonders to perform;
He plants His footsteps in the sea,
And rides upon the storm.

Deep in unfathomable mines
Of never-failing skill,
He treasures up His bright designs,
And works His sovereign will.

Ye fearful saints, fresh courage take,
The clouds ye so much dread
Are big with mercy, and shall break
In blessings on your head.

Judge not the Lord by feeble sense,
But trust Him for His grace:
Behind a frowning providence
He hides a smiling face.

His purposes will ripen fast,
Unfolding every hour;
The bud may have a bitter taste,
But sweet will be the flower.

Blind unbelief is sure to err,
And scan His work in vain;
God is His own interpreter,
And He will make it plain.[5]

---

5 William Cowper, "God moves in a mysterious way," in Adam Fox, *English Hymns and Hymn Writers* (London: Collins, 1947), 26.

Providence is comfort to the believer, not only regarding the course of his own life individually, but also regarding history in its entirety. God governs the course of history, in its minutest detail. In all that takes place, he is reaching his goal of glorifying himself in Jesus Christ by the salvation of the elect church. As all things were created for Jesus Christ unto the glory of God, so also does providence infallibly direct all things unto Jesus Christ for the glory of God (see Col. 1:16).

The truth of providence affords the believer other benefits than only consolation regarding the evils in his life. Providence enables the believer rightly to understand the developments in the world around himself and the church. The spread of false doctrine and the falling away from the truth of so many in the churches of the "Christian West" are not to him a bewildering conundrum. But he views these developments as God's righteous judgment of churches and their members who received not the love of the truth but had pleasure in "unrighteousness" (2 Thess. 2:10–11).

The shameless increase and approval of homosexuality and even of homosexual "marriage" in Western civilization are not an inexplicable descent of the West into the abyss. They are the righteous judgment of God upon peoples who have held the truth of God, which they knew, under in unrighteousness (Rom. 1:18–32). In this light also does the Reformed Christian, holding the doctrine of providence, judge the national and international plague of AIDS. It is not merely an unfortunate disease concerning which we ought only to feel pity for the sufferer and to which a society ought to react only by throwing billions of dollars at it, in order to cure it, without examining the cause of the plague—surely a most unscientific policy. But AIDS is the judgment of God, not only on individual sodomites, but also on societies that tolerate, encourage, and justify the sin of sodomy and lesbianism.

Also for the believer, providence has other benefits than only his comfort. It is also instructive, sometimes painfully so. Sometimes evils befall him as direct chastisements for sins that he has committed. This is not always the explanation of the evils he suffers, as the experience of Job shows. But this sometimes is the case. David's sin with Bathsheba and Uriah troubled his family by the providence of God (2 Sam. 12:7–14). There were sickness and death in the congregation at Corinth because of schism in the church (1 Cor. 11:17–34). These evils are not punishments for the sins. But they are direct chastisements. Believing the truth of providence, both church and believer must be open to the divine instruction in the evils that are chastisements for sins. "If we would judge ourselves, we should not be judged" (1 Cor. 11:31).

One significant benefit of providence for both church and believer is that it undergirds their prayers. Because God governs all things, prayer to him is eminently reasonable, as it is God glorifying—prayer for the repentance of a sinner; prayer for daily bread; prayer for healing from sickness; prayer for punishment of enemies of the church; prayer for the soon coming of Christ. Indeed, prayer is the practical demonstration of the sincerity of one's confession of providence.

Chapter Ten

OF THE CREATION AND FALL OF MAN, AND HIS INCAPACITY TO PERFORM WHAT IS TRULY GOOD

(ARTICLE 14)

ART. XIV. OF THE CREATION AND FALL OF MAN, AND HIS INCAPACITY TO PERFORM WHAT IS TRULY GOOD.

We believe that God created man out of the dust of the earth, and made and formed him after his own image and likeness, good, righteous, and holy, capable in all things to will agreeably to the will of God. But being in honor, he understood it not, neither knew his excellency, but willfully subjected himself to sin, and consequently to death and the curse, giving ear to the words of the devil. For the commandment of life, which he had received, he transgressed; and by sin separated himself from God, who was his true life, having corrupted his whole nature, whereby he made himself liable to corporal and spiritual death. And being thus become wicked, perverse, and corrupt in all his ways, he hath lost all his excellent gifts which he had received from God, and only retained a few remains thereof, which, however, are sufficient to leave man without excuse; for all the light which is in us is changed into darkness, as the Scriptures teach us, saying: The light shineth in darkness, and the darkness comprehendeth it not: where St. John calleth men darkness.

Therefore we reject all that is taught repugnant to this concerning the free will of man, since man is but a slave to sin; and has nothing of himself unless it is given him from heaven. For who may presume to boast that he of himself can do any good, since Christ saith, No man can come to me, except the Father which hath sent me draw him? Who will glory in his own will, who understands that to be carnally minded is enmity against God? Who can speak of his knowledge, since the natural man receiveth not the things of the Spirit of God? In short, who dare suggest any thought, since he knows that we are not sufficient of ourselves to think any thing as of ourselves, but that our sufficiency is of God? And therefore what the Apostle saith ought justly to be held sure and firm, that God worketh in us both to will and to do of his good pleasure. For there is no will nor understanding, conformable to the divine will and understanding, but what Christ hath wrought in man: which he teaches us when he saith, Without me ye can do nothing.

INTRODUCTION

Article 14 is especially rich, full of doctrines that are fundamental to the Reformed faith, that is, to the Christian religion. The article begins with the creation of man. The creation of the human race is not treated in article 12, where the divine act of creation is the topic, but is reserved for careful consideration in article 14.

As an aspect of the truth of the creation of man, there is in the article confession of man's glorious original estate "after his [God's] own image and likeness."

Even though the word "covenant" does not occur, the article raises the important, controversial matter of God's covenant with Adam in paradise before the fall. The truth of the covenant comes up in the article when it states that Adam transgressed "the commandment of life," adding that by his sin he "separated himself from God, who was his true life." The reference is to the prohibition of Gen. 2:16–17 against eating of the tree of knowledge. From this commandment, some Reformed and Presbyterian theologians have constructed a "covenant of works" in paradise prior to the fall. This raises the questions, "Was there a 'covenant of works' in the garden before the fall?" "If not, was there a covenant at all?" "If so, what was that covenant?"

The article includes as one of its main teachings the fall of Adam into sin, as recorded in Genesis 3. In our apostate age it is significant that the article presents this fall as a historical event, that is, a real fall, in distinction from the imaginary fall (which is no fall at all) of much of contemporary theology, both ostensibly liberal and reputedly conservative. Treatment of the fall necessitates consideration of the possibility of the fall in view of man's having been created good. The article addresses this issue when it states that Adam "willfully subjected himself to sin." Another aspect of the fall is the role played by the tempter: "giving ear to the words of the devil."

An element of its doctrine concerning the fall of man

is the article's teaching of the effects and consequences regarding the fall for the human race, one of which is "death." One aspect of this death is total depravity, what the creed calls "spiritual death."

In connection with the confession of total depravity, the question comes up, whether fallen men and women retain any good, any ability to please God, or to save themselves, or to cooperate in their salvation. The Confession does recognize that fallen man "retained a few remains thereof," that is, a few remains of the excellent gifts with which God created him. Are these "remains" some good left over after the fall? Many Reformed churches and theologians argue strenuously that these remains are genuine, spiritual good in the judgment of God. They are either a remnant of the image of God, which was not completely lost in the fall, or the gift to man of a "common grace" of God. They enable fallen man to perform works that please God in the realm of culture and society and even to accept God's alleged well-meant offer of salvation to all in the gospel.

Against this latter error, namely, an ability of fallen man to accept an offered salvation, the article rejects the theory of a free will of fallen sinners as heresy: "We reject all that is taught...concerning the free will of man, since man is but a slave to sin; and has nothing of himself." The rejection of free will is distinctive of the Reformed faith, identifying it as the faith of holy scripture. Other nominally Christian faiths agree with each other in affirming free will. The issue of free will is no insignificant matter. With its rejection stands or falls the gospel of grace.

In addition to all the important doctrinal content of the article, it should be noted that the article either quotes or refers to many passages of scripture. The entire second half of the article is a string of carefully chosen texts of scripture. The Reformed faith is biblical.

One other feature of article 14 is noteworthy by way of introduction. This is the relationship of the article to the articles that precede and the articles that follow. Article 14 completes the account of creation that was begun in article 12. Article 14 confesses the crowning work of the Creator: the creation of man, both male and female. Following as it does article 13 on providence, which article affirmed that God appointed all that happens in the world and that God governs all that takes place, article 14 must be understood in such a way that the fall did not take God by surprise, but rather was planned and governed by him. Deliberately, De Bres placed the article on the fall immediately after the article on providence.

Regarding what follows, article 14 sets the stage for the confession of God's great work of redeeming out of the fallen human race a church chosen to eternal life in Jesus Christ. Article 16, which confesses the origin in election of the gracious redemption of the church by Jesus Christ, opens with the words, "We believe that all the posterity of Adam, being thus fallen into perdition and ruin by the sin of our first parents, God then did manifest himself such as he is; that is to say, MERCIFUL AND JUST."

GOD'S CREATION OF MAN

It is necessary to be clear, first, as to what the Confession has in mind with the word "man" in article 14. At the outset, regarding the creation of "man," it refers to the first human, the male named Adam. It was Adam who was "created out of the dust of the earth," according to Genesis 2:7. Nevertheless, Eve, the first female, given to Adam as his wife, is not overlooked or excluded by the article. She was the complement of the male, so that the male and the female in their union in marriage are full and complete "man." Having her origin as she did from a rib of Adam, she too was originally "made and formed" with and in the male. She too was made in God's image. She too was involved in the fall, as the article suggests when it says that man gave "ear to the words of the devil." Adam heard those words only secondhand, from Eve.

So Genesis 1:26–27 uses the word "man" not exclusively of the male, but of the male and the female together in marriage: united in marriage, the male and the female are "man," just as Jesus and the church are the complete new man. "So God created man in his own image, in the image of God created he him; male and female created he them" (v. 27).

Then the view of the creed broadens out, so that later in the article by "man" is meant the entire human race. The few remains of the excellent gifts are sufficient to leave "man" without excuse. It is "man" who does not have a free will and who is a slave to sin. The explanation is that Adam was created the head of the race. He was not merely a private individual. The important implication is that our confession of the creation of "man" concerns the creation of all of us in honor. Likewise, what the article says about the fall, it says about the fall of all humans, Jesus only excepted.

At the end of the sixth day of creation week, as his last, crowning work, God made man. He made this creature differently than he had made the other creatures. Whereas he simply called the other creatures into existence, God "formed man" with his own hand. This special care gave evidence of the exalted position and high honor of man.

There were two distinct phases of God's creation of man. First, he "formed" the male—Adam—from the dust, breathing into Adam's nostrils the breath of life (Gen. 2:7). This twofold creative act is not so much to be understood as accomplishing that every human is soul and body, as it is that man is related both to the earth and to God. Man is physical, but he is also inescapably related to God and in this sense spiritual.

The second distinct phase of the creation of man was the making of a woman (v. 22). After Adam had named the animals and realized his "aloneness," God made the female—Eve—from a rib of Adam. There was the same special care in the creation of the female as there had been in the creation of the male. God did not simply call the woman into existence. He formed her also with his hand. From the rib "made he a woman" (v. 22). In the Hebrew original, "made" is "built," emphasizing the creative labor and care of the Creator with the woman.

The significance of these creative acts of God forming a male and a female to be complete "man" in marriage, as taught not only in Genesis 2, but also in 1 Corinthians 11 and 1 Timothy 2, is that (one) male and (one) female are as the rule to marry; that the life of the husband and the wife in marriage is to be intimate communion; that the husband is the head in marriage, as created first, and the wife is to be the help of the husband, as created out of him, for him, and after him; and, obviously, that it is the will of God that a male marries a female, indeed, that only the union of a male and a female is, or can be, a marriage. In AD 2017, as wickedness develops in the world, it demands to be said that the intimate, sexual relations of male with male and female with female is not and never can be marriage, but is rather perversion. This is determined not by public opinion, nor by civil courts, nor by bigotry, but by God's creation of the human race as male and female in marriage, according to the inspired, authoritative scripture.

This creation of man was a historical reality, a historical fact. It actually happened, and it happened exactly as described in Genesis 1 and 2. Denial of the historicity of the creation of man is heretical. This denial is widespread in the Reformed and Presbyterian churches. Theologians and synods wax eloquent and loquacious in denying what Genesis 1 and 2 make plain to every believing mind: there was a historical creation of a historical Adam and a historical Eve, and the opening chapters of the Bible are God's own account of this creation.

Although Reformed assemblies disgrace themselves, indeed identify their churches as false churches, by their arduous efforts to judge these denials of the historicity of Genesis 1 and 2 as within the bounds of orthodoxy, if not God's own truth, it is plain on the very face of the denials that the denial of the historicity of the creation account in Genesis 1 and 2 is grievous surrender of the Christian faith to the unbelief of higher criticism of holy scripture and of evolution. To set aside the account of the creation of man in Genesis 1 and 2 as unhistorical (mythical!) is to deny the clarity and authority of scripture, which is an attack on the inspiration of scripture. Thus is denied in Reformed circles everything that the Belgic Confession has confessed about scripture in articles 2–7.

At stake in the denial of the historicity of the account of the creation of man in Genesis 1 and 2 is the historicity of the account of the origin of the new human race in the opening chapters of the gospels. First, if there was no historical creation as revealed in Genesis 1 and 2, neither does Genesis 3 reveal a historical fall. In this case, there is no need for the Jesus of the gospels. If Adam the first is mythical, so also is Adam the second mythical. Second, the same unbelief that doubts the origin of Adam also, and all the more, doubts the origin of Jesus. The mind that stumbles over the account of the creation of Adam out of the dust must find absurd the account of the forming of Jesus in the womb of a virgin.

This exposure of the wickedness of denying the historicity of the biblical revelation of the creation of man says nothing yet of the evil of Reformed theologians and Reformed assemblies contradicting their own, authoritative creeds. Lord's Day 3 of the Heidelberg Catechism and article 14 of the Belgic Confession bind Reformed theologians and Reformed church assemblies to the confession of a historical creation of man as revealed in Genesis 1 and 2.

Going on at length in defense of the historicity of scripture's revelation of creation (and the fall—and the origin of Jesus!) is not necessary for the Reformed believer and the soundly Reformed church. If this defense is necessary in a church, the church is so far gone in apostasy that its state is hopeless. What it needs is not an extended defense of creation (and the fall), but reformation.

What interests the Reformed believer is the meaning of the grand event of the creation of man, that is, the word of God to him or her in this reality.

The main truth about man as originally created was that he was made "in his [God's] image" (Gen. 1:26). Other truths are also important. God created man as king of the earth and all it contained: "have dominion" (v. 28).

As was already noted, man was created to be married,

indeed, *as* married. It is a weakness of this article on creation and of the three forms of unity generally that so little is confessed and taught concerning this fundamental aspect of the Christian human life. Marriage was an outstanding aspect of the creation of man in the beginning. Its importance to social life in a nation is abundantly evident from the destructive consequences in a society when marriage and the home (to which marriage is basic) are no longer held in honor. In addition, marriage is of fundamental importance to the Reformed, Christian life and experience. It is the means for the birth and godly rearing of children, whom God includes in his covenant of grace. It is the living symbol of the covenant of grace, which is the real marriage, the marriage of Jesus Christ and his church (see Eph. 5:22–33). Its bliss foreshadows the nature and delight of the coming salvation, which will be the marriage of the Lamb and his bride (Rev. 19:7–9; 21:9).

If Reformed churches worldwide were sound enough regarding the truth of marriage, it would be profitable to call an international synod to formulate an addition to article 14 of the Belgic Confession setting forth the truth of marriage. But to their shame, many of the churches corrupt the doctrine and practice of holy marriage. They regard marriage as a contract that is as fragile and breakable as marriage in the world of the ungodly. They approve divorce on other grounds than fornication. They legitimize remarriage while the original mate still lives, which remarriage the God of the institute of marriage condemns as adultery (Mark 10:11–12; Luke 16:18; Romans 7:2–3; 1 Corinthians 7: 10–11, 39).

One vitally important aspect of the creation of man is reserved for article 15 of the Confession, namely, Adam's headship of the human race. This headship is basic to the reality of original sin.

AFTER HIS OWN IMAGE

The "honor" and "excellency" of man as created that article 14 speaks of were that God made him "after his own image and likeness." Generally, the meaning is that Adam and Eve resembled God as children resemble their parents. And they were children of God. Of Adam, Luke 3, tracing the genealogy of Jesus through his adoptive father, declares that he was "*the son* of God" (Luke 3:38; emphasis added). Specifically, the image of God in Adam was that he was spiritually good. This is the identification of the image by the Confession: "good, righteous, and holy, capable in all things to will agreeably to the will of God." That the Confession conceives the image as Adam's spiritual goodness is evident also in its description of the loss of the image: "being thus become wicked, perverse, and corrupt in all his ways." This confessional identification of the image and likeness as Adam's original spiritual goodness is based on scripture's description of the restoration of the image as the bestowal upon the elect of "knowledge," "righteousness," and "holiness" (Eph. 4:24; Col. 3:10).

To bear, or be, this image, man had to have a mind and a will with which he could consciously and deliberately be related to God, the divine original that he imaged. Adam had to be human. But the image was Adam's spiritual goodness. This goodness was goodness of nature, goodness of what he was in body and soul. His goodness was not merely in deeds, nor in the decisions of his will. Accordingly, loss of the image was corruption of "his whole nature." The misery of fallen Adam, accordingly, was not only that now he thinks wicked thoughts, wills evil desires, and performs sinful deeds. But "being thus become wicked, perverse, and corrupt in all his ways, he hath lost all his excellent gifts which he had received from God," according to the Confession.

Identification of the image in which Adam was created as something other than his original spiritual goodness of nature is serious doctrinal error. It underestimates the gravity of the fall: the loss of the spiritual likeness to God. Invariably, error concerning the image entails the notion that fallen man retained the image, or at least part of the image. This, in turn, involves the false doctrine that fallen man is still somewhat pleasing to God and even that he can contribute to his salvation, usually by a free will that he is thought to have retained. Retention of even a small portion of the image implies that fallen, unsaved man is still somewhat pleasing to God and capable of some good. Thus fallen man escapes the devastating judgment of the gospel upon him: *dead* in sin, incapable of *any* good.

Neither is it Reformed orthodoxy, as outlined by article 14 of the Confession, to speak of the image in a "wider and narrower sense." This is common in Reformed circles, but wrongly. The thought is that man lost the image in the narrower sense, with reference to his original goodness, but retained the image in the broader sense, with reference to his mind and will. First, there is no creedal basis for this distinction. Second, the distinction teaches, and is intended to teach, fallen man's retention of the image in some important respect. Since the image is obviously good and capable of willing and doing good, the result of the distinction, if not its purpose, is to teach that fallen man retains some good and some capability for good. Thus is denied total depravity. Thus is asserted fallen man's retention of a free will upon which his salvation depends, to the denial of the gospel of grace.

From his thesis that all humans retain, or are, the image of God, Christian Reformed theologian Harry Boer drew the conclusion that all humans were redeemed by Christ and will likely be saved in the end, that is, sheer universalism.

> It is that Man as imago Dei [image of God]—and therefore all participants in the imago, that is, all members of the human race—has the competence to respond affirmatively to the proclamation of the gospel. Every hearer of the gospel has the spiritual resource to believe the gospel and become a living member of the body of Christ. In this sense, he can decide to be born again.[1]

In this universal retention of the image of God is found the "possibility" (and for Boer, reality) "of salvation outside the church and knowledge of the gospel."[2]

From this universal retention of the image of God, Boer deduces the possibility (and for Boer, reality) of universal redemption. "Did Christ die only for those who come to know him and believe in him? Did he not die for the sins of the whole world?"[3] But this universal redemption

---

1 Harry R. Boer, *An Ember Still Glowing: Humankind as the Image of God* (Grand Rapids, MI: Eerdmans, 1990), 85. Here, Boer recognizes and affirms that retention of the image implies that salvation, indeed the new birth, depends upon the will of the sinner. Thus is denied total depravity and, indeed, all of the gospel of salvation by grace alone.
2 Ibid., 121.
3 Ibid., 123.

is grounded in the retention of the image of God by all humans without exception:

> In Christ Man is restored to his true self, that is, to being again the true and full image of God...The redemption of mankind is the redemption of the imago Dei...As we have all been created in Adam, so we are created anew in Christ, who is the image of God in the new creation.[4]

The conclusion is that the doctrine of the retention of the image by all humans implies the very real possibility of universal salvation. "Does God redeem the entirety of mankind, person for person?...We therefore await the revelation of God's possibility."[5] On the basis of his doctrine that all humans share still the image of God and in light of his open, vehement denial of the creedal, Reformed doctrine of reprobation, there can be no doubt that "God's possibility" is Boer's reality.

In his teaching of the retention of the image by fallen humankind, with its implication of a will that is capable of choosing God and the good, Boer contradicts article 14 of the Belgic Confession: "We reject all that is taught repugnant to this concerning the free will of man, since man is but a slave to sin; and has nothing of himself unless it is given him from heaven."

The significance of God's having created man in his own image is that it reveals God's great goodness to man. God kept nothing back from man but deity itself. Man was "in honor." Indeed, as the image of God, man was God's child. Although this is often overlooked, it is the implication of man's having

---

4 Ibid., 159.
5 Ibid., 185, 187.

been created in the image of God. As a human child is the image of his earthly parents, Adam and Eve were the image of their heavenly Father. Because Adam was created in God's image, Luke 3:38 can call him "the son of God."

His having been created as God's image aggravates man's wickedness in the disobedience of his original sin. Man's disobedience was sheer, outrageous ingratitude. "Being in honor, he understood it not, neither knew his excellency, but willfully subjected himself to sin."

In his fall, man lost the image completely. He remains man; always he remains human. In hell, men and women are humans. But now, as fallen, man is unlike God and like the devil, spiritually. How the Confession asserts the complete loss of the image of God by fallen man! "Having corrupted his whole nature...being thus become wicked, perverse, and corrupt in all his ways...all the light which is in us is changed into darkness...there is no will nor understanding, conformable to the divine will and understanding."

Rather than being the image of God in any degree or respect whatever, retaining something of their original knowledge, righteousness, and holiness, fallen humans are "the children of wrath," "dead in trespasses and sins" (Eph. 2:1–3). The salvation of fallen man, therefore, as the Confession declares, must be "given him from heaven." Salvation cannot come from man himself, that is, out of or depending upon his own will or working. Salvation can only come from God, that is, out of, depending upon, and being worked by grace.

THE COVENANT WITH MAN

Created in the image of God, man lived in a definite covenantal relationship with God his creator from the moment of his creation. Although the word "covenant" is not used, article 14 of the Confession strongly suggests a covenant of God with man. It speaks of a "commandment of life." The reference is to Genesis 2:16–17: "And the LORD God commanded the man, saying, Of every tree of the garden thou mayest freely eat: But of the tree of the knowledge of good and evil, thou shalt not eat of it: for in the day that thou eatest thereof thou shalt surely die." The Confession also describes the effect of the fall as man's separating himself from God, who was his true life. Separation from God is, in fact, the Confession's description of the breaking of the covenant with Adam. By implication, the covenant with Adam was his communion with God.

Here in article 14 is the opportunity, if not the requirement, for the Reformed faith to express its unique and fundamental doctrine of the covenant, a truth that all the Reformed creeds leave woefully, if understandably, undeveloped. Development of the doctrine of the covenant has come late in the history of the church.

Very early in the tradition, Reformed theologians came to describe man's relationship to God in the Garden of Eden as a covenant. The Reformed tradition has understood that God made man in his image, for the sake of the covenant between himself and man.

By many in the Reformed churches, this covenant is understood to have been a "covenant of works." This name and understanding of the covenant with Adam are based on the prohibition of Genesis 2:17, quoted above. The conception of the covenant of God with man in paradise accordingly is as follows. The covenant was an agreement between God and Adam, made by God sometime after the creation of Adam. The agreement was conditional. Adam must obey the prohibition of Genesis 2:17. If he did, God would reward Adam with eternal life, that is, the higher life in heaven that the saints now enjoy through the work of Jesus Christ. Adam would earn this higher life by his obedience. Should Adam disobey the prohibition, he would lose the perfect, but merely earthly, life he enjoyed in paradise and suffer death.

This conception of the covenant with Adam as a conditional contract in which Adam might have obtained a higher, eternal life by his obedience is the basis of the contemporary heresy in Reformed and Presbyterian churches that calls itself the federal, that is, covenantal, vision. According to this heretical theology of the covenant of grace in Christ Jesus, the New Testament covenant is a conditional contract with believers and their children. In it justification is by faith and works. By fulfilling the conditions of believing and performing good works, believers and their children must maintain the covenant with themselves. Failing to fulfill the conditions, which is a real possibility, believers and their children will forfeit the covenant and lose their salvation. The covenant of grace (which is a covenant of works in federal vision theology) and its salvation depend upon the works of believers and their children.[6]

For this conception of the covenant with Adam in paradise as a conditional contract, by which Adam might have merited or otherwise obtained eternal life, there is no

---

6 For the federal vision theology of the covenant, see Norman Shepherd, *The Call of Grace: How the Covenant Illuminates Salvation and Evangelism* (Phillipsburg, NJ: P&R, 2000). For the Reformed critique of the federal vision, see David J. Engelsma, *Federal Vision: Heresy at the Root* (Jenison, MI: Reformed Free Publishing Association, 2012).

biblical basis whatever. Genesis 2:17 does prohibit Adam from eating the fruit of one tree in the garden and does threaten death upon disobedience, but that this was the establishment of the covenant with Adam and that by this covenant Adam might have obtained a higher life are the reading of a theory into the text.

The truth is that man can never merit with God, not even in the state of innocence. Obtaining a higher life by fulfilling a condition is essentially meriting. Jesus' word in Luke 17:10 applies to Adam in paradise: "When ye shall have done all those things which are commanded you, say, We are unprofitable servants: we have done that which was our duty to do." Nor can God condescend to the creature in such a way as to permit man to earn the higher life by fulfilling a condition. This would put God in debt to man. Theoretically, at least, the Adam who fulfilled the condition and the human race in him would have been able to sing in heaven, "We are here and enjoy the glories of eternity by our own work, by our own performance of the condition." Even theoretically, this would be a song jarringly out of tune with the glory of God.

In addition to all this, Adam could never earn and obtain the higher life that Christ has earned for the elect church merely by not eating of the forbidden fruit. "The first man is of the earth, earthy" (1 Cor. 15:47). As such he cannot by any means, including some gracious provision of God, attain for himself and the human race the heavenly. The capabilities of earthy Adam extended no higher than the earth and the earthy. By not eating of the forbidden tree, Adam could only assure the everlasting earthly life of himself and his posterity. Only the "second man," who is "the Lord from heaven," can earn and obtain for himself and for the human race of the elect out of all nations the higher, heavenly, eternal life (v. 47). The abilities of the Lord from heaven are greater than those of Adam the first.

What ought finally to open the eyes of the Reformed churches to the serious error of the traditional conception of the covenant with Adam is the development of this conception by the federal vision heresy. The federal vision views the covenant of grace in Jesus Christ as also a conditional agreement between God and believers. By fulfilling the conditions of believing and working, believers themselves obtain eternal life. Obtaining amounts to earning. But by failing to fulfill the conditions, believers may very really forfeit the salvation they have begun to enjoy and plunge themselves into perdition. This covenantal conception is the perversion of the gospel of grace. It bases itself largely on its view of the covenant with Adam as a conditional contract.

Even though article 14 of the Confession does not use the word *covenant* in its account of the creation of man, the reality of the covenant is suggested in the article, if only the nature of the covenant as a relationship of friendship between God and man is understood. The article calls the prohibition of Genesis 2:17 "the commandment of life." It continues by describing the sin of man as the act by which "he separated himself from God, who was his true life." The prohibition of Genesis 2:17 was not the establishment of a covenant with Adam. It was a negative command that implied a covenant of life that already existed between God and Adam. An aspect of the covenant was that God commanded his covenantal friend to carry out his part in that covenant, namely, not eating of the forbidden fruit. The nature of the covenant with Adam is indicated by the Confession's description of the fundamental effect of Adam's sin: he "separated himself from God." The covenant of God with Adam was union and communion of God with his creature man.

Although Genesis 1–3 does not use the word *covenant,* scripture elsewhere does describe the relationship of Adam with God, by virtue of Adam's creation in the image of God, as a covenantal relationship. Hosea 6:7 explicitly refers to the covenant of God with Adam: "But they like men have transgressed the covenant: there have they dealt treacherously against me." In the Hebrew original of Hosea 6:7 the word translated "men" in the Authorized Version is "Adam." The reference is to the first man, Adam. His sin was transgression of a covenant with God. Even if one insists on translating the word as "man," the text still refers to the transgression of the covenant by Adam in paradise. The text compares Israel and *Adam.* It makes no sense to compare Israel to humankind. This would amount to declaring that men transgress like men. The prophet has the first father of the race in view. His sin was transgression of a covenant. The sin of Israel was similarly transgression of a covenant.

Romans 5:12–21 also teaches that Adam was created in a covenantal relationship with God. The apostle compares Adam with Christ. The comparison is specifically their headship in a covenant, so that the sin of the one rendered all his posterity sinful and subject to death. Similarly, the obedience of the other rendered all those whom he represented righteous and worthy of life. But Christ's relationship to his church is that of headship in the covenant of grace. Necessarily, Adam's relationship to the human race is similarly headship in a covenant.

The nature of the covenant with Adam was that it was a living relationship of fellowship between God and Adam. This relationship was established by God in Adam's creation in the image of God. As image of God, Adam and Eve were children of God, who was their father. The relationship between children and their father is not that of a conditional contract. It is a relationship of close communion and intimate fellowship. This fellowship, the children of God enjoyed in a special way when God walked with them in the garden in the cool of the day (see Gen. 3:8). Covenantal fellowship with God was man's very "life," as the Confession states, so that when the fall into sin "separated" man from God, man died. Of the covenantal communion with God before the fall into sin, the tree of life was the sacramental sign and seal, as the sacrament of the Lord's supper is the sign and seal to the church today of the covenant of grace.

The command of Genesis 2:17 was the expression of God's sovereignty in the covenant and of the duty, or part, of man in the covenant. In the way of obedience, man would continue to live, *on the earth.* Therefore, the Confession rightly speaks of the prohibition as the "commandment *of life.*" Obedience to God's command was man's part in the covenant, just as God's covenantal friends have a part in the covenant of grace, according to the Reformed form for baptism: "Whereas in all covenants there are contained two parts, therefore are we by God, through baptism, admonished of and obliged unto new obedience."[7]

Since the Adamic covenant was a type of the covenant

---

7 [Reformed] Form for the Administration of Baptism, in *Confessions and Church Order*, 258.

of grace in Jesus Christ, even as Adam was a type of Christ (Rom. 5:14), there are important similarities between the covenant with Adam and the covenant with Christ. In both instances, the covenant consists of fellowship with God. The covenant is the friendship of God with man. Therefore, in both covenants marriage plays a prominent role (compare Gen. 2:18–25 and Eph. 5:22–33), mirroring and symbolizing the friendship of the covenant.

God establishes both covenants unilaterally. In the case of the covenant with Adam, God established the covenant with his creation of Adam in his image. In the case of the covenant with Christ, God established it with Christ and all the elect in him in the eternal decree of the covenant.[8] The establishment of both covenants resides in the free goodness of God. Both are gracious in their making. In both are man's life and blessedness. As the Psalter puts it, "To live apart from God is death, / 'Tis good His face to seek."[9]

There are also differences, distinguishing the type and the reality. The covenant with Adam was not made in Jesus Christ, the mediator. The covenant with Adam could be broken, just as the first Adam could fall, whereas the covenant in Christ is unbreakable. The covenant with Adam was not made in the grace that forgives sin in the cross, but simply by the goodness of God in creation. The covenant with Adam merely gave man earthly life in paradise, earthly life that was blessed to be sure, earthly life that would be

---

8 On the eternal decree of the covenant of grace in Jesus Christ, see David J. Engelsma, "The Counsel of the Covenant," in *Gospel Truth of Justification* (Jenison, MI: Reformed Free Publishing Association, 2017), 294–321.

9 No. 203:5, in *Psalter with Doctrinal Standards.*

everlasting, if man would be obedient, but for all this only earthly. The covenant in Christ gives humans a higher, better, heavenly life, a life that is eternal in Jesus Christ.

Such are the differences that the church ought to distinguish the covenant with Adam from the covenant of grace in Christ by calling the covenant with Adam "the covenant of creation." For the covenant in Christ is reserved the name "covenant of grace."

According to God's eternal decree to bless the human race and to glorify himself in Jesus Christ, as revealed in Romans 5:12–21 and in Colossians 1:13–29, the covenant with Adam gave way to the better covenant of grace in Jesus Christ. Covenantal head Adam was created as a "figure of him that was to come" (Rom. 5:14). Covenantal head Jesus Christ is the "firstborn of every creature" (Col. 1:15). "All things were created...for him" (v. 16).

The Reformed faith recognizes two different covenants in history: the covenant of creation with the first Adam in paradise and the covenant of grace with the second Adam, Jesus Christ. The covenant of grace has several phases, or administrations, including the covenant with Noah, the covenant with Abraham, the Sinaitic covenant with Israel, the covenant with David, and the new covenant with Jesus Christ, which is the fulfillment of the covenant of grace. The covenant with Jesus Christ is also the reality of the typical covenant with Adam. Such was the significance of the form of the covenant of grace with Israel in the Old Testament that it is viewed in Jeremiah 31:31–34 as the "old covenant" in distinction from the "new covenant" that God would make in Jesus Christ (see also Heb. 8–9).

The source of the covenant is the eternal decree of the triune God to glorify himself in Jesus Christ as head of the covenant and as the counsel of the covenant (Ps. 89). Ultimately, the source of the covenant is God's own triune life as the fellowship of Father and Son in the Holy Ghost.[10]

THE FALL OF MAN

Article 14 of the Confession treats also of the fall of man. An aspect of the Reformed confession of the fall of the human race into sin by the disobedience of Adam that may not be overlooked in the beginning of the twenty-first century is that the fall of man described in Genesis 3 was historical. It actually happened in time and space, and it happened exactly as Genesis 3 describes it. Genesis 3 is history, not myth: real people, Adam and Eve; real tree and fruit; a real, speaking serpent.

The historicity of Genesis 3 is confessional for the Reformed churches and members. This confession requires every Reformed church member and especially every Reformed officebearer to believe and teach the historicity of the fall of man as revealed in Genesis 3. Article 14 teaches that the man, who was created "out of the dust of the earth," "subjected himself to sin, and consequently to death and the curse, giving ear to the words of the devil."

Later articles in the Confession reinforce the historicity of the fall according to the Reformed faith. Article 15 explains original sin "through the disobedience of Adam." Article 16 accounts for the universality of sin thus: "All the posterity of Adam, being thus fallen into perdition and ruin by the sin of our first parents." Article 17 locates the source

---

10 For a fuller account of the origins of the covenant of grace in the triune life of God, see David J. Engelsma, *Trinity and Covenant: God as Holy Family* (Jenison, MI: Reformed Free Publishing Association, 2006).

of the gospel of grace in God's seeking out Adam "when he trembling fled from his presence, promising him that he would give his Son."

It is impossible for even the subtlest theologian to deny that the Confession of the Reformed churches teaches the historicity of the account of the fall in Genesis 3. It is also impossible for anyone to question whether the Confession regards this historical fall as of essential importance. The historicity of the fall, therefore, may not be challenged in a Reformed church. For theologians and ministers, who have signed the Formula of Subscription binding them to the creeds, to challenge or question the historicity of the fall as revealed in Genesis 3, scoffing at a "speaking serpent," is violation of their solemn vow. It is ground for church discipline. For churches to permit their officebearers to challenge the historicity of Genesis 3 is dereliction of duty and evidence that, name notwithstanding, the churches are no longer Reformed in reality. Indeed, they are not Christian. What these theologians and churches deny is fundamental *Christian* doctrine. It is basic to the gospel of grace: no Adam, no Christ.

Genesis 3 presents itself as history. The New Testament clearly, repeatedly, and authoritatively declares the historical nature and reality of Genesis 3. It does so in contexts that indicate the importance of the historical fall for original sin, the covenantal headship of Jesus, the hope of the resurrection of the body, restriction of office in the church to qualified males, and more (John 8:44; Rom. 5:12–21; 1 Cor. 15:22; 1 Tim. 2:14).

What can be a question for the Reformed believing mind is the possibility of the fall in view of man's creation as good, indeed as the image of God. How could the good man, created in God's image, possibly sin? This goodness of man's very nature, body and soul, made it necessary that there be an external tempter—the devil himself tempting Eve and Eve tempting Adam. In man in the image of God, the thought and will of disobedience could not have risen of themselves. The Confession recognizes the role of the powerful, seductive external tempter: "giving ear to the words of the devil."

In response to the difficult question of the possibility of Adam's sinning, it can be said that God made Adam able to sin, whereas in the new world the saved elect will not be able to sin. Thus is Christ Jesus, the second Adam, superior to the first Adam.

But it must also be said, as article 13 of the Confession intimated, that God ruled and governed the fall according to his holy will, so that it did not happen without his appointment. God decreed the happening of the fall and then ruled and governed its occurrence with the purpose of gathering together all things in Jesus Christ, so that in all things Jesus might have the preeminence (see Eph. 1 and Col. 1). Not the first Adam and the race and creation in him, but the second Adam and the race and creation in him were the eternal counsel and good pleasure of God. The fall of Adam did not take God by surprise, nor did it spoil his plan.

Such was the mysterious bearing of the decree and providential government upon the fall of Adam that the fault of the fall was man's and man's only. God's sovereign government of the fall by his providential decree and rule in no way detracts from man's guilt. Nor does it cast any blame for the fall upon God. Article 13, on God's providence, which affirms God's appointment and government of the fall, continues: "Nevertheless, God neither is the author of, nor can be charged with, the sins which are committed." The reason is that, regardless of his government of sin, particularly the fall of Adam, "he orders and executes his work in the most excellent and just manner even when the devil and wicked men act unjustly."

Without reservation, therefore, the Reformed faith blames man, and man only, for the fall. Its confession of divine sovereignty does not mitigate, much less deny, this responsibility of man regarding the fall into sin. The Confession expresses this blameworthiness of man. Regarding responsibility, the fall was simply that man "transgressed" the commandment of life. Article 15 analyzes the fall as "the disobedience of Adam."

This transgression entailed enormous guilt. Man inexcusably refused to esteem his "honor," in his envy of and lust for the honor that belongs to God only: "Being in honor, he understood it not." "He...willfully subjected himself to sin." Adam gave "ear to the words of the devil." Although the devil also bears responsibility for the fall, his clever, powerful role in no wise minimizes man's guilt. Man gave the outspoken opponent of God ("yea, hath God said?") his ear. Man actively "separated himself from God," deliberately despising and renouncing the covenant, transferring his allegiance to God's enemy. He "corrupted his whole nature." "He made himself liable to corporal and spiritual death." He squandered "all his excellent gifts which he had received from God." A stronger, fuller description of man's responsibility in the fall is inconceivable. The canard that the Reformed confession of the sovereignty of God fails to do justice to the responsibility of man is given the lie in article 14 of the Belgic Confession.

Just as man is fully responsible for the deed of disobedience of transgressing the commandment of life, so also is man responsible for the consequences of that deed. That Adam and the entire race, Jesus only excepted, are subject to sin and death; are separated from God our life; and are lacking the excellent gifts in which God created us are our guilt. For this dreadful, miserable, sinful state, we are responsible and worthy of punishment.

Specifically, man's corrupt nature with its sinful lusts is not reason for God to feel sorry for his human creature, or for the human creature to feel sorry for himself. The corrupt nature with which man is conceived and born is certainly not justification for man's putting the nature into practice in deed. Rather, it is reason for God to punish man and reason for humans to repent. For example, homosexual nature and desire are sin. It is idle for ecclesiastical committees to speculate whether the homosexual inclination derives from one's genetic make-up or from example. The nature of fallen man is sinful, including, in some, homosexual sinfulness. "In sin did my mother conceive me" (Ps. 51:5). Sin is not only in the deeds. It is also in the nature itself, whence the deeds spring. The Confession accuses fallen man of "having corrupted his *whole nature.*"

The consequences of the disobedience of Adam were enormous. The only act by a man with greater consequences for humanity is the obedience of Jesus Christ.

The effect of the fall of man was the introduction of the curse of God and death into the entire earthly creation (Gen. 3:17–19; Rom. 8:19–22). Prior to the fall of man, there was no death either in man or in the creation at large. There was no curse of God either upon man or upon the earthly creation of animals, plants, and other creatures.

There was only the word of blessing. This important truth is necessarily denied by all forms of the scientific theory of an old earth, whether theistic evolution or atheistic evolution. One evil implication of this theory is that it makes God himself responsible for death in the human race and in the wider creation.

It is especially that Adam's disobedience brought sin and death into the world of humans that constitutes the enormity of his deed, according to the Confession: "[Adam] willfully subjected himself to sin, and consequently to death and the curse...he made himself liable to corporal and spiritual death." The Confession here expresses the teaching of the apostle in Romans 5:12–21: "By one man sin entered into the world, and death by sin; and so death passed upon all men" (v. 12). God did not create man sinful and dying. Death is the "wages of sin" (6:23).

TOTAL DEPRAVITY

The full reality of the death into which man plunged himself by his disobedience includes "spiritual death," according to the Confession: "He made himself liable to corporal *and spiritual death.*" This is the corruption of man's *nature*, that is, what man is, body and soul. The extent of this spiritual corruption is total, as is already indicated by the description of it as "death." One does not die partially.

The Confession teaches the total depravity of fallen man. It emphasizes total depravity in several expressions of this total depravity: "having corrupted his whole nature"; "liable to...spiritual death"; "having become wicked, perverse, and corrupt in all his ways"; "all the light which is in us is changed into darkness."

It is the teaching of the Confession not only that sin

infects every part of fallen man, but also that every part of fallen man is completely sinful. This truth is not to be confused with the notion that every sinner is as evil as he can possibly be, for there is development of wickedness in the sinner's own life. At birth, Judas Iscariot was as wicked as he could be *extensively*. When he betrayed Jesus, Judas was more wicked *intensively* than he had been as a child. But there was no good in him as a child. One must not confuse total depravity with absolute depravity. By its clear and strong expressions of total depravity, the Confession makes plain that man has lost the image of God, and lost it completely. There is nothing left in him of the righteousness, knowledge, and holiness with which God created Adam and Eve in the beginning.

One crucially important aspect of the doctrine of total depravity taught by the Confession is the denial of the "free will" of fallen mankind. The Confession itself calls attention to this implication of total depravity: "Therefore we reject all that is taught repugnant to this [truth of total depravity] concerning the free will of man, since man is but a slave to sin; and has nothing of himself unless it is given him from heaven."

By "free will" is meant an ability of fallen man to choose or desire or seek God, Christ, and salvation. In general, it is the alleged ability of fallen man to will the good. The Reformation fought with the Roman Catholic Church over this issue—a fundamental issue, if not *the* fundamental issue, of the sixteenth-century Reformation of the church. Luther wrote his monumental *The Bondage of the Will*.[11] Against the

---

11 Martin Luther, *The Bondage of the Will*, trans. J. I. Packer and O. R. Johnston (London: James Clarke, 1957).

Roman Catholic theologian Pighius, John Calvin wrote *The Bondage and Liberation of the Will.*[12] In the early seventeenth century, the Reformed churches, meeting in the ecumenical Synod of Dordt, defended the truth of the bound will against the Arminian heresy of the freedom of the will of fallen humans.[13]

The confessional, official Reformed position on the issue of the freedom or bondage of the will of fallen humans is that the teaching of free will is false doctrine. As article 14 of the Belgic Confession states, "Man is but a slave to sin." The fallen sinner freely chooses sin, but by virtue of his condition of total depravity he cannot do anything else but choose sin.

Man's total depravity affects more than only the faculty of willing. The Confession describes in detail the full extent of the depravity of fallen mankind. Fallen man is unable to *do* any good, particularly the good of coming to Christ for salvation: "Who may presume to boast that he of himself can do any good, since Christ saith, *No man can come to me, except the Father which hath sent me draw him?*" Fallen man has no good knowledge or capability of knowing rightly: "Who can speak of his knowledge, since *the natural man receiveth not the things of the Spirit of God?* In short, who dare suggest any thought, since he knows that *we are not sufficient of*

---

12 John Calvin, *The Bondage and Liberation of the Will: A Defense of the Orthodox Doctrine of Human Choice against Pighius,* tr. G. I. Davies, ed. A. N. Lane (Grand Rapids, MI: Baker, 1996).

13 See the Canons of Dordt, in Schaff, *Creeds of Christendom,* 3:581–97. For the Dordt synod's important rejection of errors, which are not given in Schaff, see *Confessions and Church Order,* 153–80. The Reformed creed rejects the error "that the will of itself is able to will and to choose, or not to will and not to choose, all manner of good which may be presented to it" (Canons of Dordt, 3–4, Rejection 3, in *Confessions and Church Order,* 171).

ourselves to think any thing as of ourselves, but that our sufficiency is of God?"

Should there remain any possibility of doubting that the Confession teaches total depravity or that "total" for the Confession means total, the conclusion of article 14 demolishes that doubt: "For there is no will nor understanding, conformable to the divine will and understanding, but what Christ hath wrought in man: which he teaches us when he saith, *Without me ye can do nothing.*"

Mind, will, and deeds, fallen mankind is utterly incapable of any good and prone by nature to evil. Here, the Reformed faith stands alone in defense of total depravity and thus in defense of the gospel of salvation by grace alone. But it stands on the basis of the word of God. For every aspect of its insistence on total depravity, the Confession quotes passages of scripture.[14]

The issue concerning free will that is raised in the second half of article 14 of the Confession is fundamental. First, if this is the truth, namely, that the sinner has no free will, the theology and preaching of many in our day are exposed as false. This is the theology and preaching that proclaim that God loves all, Christ died for all, and God desires to save all, but that the salvation of the sinner depends squarely on his exercise of his free will, in choosing to believe on Jesus.

Second, such is the seriousness of this issue that the teaching, the "gospel," of free will is a false gospel, is the lie, is an enemy of the true gospel of salvation by grace alone. The Confession points out this seriousness of the issue. It

---

14 These passages are the lines in italics in the Confession. In order they are John 6:44; 1 Corinthians 2:14; 2 Corinthians 3:5; and John 15:5.

accuses those who hold free will of "boasting" and of "glorying": "Who may presume to boast...Who will glory in his own will?" Boasting and glorying regarding salvation is heinous sin! The one who is guilty of this is lost! The saved sinner must, and will, "glory in the Lord" (1 Cor. 1:31).

The Confession also shows the fundamental importance of the issue of the bound or free will when it contrasts the error of free will with the truth of gracious salvation: the Reformed faith rejects the lie of a free will on behalf of the truth of the gospel, that all of salvation "is given [to the saved sinner] from heaven." All the way through the second section of article 14, the Confession contrasts the error of free will with the gospel of salvation by grace. In this way, the Confession identifies the false doctrine of free will as a form of the false gospel of salvation by man's own worth and working.

The Reformed creed the Canons of Dordt supports the judgment of the Belgic Confession upon the doctrine of salvation by the free will of the sinner. The Canons condemn the message of free will, as taught by the Arminian heresy, as a "bring[ing] again out of hell the Pelagian error."[15]

Rejection of the error of free will as the corruption of the gospel of grace is the teaching of the Bible. In addition to all the passages adduced in article 14 of the Belgic Confession, Romans 9:16 expressly condemns the theology of free will as a form of the false "gospel" that always attempts to overthrow and replace the gospel of grace in the church: "So then it [salvation] is not of him that willeth, nor of him that runneth, but of God that sheweth mercy."

The heresy of free will is today no longer outside the camp of the Reformed and Presbyterian churches. It is not

---

15 Canons of Dordt 2, error 3, in *Confessions and Church Order*, 165.

to be found only in those churches that honestly identify themselves as Arminian and Pelagian free will churches. It is found today within churches that claim to be Reformed, formally having the Belgic Confession and the Canons of Dordt as their creeds. The free will heresy now takes the form of the doctrine of the well-meant offer of Christ and salvation. This is the doctrine that God loves all humans and, in this common love or grace, offers all humans salvation in the sincere desire that they accept the offer and be saved. Necessarily implied by this doctrine is that salvation depends upon the will of the sinner, who accepts the offer. Salvation in this theology does not depend upon the grace and will of God, inasmuch as God is gracious to all alike and wills, or desires, the salvation of all alike.

It is nothing less than astounding that this doctrine of the well-meant offer passes for Reformed and Presbyterian orthodoxy today, contradicting as it does not only article 14 of the Belgic Confession and heads 2 and 3 of the Canons of Dordt, but also everything that the Reformed creeds teach about predestination, reprobation as well as election. It is hardly less astounding that churches that faithfully subscribe to what article 14 of the Confession teaches about the bondage of the will are well-nigh universally regarded and vilified as hyper-Calvinists.

A "FEW REMAINS"

Controversial is what the Confession states concerning fallen man's retention of a "few remains" of the excellent gifts that Adam had received from God at his creation. Similarly, the Canons of Dordt affirms that "there remain...in man since the fall, the glimmerings of natural light."[16] Many Reformed theologians eagerly seize on these phrases to negate everything that article 14 of the Confession teaches concerning the total depravity of fallen man, as though the "few remains" were spiritually good.

The remains after the fall are not some remnants of the image of God. But they are a few remains of the "excellent gifts" with which God honored man as man at his creation. They are his mind, his will, and other natural powers—his humanity. The Canons of Dordt identifies what it calls the "glimmerings of natural light" and what the Belgic Confession calls "remains" of man's "excellent gifts": "some knowledge of God, of natural things, and of the difference between good and evil, and discovers some regard for virtue, good order in society, and for maintaining an orderly external deportment."[17]

The remains of the excellent gifts belong to man's humanity, not to the image of God.

Not many gifts are left to fallen man, merely a "few remains." Man as man is not nearly what he once was. He is only a pitiful vestige of his former self, wreckage after his fall.

Such was the effect of the fall even upon these few remains that they are no longer good. Nor do they enable man to do the good. Those Reformed theologians and churches that run with the few remains and glimmerings of natural light in fallen man from the theology of total depravity into a theology of remaining goodness that enables fallen man to do good in the judgment of God in

---

16 Canons of Dordt 3–4.4, in Schaff, *Creeds of Christendom*, 3:588.
17 Canons of Dordt 3–4.4, in ibid.

culture and even to accept an offered salvation err greatly, and they do so in inexcusable disregard of article 14 of the Belgic Confession.

This was the error of the Arminians in the early seventeenth century. By "the light of nature," or "the gifts left him [fallen man] after the fall," which the Arminians regarded as "common grace," these heretics understood the ability in fallen man to:

> gradually gain by their good use a greater, namely, the evangelical or saving grace and salvation itself. And that in this way God on his part shows himself ready to reveal Christ unto all men, since he applies to all sufficiently and efficiently the means necessary to conversion.[18]

The "few remains" are not some remaining goodness in fallen man. Much less are they remnants of the image of God. They do not enable man to perform good works. Least of all do they make possible man's acceptance of a well-meant offer of salvation. Article 14 of the Confession condemns all such thinking about the "few remains." The natural "light" possessed by fallen man, which the "few remains" are, is spiritual "darkness": "All the light which is in us is changed into darkness." In support of this devastating judgment, the Confession appeals to and quotes John 1:5: "The light shineth in darkness; and the darkness comprehended it not." The "few remains" of the excellent gifts with which God created man serve only "to leave man without excuse." According to the Confession, fallen men *are* "darkness."

---

18 Canons of Dordt 3–4, error 5, in *Confessions and Church Order*, 171.

Neither does any good remain in man after the fall, nor is there any good, or capacity for good, in fallen man by an imaginary "common grace" of God. The sole possibility of goodness in fallen man is the regenerating, saving, particular grace of God in Jesus Christ: "what Christ hath wrought in man." In conclusive support of this doctrine, the Confession quotes Christ's words in John 15:5: "Without me ye can do nothing."

SAVING SIGNIFICANCE OF THE DOCTRINE OF TOTAL DEPRAVITY

The implications of the Confession's doctrine of total depravity are profound. The Reformed believer humbles himself deeply as sinner, and only sinner, and as sinner by his very nature, that is, all that he himself is. He places no confidence whatever concerning his salvation in himself or in mankind. For his salvation in its entirety, he depends solely upon God's grace in Jesus Christ. Salvation is, and must be, God's work alone. He is grateful to God, therefore, for forgiving grace and for renewing power. The will to do the good is to him evidence of his salvation, as Philippians 2:13 indicates, a text quoted by the Confession in article 14: "It is God which worketh in you both to will and to do of his good pleasure." Such a will and such working are not, and cannot be, of the sinner himself.

Of the greatest importance, both to the saved sinner and to God, is that the doctrine of total depravity glorifies God for all the salvation of humans. The heresy of free will glorifies the sinner himself. The gospel truth of the bondage of the will glorifies God. For this reason more than any other, Reformed Christians confess and contend for the bondage of the will of fallen man. They do so in article 14 of the Belgic Confession.

Chapter Eleven

OF ORIGINAL SIN

(ARTICLE 15)

ART. XV. OF ORIGINAL SIN.

We believe that, through the disobedience of Adam, original sin is extended to all mankind; which is a corruption of the whole nature, and an hereditary disease, wherewith infants themselves are infected even in their mother's womb, and which produceth in man all sorts of sin, being in him as a root thereof; and therefore is so vile and abominable in the sight of God that it is sufficient to condemn all mankind. Nor is it by any means abolished or done away by baptism; since sin always issues forth from this woful source, as water from a fountain: notwithstanding it is not imputed to the children of God unto condemnation, but by his grace and mercy is forgiven them. Not that they should rest securely in sin, but that a sense of this corruption should make believers often to sigh, desiring to be delivered from this body of death. Wherefore we reject the error of the Pelagians, who assert that sin proceeds only from imitation.

INTRODUCTION

Article 15 of the Confession is closely related in thought to the preceding article. Article 14 confesses God's creation of man; man's fall into sin; and the consequences of the fall for man, particularly total depravity. Article 15 teaches that the fall of Adam in paradise had consequences for the entire human race and that these consequences are the original sin of every member of the race, Jesus only excepted. The preceding article did not *state* this. It only spoke of *man's* being created; of *man's* fall; and of *man's* becoming corrupt. Nor did the preceding article mention "original sin."

Two passages of scripture are of fundamental importance for the truth taught in this article. The first is Romans 5:12–21. The main thought of article 15, namely, that the result of Adam's disobedience is the extension of sin to all humans, rests squarely on this passage. That the truth of the article derives from and depends on Romans 5 is evident from verse 12: "Wherefore as by one man sin entered into the world, and death by sin; and so death passed upon all men, for that all have sinned."

The second biblical passage that is fundamental to the article is Romans 7:7–25. This passage teaches that every human has a sinful nature: "Sin...dwelleth in me" (v. 17). It teaches that this spiritual disease, this disorder of our nature, is truly *sin*: it is "sin" that dwells in us, not merely a tendency to sin, or a weakness that could lead to sin, if we are not on our guard. This sinful nature is ours after regeneration, until we die: says the apostle of himself near the very end of his sanctified life, "O wretched man that I am!" (v. 24). What this lifelong wretchedness is, and how evil, the apostle confesses in verse 14: "I am carnal, sold under sin."

To Romans 7:7–25, the Confession plainly refers when it declares: "A sense of this corruption should make believers often to sigh, desiring to be delivered from this body of death." This is the sigh of the apostle in verse 24: "Who shall deliver me from the body of this death?"

ORIGINAL SIN

Original sin is the corruption, or pollution, or depravity, of human nature, soul and body, with which every person is conceived and born. It is "original" in distinction from the actual sins of thought, desire, word, and deed that every person commits consciously as soon as he becomes old enough to have these wicked thoughts and desires, speak these wicked words, and perform these wicked deeds.

The relationship between "original" sin and all a person's actual sins is that original sin produces the actual sins. Original sin is the root underground from which the visible, sinful plants sprout: "[Original sin] produceth in man all sorts of sin, being in him as a root thereof." Using the figure of "an heredity disease", original sin is the hidden sickness in the blood and within the body, whereas the actual sins are the sores and pus, resulting from the inner sickness, that appear upon the outer surface of the body.

It is the doctrine of original sin that man sins because he *is* a sinner. He does not become a sinner because he sins. Another figure employed by the Confession to describe the relationship between a man's sins and original sin is that of water flowing from a fountain. "Sin always issues forth from this woeful source, as water from a fountain." Every sinful thought, every vile desire, every curse that is on the tip of our tongue when something goes contrary to our will, is powerful witness to us of our original sin.

Every human is conceived and born with original sin: "Infants themselves are infected even in their mother's womb." This is the confession of David in Psalm 51:5, concerning the cause and source of his adultery and murder: "Behold, I was shapen in iniquity; and in sin did my mother conceive me."

Although this is not the thought or purpose of the Confession, drawn up and adopted as it was before the godless, lawless, murderous twenty-first century, the affirmation of the original sin of unborn infants implies that these infants, yet unborn, are responsible persons. To abort them is murder of persons. The God who hates murder will take vengeance upon the murderous mother, the murderous doctor who performs the abortion, and the murderous state that approves this murder, as well as the murderous (false) church that sanctions this abomination.

Original sin is universal: "[It extends] to all mankind."

It is total, that is, it is a "corruption of the whole nature." It affects both soul and body. The previous article has confessed that this wickedness of nature is total in the sense of completely corrupting human nature. Not even the smallest part of the nature of the human escapes the corruption. All is sinful.

This original sin is "vile and abominable in the sight of God." We ourselves come to know the vileness of our original sin by experience of its motions and expressions within ourselves. We are grateful that our fellow churchmen do not know our secret thoughts and desires. What we often forget is that God can and does know.

What a torrent, indeed flood, of evil words and deeds proceeds from original sin in all the human race!

Scripture calls original sin "sin." "Sin...dwelleth in me" (Rom. 7:17); "the law of sin which is in my members" (v. 23).

ORIGINAL SIN AS GUILT

Original sin in humans, in the sense in which the Confession speaks of it, namely, the corruption of nature, makes every human guilty before God and worthy of condemnation. This is true altogether apart from any actual sin that the human commits. Since we are conceived and born with original sin, we come into existence, into the world, exposed to just damnation. Every human enters the world at birth exposed to the wrath of God. This is why children are subject to death. This is why infants are justly exposed to the ravages of illness, the agonies of starvation and war, the brutalities of other people. Children are not innocent but damnworthy.

The Christian church acknowledges the guilt of children at birth and in infancy on account of original sin by her baptism of infants. The Reformed baptism form begins:

> We with our children are conceived and born in sin, and therefore are children of wrath, in so much that we cannot enter into the kingdom of God except we are born again. This the dipping in or sprinkling with water teaches us, whereby the impurity of our souls is signified, and we admonished to loathe and humble ourselves before God, and seek for our purification and salvation without ourselves.[1]

---

1 [Reformed] Form for the Administration of Baptism, in *Confessions and Church Order*, 258.

The question is, how is the child of God delivered from original sin? The Confession denies that the deliverance occurs by baptism, as though the sacrament abolishes original sin: "Nor is it by any means abolished or done away by baptism." That the sacrament abolishes original sin is the doctrine of the Roman Catholic Church. Rome acknowledges that everyone is born with original sin. The sacrament of baptism, administered by a Roman Catholic priest or, in an emergency, by a Roman Catholic lay person, has the efficacy to abolish original sin. The effect of baptism is that there is no longer in the baptized person indwelling sin. What remains is only a certain tendency to sin. Rome calls this tendency "concupiscence." Concupiscence is not itself sin. If one resists concupiscence, as is theoretically possible, he could lead a sinless life.

> If any one...asserts that the whole of that which has the true and proper nature of sin is not taken away [in baptism]...let him be anathema...In the baptized there remains concupiscence, or an incentive (to sin); which...can not injure those who consent not, but resist manfully by the grace of Jesus Christ...This concupiscence...the Catholic Church has never understood it to be called sin, as being truly and properly sin in those born again.[2]

Against the Roman doctrine of the abolishing of original sin by baptism, according to the Confession, is experience: "Sin always issues forth from this woeful source, as water from a fountain." This experience of every

---

2 The Canons and Decrees of the Council of Trent, Fifth Session, "Decree concerning Original Sin," in Schaff, *Creeds of Christendom*, 2:87–88.

human corroborates the testimony of scripture. In Romans 7 the baptized and born-again apostle laments concerning himself, as to his very nature, "I am carnal, sold under sin"; "Sin...dwelleth in me"; "The law of sin...is in my members"; "O wretched man that I am" (vv. 14, 17, 23–24).

The deliverance of the believing child of God from original sin, according to the Confession, is that this sin is not imputed to him, but forgiven: "Notwithstanding [that original sin is not abolished by baptism] it is not imputed to the children of God unto condemnation, but by his grace and mercy is forgiven them." An important part of the prayer of the believer, daily, must be the request for the forgiveness of original sin. The Heidelberg Catechism has the Reformed Christian making this part of his petition for the forgiveness of his debts in the model prayer: "Be pleased, for the sake of Christ's blood, not to impute to us, miserable sinners...the evil which still always cleaves to us."[3]

Baptism is a means to this deliverance from original sin in that baptism assures the believer that his original sin is covered in Jesus' blood, so that God cannot see that filthy mass of sinfulness in the believer. Baptism is a sign and seal to the believer of the forgiveness of original sin.

To what the Confession says about deliverance from original sin, that is, its being not imputed to the children of God but forgiven, may be added that the Holy Ghost, who dwells in the children of God, sanctifies them, so that they hate and fight against original sin. Thus even though original sin remains in them, original sin does not reign in their life. They obey the exhortation of Romans 6:12: "Let not sin...reign in your mortal body, that ye should obey it

---

3 Heidelberg Catechism Q 126, in Schaff, *Creeds of Christendom*, 3:353–54.

in the lusts thereof." The result is that "sin shall not have dominion over you" (v. 14).

ORIGINAL SIN AND ADAM

The Confession asserts a relationship between the original sin of all humans and the disobedience of Adam: "Through the disobedience of Adam, original sin is extended to all mankind." The relationship is that of cause and effect. Adam's disobedience regarding the forbidden tree in paradise is the cause of the original sin with which all humans are born. This is the teaching of Genesis 3–11. Adam's disobedience resulted not only in his own sinfulness, but also in the sinfulness of his firstborn son, Cain, who murdered his brother, and of the world before the flood. Before the disobedience of Adam, man was good, naked, without shame, walking fearlessly with the holy God. After his disobedience, man was depraved, needing clothing, ashamed of himself, and hiding from God.

Soon, humanity "was corrupt; for all flesh had corrupted his way upon the earth," so that God said, "The end of all flesh is come before me; for the earth is filled with violence through them; and, behold, I will destroy them with the earth" (Gen. 6:12–13). Romans 5:12 and 19 explain this fact of history after the disobedience of Adam: "By one man sin entered into the world"; "By one man's disobedience many were made sinners."

Negatively, the explanation of the relationship between Adam's disobedience and original sin is not that Adam set the first, bad example and that the whole human race has imitated him. This explanation was the heresy of the fourth-century teacher Pelagius. Pelagius denied original sin. He taught that all are conceived and born, if not good, then neutral regarding holiness and sinfulness. All persons sin by choosing bad role models, by imitating bad examples, going back ultimately to the bad example Adam. Sin for Pelagius is only in the deliberate deed, not in the nature of man. In Romans 5, the Holy Ghost means only that Adam caused others to sin by setting a bad example for his descendants.

Augustine, Pelagius' orthodox antagonist, astutely pointed out that, if this is the case with the relationship between Adam and his descendants, also Christ saves his people merely by his example, for Romans 5 compares the destroying deed of Adam and the saving deed of Christ. Following the great African theologian, the Confession "reject[s] the error of the Pelagians, who assert that sin proceeds only from imitation."

Positively, the explanation of the relationship between Adam's disobedience and original sin is that Adam was not merely a private individual, whose sin affected only himself. Rather, he was the father of the race, who passes his own nature on to all his children, who are all members of the race, Christ only excepted. Since Adam corrupted his own nature, he passes this corrupt nature on to all humans. Sin, according to the Confession, is a "hereditary disease." In some mysterious way, the sexual propagation of the race passes on to every child the spiritually corrupt nature of Adam by means of the parents, which is not a pronouncement that sex is inherently corrupt.

> Man after the fall begat children in his own likeness. A corrupt stock produced a corrupt offspring. Hence all the posterity of Adam, Christ only excepted, have derived corruption from their original parent, not

by imitation, as the Pelagians of old asserted, but by the propagation of a vicious nature.[4]

But this raises a question, a question the Confession does not address: how can it be just of God that the children suffer for the father's disobedience? The answer is that Adam was not only the father of the race, but also the representative head in the covenant, so that his disobedient act is imputed to all his posterity. The entire human race is guilty for Adam's transgression. This too is original sin. Original sin is not only the total depravity of nature with which every human is conceived and born, what the Confession calls "corruption of the whole nature." But original sin is also the guilt for Adam's disobedience that is borne by every member of the race.

This is the full doctrine of original sin in Romans 5. Adam's disobedience constituted all members of the race sinners *legally*, just as Christ's obedience rendered all who are his by election righteous *legally*, that is, in the just judgment of God.[5] Original sin therefore is twofold. It is original corruption of nature. It is also original guilt, that is, guilt regarding the disobedience of Adam. The latter, that is, original guilt, is the cause of the former, that is, original corruption. God is just in the judgment of punishing all humans with corruption of nature from conception and

---

4 Canons of Dordt 3–4.2, in ibid., 3:588.
5 "Rendered" and "constituted" are the correct translations of the same Greek verb misleadingly translated "made" in the Authorized Version in both instances in Romans 5:19. In the Greek, the verb is *kathisteemi*. Thayer's *Greek-English Lexicon* translates the verb as "constitute," that is, "render." In Romans 5:19, the subject is not that of making sinners and making righteous as to their actual condition, but of constituting sinners and righteous as to their legal state in the judgment of God.

birth, because all are guilty, and therefore worthy of this dreadful condition, with the guilt of Adam's disobedience.

The original, Latin version of the Canons of Dordt gave expression to the truth of original guilt, as well as to the relationship of original guilt and original corruption of nature, in a phrase that unfortunately has been omitted in the English translations of the Canons. In the article that confesses original sin as the propagation of a vicious nature, the Canons explains, "*justo Dei judicio,*" that is, "in consequence of a just judgment of God."[6] The totally depraved nature with which every human is born is divine judgment upon him for his guilt in the disobedience of Adam.

APPLICATION OF THE DOCTRINE OF ORIGINAL SIN TO THE REFORMED BELIEVER

An implication of the Reformed, Christian doctrine of original sin is that the worst punishment of sin is *sin*, not lightning bolts or cancer, but the divine act of giving guilty sinners over to the ruling, shaming power of sin in their lives. This is the word of God in Romans 1:18–32. The wrath of God that is revealed from heaven against all ungodliness and unrighteousness of men takes form in God's giving these humans up to uncleanness through the lusts of their own hearts. Specifically, in the extreme expression in history of this wrath against sinful mankind, the divine punishment of sin with sin is that God gives men and women up unto the vile affections of sodomy and lesbianism. Thus his punishment of sinners is his giving them over to a reprobate mind to do those things that are not convenient.

Original sin announces that the condition of fallen man

---

6 Canons of Dordt 3–4.2, in Schaff, *Creeds of Christendom,* 3:564.

is desperate and utterly hopeless so far as the sinner himself is concerned. He is conceived and born sinful, which condition is a "corruption of the whole nature." This spiritual condition, itself "vile and abominable in the sight of God," is the sinner's misery in the just judgment of God. Deliverance from original corruption, therefore, is a matter of satisfying the justice of God.

The only possible deliverance of the sinner is the grace of God in Jesus Christ. Such is the truth proclaimed by the apostle in Romans 7:24–25: "Who shall deliver me from the body of this death? I thank God through Jesus Christ our Lord." This gracious deliverance has its origin in election. This is the subject of article 16 of the Belgic Confession.

Deeply humbling though the truth of original sin is, there is also something consoling about it, particularly its message that a corrupt nature remains with the saved child of God as long as he lives. The presence and power of a corrupt nature do not cast the believer into despair, as though, having such a sinful nature, he was not, and could not be, a born-again, believing, sanctified child of God. The Wesleyan perfectionist must live always on the brink of despair, professing that salvation in this life consists of sinlessness, while experiencing daily that he is carnal, "sold under sin", as the apostle writes in Romans 7:14. The Reformed believer wars daily with indwelling sin in the knowledge that "even the holiest men, while in this life, have only a small beginning of this obedience."[7]

Nevertheless, the experience of the reality of original sin causes the Reformed, Christian believer to sigh and groan for deliverance from this evil. There is the daily

---

7 Heidelberg Catechism Q 114, in ibid., 3:349.

deliverance of pardon. There is also the hope of final deliverance from the evil through death. At death, original sin is abolished: "Our death is…only a dying to sins."[8] With an eye on Romans 7:24, article 15 concludes, therefore, with an implied exhortation: "A sense of this corruption should make believers often to sigh, desiring to be delivered from this body of death."

---

8   Heidelberg Catechism Q 42, in ibid., 3:320–321.

Chapter Twelve

OF DIVINE PREDESTINATION AND OF THE RECOVERY OF FALLEN MAN

(ARTICLES 16 AND 17)

ART. XVI. OF ETERNAL ELECTION.

We believe that all the posterity of Adam, being thus fallen into perdition and ruin by the sin of our first parents, God then did manifest himself such as he is; that is to say, MERCIFUL AND JUST: MERCIFUL, since he delivers and preserves from this perdition all whom he, in his eternal and unchangeable council, of mere goodness hath elected in Christ Jesus our Lord, without any respect to their works: JUST, in leaving others in the fall and perdition wherein they have involved themselves.

ART. XVII. OF THE RECOVERY OF FALLEN MAN.

We believe that our most gracious God, in his admirable wisdom and goodness, seeing that man had thus thrown

*himself into temporal and spiritual death, and made
himself wholly miserable, was pleased to seek and comfort
him when he trembling fled from his presence, promising
him that he would give his Son, who should be made of a
woman, to bruise the head of the serpent, and would make
him happy.*

INTRODUCTION

Yet again, and again, the Reformed Confession repeats the
biblical and Reformed judgment upon the fallen human
race. The judgment is repeated in articles 16 and 17. The
judgment is universal and searing. Article 16 confesses that
"all the posterity of Adam...[is] fallen into perdition and
ruin by the sin of our first parents." This fall of the race
occurred "thus," that is, by the disobedience of Adam. Article 17 declares that by this disobedience of Adam "man had
thus thrown himself into temporal and eternal death, and
made himself wholly miserable."

The plight and misery of the human race, apart from
the grace of God in Jesus Christ, are dreadful and hopeless. "Perdition" is eternal damnation under God's burning
wrath. "Ruin" is utter spiritual destruction and therefore
the complete incapability of fallen humans of saving
themselves.

Article 17 passes judgment upon the condition of fallen
man as that of death—not sickness, but death. This death
is both temporal and eternal. Both the horror and the
helplessness of fallen man are expressed by this damning
judgment. As for the effect of this condition, it is one of
being "wholly miserable." That fallen man yet laughs and
plays under this judgment is the hollow gaiety of the grave-
yard, a bizarre gallows humor. That Reformed churches

yet find some good in fallen man, minimizing his dreadful condition and state, is sheer rebellion against the authority of the Belgic Confession, blatant violation of the vow of the officebearers to uphold the doctrine of the Confession, and treacherous undermining of the gospel of gracious salvation.

Articles 16 and 17 do not simply repeat in other words the misery of fallen man that was stated in articles 14 and 15. But they assert this misery in different contexts and with different purposes.

Article 16 declares the misery of fallen man in order to underscore that God's salvation of fallen, damnworthy, and ruined humans is due solely to the mercy of God, a mercy that has its origin only in God's gracious election and that is not at all due to the worthiness of these humans. There is no worthiness of fallen humans.

Article 17 advances the argument of article 16. Fallen man being dead and "wholly miserable," the promise of the gospel of Jesus Christ originates in and is due to the grace of "our most gracious God," not to anything in fallen humans.

The full reality of the misery of fallen man is the background of the full reality of grace in the saving work of God in Jesus Christ. Whatever doctrine denies or minimizes the full reality of the misery of fallen man denies or minimizes the reality of the gospel of salvation by the grace of God alone.

Thus articles 16 and 17 introduce the following articles concerning Jesus Christ and his saving work, beginning with article 18 on the incarnation of the Son of God. Jesus Christ and his saving work arise out of the gracious decree of election and out of the gracious promise of the gospel, which itself has its origin in election. Accounting as they do for the gift of Jesus Christ and all his saving work, as well as for the promise of the gospel that reveals and effects salvation, these articles of the Confession are of vital importance. By the very placement of the doctrine of election, with the accompanying doctrine of reprobation, between the truth of the fall and the truth of Jesus Christ, the Confession attributes to election the importance that the doctrine has in scripture as the "fountain of every saving good."[1]

PREDESTINATION IN THE CONFESSION

In article 16, the Reformed churches and believers confess the doctrine of predestination. Both because of the inherent importance of the doctrine in the Christian religion and in the faith of the Reformed Christian and because of the controversial nature of the doctrine, this article of the Confession is of extraordinary importance. Only here does the Belgic Confession treat this doctrine.

It is obvious at a glance that the treatment of predestination by the Confession is very brief. In fact, the treatment is too brief to do justice to the great doctrine or to ward off the errors that threaten the doctrine. This became evident in the history of the Reformed churches, in that about sixty years after the composition of the Belgic Confession these churches more fully developed the truth of predestination in the Reformed creed the Canons of Dordt. In the Canons, four large heads, or chapters, are devoted to predestination and related doctrines, in positive and negative

---

1 The description of election in the Canons of Dordt 1.9, in Schaff, *Creeds of Christendom*, 3:583.

sections. The Canons of Dordt is a much fuller explanation of the doctrine so briefly stated in article 16 of the Belgic Confession.[2] In addition, the Canons describes and condemns the errors that oppose the truth of predestination in every age.

Nevertheless, the Canons is only an explanation of the truth found in the Belgic Confession, as the Reformed Formula of Subscription for officebearers states. With reference to the Belgic Confession and the Heidelberg Catechism, the formula describes the Canons of Dordt, particularly its doctrine of predestination, as "the explanation of some points of the aforesaid doctrine."[3] The Canons adds nothing new to the doctrine of predestination in the Confession. It only develops what is found in the Confession, as the tree develops the acorn. The Canons also defends the biblical teaching of predestination against attacks upon it, particularly by the Remonstrants, or Arminians.

So much is it the case that the truth of sovereign predestination is clearly and adequately (although not fully) taught in article 16 of the Confession that the enemies of predestination in the Dutch Reformed churches in the late 1500s and early 1600s—the Arminians—opposed especially this article of the Belgic Confession. The Arminians opposed both the Heidelberg Catechism and the Belgic Confession regarding the brief doctrine of predestination in both these Reformed creeds. Especially did they oppose

---

2 For the positive sections of the Canons, see Schaff, *Creeds of Christendom*, 3:581–97. For the negative sections as well as the positive, see *Confessions and Church Order*, 153–80. The Canons contain "four" heads or chapters inasmuch as the third and fourth heads of doctrine are combined in one section, or chapter.

3 Ibid., 326.

the phrase in the Confession that teaches reprobation: "JUST, in leaving others in the fall and perdition wherein they have involved themselves."

Therefore, a commentary on article 16 of the Confession need not, and ought not, deliver a complete exposition of the Reformed doctrine of predestination. Rather, it can content itself with a brief explanation of predestination as predestination is confessed in article 16 of the Belgic Confession. Such an explanation will do justice to the fundamental aspects of the doctrine.

THE DOCTRINE OF ELECTION

As the Confession shows by the relative length of its explanation of the two elements of God's predestination, election is the more important aspect of predestination. Indeed, reprobation serves election. This is not to imply that reprobation is unimportant. On the contrary! Reprobation is one decree with election. Such is the importance of reprobation that the denial or loss in the church's confession and preaching of reprobation is necessarily the denial or loss of election. But that reprobation serves election is to acknowledge that scripture teaches that election is the "heart of the church," not the distinct aspect of predestination that consists of reprobation, and that election has primacy in the preaching of the gospel by the church, whereas reprobation is secondary, appearing in the preaching not as a truth of independent significance, but as a truth that has its significance in the service of election.

Election is God's choice in love of some sinners, to be delivered from the "perdition and ruin" of sin and death and to enjoy the bliss of his fellowship forever, which is salvation. Election means choice. Passages in scripture that use the term and teach the doctrine include Deuteronomy 7:6–8 in the Old Testament and Ephesians 1:4 in the New Testament. Concerning Israel in the Old Testament, God locates his redemption and salvation of that people, in distinction from all the other nations, in his election of them. In Deuteronomy 7, contrary to the wisdom that cries that election is not to be preached or cannot be preached, Moses preached their election to Israel:

6. For thou art an holy people unto the LORD thy God: the LORD thy God hath chosen thee to be a special people unto himself, above all people that are upon the face of the earth.
7. The LORD did not set his love upon you, nor choose you, because ye were more in number than any people; for ye were the fewest of all people:
8. But because the LORD loved you, and because he would keep the oath which he had sworn unto your fathers, hath the LORD brought you out with a mighty hand, and redeemed you out of the house of bondmen, from the hand of Pharaoh king of Egypt.

In Ephesians 1:4–5 the apostle proclaims his and their election to the church in all ages: "According as he hath chosen us in him [Jesus Christ] before the foundation of the world, that we should be holy and without blame before him, in love having predestinated us unto the adoption of children by Jesus Christ to himself, according to the good pleasure of his will."[4]

---

4 This translation of the two verses is preferable to that of the Authorized Version. The phrase "in love" describes the following words in

However, the Bible teaches election in other words than "election" or "choice." John teaches election as God's giving certain persons to Christ to be his and to be saved by him (John 6:37; 17:6, 9, 11). Also, in scripture the term "predestination" always refers to election, not to election *and reprobation* as the term is generally used in theology, for example, Ephesians 1:5 and 11. "Predestination," then, is God's choice of some to salvation, viewed as God's determining beforehand their eternal destiny of salvation from sin and death unto righteousness and life.

For all its brevity, the Confession teaches all the essential aspects of election. First, election is an eternal decree of God, that is, a decision that God took in eternity: "In his eternal...council...[God] hath elected." Election is not a decision or act of God in history, after man was created and fell and after persons live and die. Election is not a temporal decision. As is the case with the whole of the Confession's explanation of the Reformed doctrine of election, this fundamental characteristic of election is biblical. Ephesians 1:4 places God's election "before the foundation of the world." About election, 2 Timothy 1:9 says that God has saved us "according to his own purpose and grace, which was given us in Christ Jesus *before the world began*" (emphasis added).

Second, God's election of his people was gracious. That is, in choosing some humans God showed favor to them, which favor was undeserved. The Confession expresses the grace of election when it accounts for this election by attributing it to God's "mere goodness" and when it adds that God elected "without any respect to their works." The

---

the passage, rather than the preceding words. Specifically, "in love" identifies the source and motive of God's predestination.

choice was not due to anything in those chosen; it did not depend upon any worthiness in those chosen; it cannot be accounted for by any loveliness or goodness in those chosen.

Again in this aspect of election, the Confession is solidly grounded in scripture. God's election of Jacob, in distinction from Esau, whom God reprobated, was a reality when the two boys were "not yet born, neither having done any good or evil, that the purpose of God according to election might stand, not of works, but of him that calleth" (Rom. 9:11). Specifically, contrary to a common heresy in both the sixteenth and the twenty-first centuries, election is not based on foreseen faith in those whom God has chosen, in which case election would not be gracious. The Bible explicitly states that election is not due to faith, but that faith is due to election: "As many as were ordained to eternal life believed" (Acts 13:48). Denied by the text is that as many as believed were ordained to eternal life. Therefore, election is gracious.

Another way of expressing the grace of election is the confession that election is unconditional. Although the Confession does not use the term, its insistence on the grace of election implies the unconditionality of the decree. The choice of some did not depend upon, or was not conditioned by, anything whatever in those whom God chose. A conditional decree would be a decree that is non-gracious.

Third, election is the choice of a certain number of specific persons. It is not a general decree to save all those who may eventually believe, whether many, or few, or none at all, as the case may be. The Confession affirms election as the choice of a certain number of definite persons when it describes the objects of election as "all whom" and when it goes on to contrast with them "others" whom it pleased God to leave in their fall and perdition. In a powerful description of the decree of election, Jesus taught that God wrote the names of particular persons in heaven (Luke 10:20). Revelation 13:8 assures believers that those whose names are "written in the book of life of the Lamb slain from the foundation of the world" will not worship the beast, who is antichrist. Election of particular persons assures, indeed effects, faith and faithfulness in those who are elected.

Fourth, as Revelation 13:8 indicates, election is God's choice of specific persons *to be saved*. The Confession teaches that when God carries out the decree of election he "delivers and preserves from this perdition." Delivering from perdition is election as to its purpose and goal. Ephesians 1:4–14 makes election known as the decree of God appointing the elect unto redemption through the blood of Jesus Christ, unto the eternal inheritance, and unto being to the praise of God's glory. This is election unto salvation. Thus is exposed the deceptive doctrine that there is an eternal election but that it merely consists of choice unto service.

Fifth, election is effectual. All those, and every one of those, who are chosen are also saved. Not one of the elect will or can go lost. This is emphasized in the Confession: "He delivers and preserves from this perdition all whom he...hath elected in Christ Jesus our Lord." As article 17 teaches, God saves the elect by the promise of the gospel of Jesus Christ, which promise is believed by the elect. But he saves all the elect. Revelation 13:8 denies that any whose name has been written in the book of life of the Lamb will fall away in the hard days of the antichrist. Acts 13:8 affirms that all those ordained to eternal life will believe and thus be saved.

Sixth, election is "unchangeable." This important characteristic of election, according to the Confession, is grounded upon the unchangeableness of God and his counsel: "all whom he, in his eternal and unchangeable counsel...hath elected in Christ Jesus." The unchangeableness of election is due, first, to the unchangeableness of God himself, which unchangeableness the creed confessed already in article 1. Second, the choice of some to salvation is unconditional. It simply does not depend on those whom God has chosen. It does not depend on them for the making of the decree. It does not depend on them for the maintaining of the decree. It does not depend on them for the realizing of the decree. It depends solely upon the God who is unchangeable in wisdom, might, and grace.

It is remarkable that the Confession taught that election is unchangeable long before the Arminian controversy erupted in the Reformed churches in the Netherlands. Arminian theology taught, and teaches still today, a changeable, and changing, decree of election. According to this theology, God chooses a man unto salvation today, depending on his faith and obedience, but may very well reject the same man tomorrow, because of his turning from faith to unbelief and from obedience to disobedience. This is the terror of everyone who believes the Arminian heresy. Salvation can be lost, because election is changeable, dependent as it is on the fickleness of the human will.

The unchangeableness of election is comfort for the Reformed believer. Knowing himself an elect, by his faith in Jesus Christ, the Reformed Christian is certain of his

THE BELGIC CONFESSION: A COMMENTARY

everlasting salvation, since God will not change the decree, upon which salvation depends, from election to reprobation. In its great controversy with the Arminian heresy, the Reformed churches laid heavy emphasis on this practical difference between the two religions, exactly locating the difference in the doctrine that God is unchangeable. The Reformed churches took note of the Arminian error "that not every election unto salvation is unchangeable, but that some of the elect, any decree of God notwithstanding, can yet perish and do indeed perish."[5] This error concerning an unstable salvation, the Reformed churches rejected:

> By which gross error they make God to be change-able, and destroy the comfort which the godly obtain out of the firmness of their election, and contradict the Holy Scripture, which teaches that the elect cannot be led astray (Matt. 24:24); that Christ does not lose those whom the Father gave him (John 6:39); and that God hath also glorified those whom he foreordained, called, and justified (Rom. 8:30).[6]

Even though the word itself is not used in article 16, the article's explanation of election implies clearly that God's election of some humans to salvation is *sovereign*. It is a decree of God that is the free exercise of his absolute, unchallengeable authority over his creatures. Especially the sovereignty of divine election is the message of the apostle in Romans 9, particularly the sovereignty of election in relationship to the accompanying decree of reprobation.

---

5   Canons of Dordt 1, error 6, in *Confessions and Church Order*, 161.
6   Ibid.

The hard question for the churches that oppose the Reformed doctrine of predestination as confessed in article 16 of the Belgic Confession is how God's election of some in distinction from others, who are reprobated, can be explained and justified. Their response to the doctrine invariably takes the form of a question, which is not in reality a question at all, but a challenge to the doctrine. The apostle states this question/challenge to the doctrine of predestination in Romans 9:19: "Why doth he yet find fault? For who hath resisted his will?"

For the apostle and for the Reformed church, the question is not a hard question at all. The ready answer to the question is the sovereignty of God: "Nay but, O man, who art thou that repliest against God? Shall the thing formed say to him that formed it, Why hast thou made me thus? Hath not the potter power over the clay, of the same lump to make one vessel unto honour, and another unto dishonor?" (vv. 20–21).

"Power" in the English translation of verse 21 is the translation of the Greek word *exousia,* which literally means authority. Such is the sovereign authority of God that he has the divine right to elect whom he pleases and to reprobate whom he wills. This is what it means to be God. No human may question, much less criticize, predestination as being unrighteous or unfair. When God himself makes known that he "will have mercy on whom I will have mercy and that I will have compassion on whom I will have compassion," in distinction from others upon whom he wills not to have mercy (v. 15), churches, theologians, and believers may confess that they find the decree of predestination incomprehensible—not unknowable, but incomprehensible. But they may not challenge the decree as unrighteous.

Clay may not challenge the Potter. Clay may certainly not challenge the Potter in order to attribute the honor of some vessels to the vessels themselves. This is invariably the case when critics of predestination arrogantly question the righteousness of predestination. The result is a theology of predestination that has God choosing some in distinction from others because of the worthiness of these humans to be elected, whether their faith or their good works. Election, then, is no longer gracious. Because all of salvation has its source in election, the result is that salvation is no longer gracious.

In article 16 the Reformed faith confesses an essential truth of election that is often overlooked. This is the truth that God elected in Jesus Christ: "[God] hath elected in Christ Jesus our Lord." The Confession took this phrase about election in Jesus Christ directly from scripture. Ephesians 1:4 states that the triune God "hath chosen us *in him*," that is, in "our Lord Jesus Christ," mentioned in verse 3. The text does not merely state that after God elected his people Jesus Christ carries out the decree by his work of salvation, which is true. But the text and the Confession on the basis of this passage teach that God's election of the church was made in eternity, *in Jesus Christ, for the sake of Jesus Christ*, and *not apart from Jesus Christ*. The apostle and the Confession are describing a decree in eternity, before the world was created, and before Jesus was born.

The meaning is that God decreed Jesus Christ first, prior to the election of the church, indeed, before the decree of creation, the decree of the fall, and the decree of history. This order cannot be temporal, because time does not qualify the eternal decree. Rather, the order is that of priority of importance in the mind and will of the decreeing God. Christ Jesus is first in the counsel of God as the one who is most precious to God and as the one in whom God would glorify himself. The church with all its members is second as the body and bride of Christ, serving Christ and manifesting the glory of Christ, to the ultimate glory of God. The election of the church and her members is subordinate to the election of Christ Jesus.

This is not the order of election as commonly conceived even in Reformed thinking. The common conception is that God first elected his people. Then he decreed Christ Jesus as the savior in order to carry out the salvation of God's elect people. First the church, then Christ Jesus.

The Confession corrects this common notion about election: God "hath elected in Christ Jesus our Lord." In the counsel of God, Christ Jesus is first and paramount. All else, including the election of the people of God, is second—for the sake of Jesus Christ. The Bridegroom is first; the bride is chosen for the sake of the Bridegroom. The Head is first; the body is chosen for the sake of the Head. The order, ultimately, is not Christ Jesus for the sake of the church, but the church for the sake of Jesus Christ. This doctrine of the order of the decree of election is uniquely Reformed, although even among the Reformed it is widely overlooked.

The biblical basis of the primacy of Christ Jesus in the counsel of the electing God is especially Colossians 1:13–29. In the counsel of God, Christ Jesus is the "firstborn of every creature" (v. 15). "He is before all things" in the eternal counsel (v. 17). Regarding the church, in the counsel of God Jesus is the "beginning." Indeed, everything that exists, or has ever existed, or will exist, are by God's appointment in his counsel "for him," that is, for Jesus Christ. Eternally, it "pleased the Father that in him [Jesus Christ] should all fulness dwell" (v. 19). Particularly regarding the church and her members, Jesus Christ is *the* Elect.

Therefore, denial of the decree of election, as election is presented in the Belgic Confession and preached by the Reformed faith, is to deny Jesus Christ and to oppose the main purpose of God regarding creation, salvation, and history. Nothing less than this is the gravity of the rejection of the Reformed doctrine of predestination.

There is, in addition, another important implication of election in Christ Jesus. This is that elect humans are united with Christ already in eternity, in the decree of election. They are never separated or independent from Christ. The beautiful confession of the Heidelberg Catechism that the only comfort of the believing child of God is that he or she belongs to his or her Savior Jesus Christ does not only apply to this earthly life.[7] It is also true from eternity: "elected in Christ Jesus." Never, from eternity past to eternity future, is the child of God apart from Jesus Christ.

Election in Christ Jesus is also instructive regarding one's knowledge of his own election personally. Knowledge of one's own personal election is possible, is necessary, is urgent. Jesus exhorts believers to "rejoice, because your names are written in heaven" (Luke 10:20). Peter admonishes those who "have obtained like precious faith" with himself to "give diligence to make your calling and election sure," that is, to be certain of their election (2 Pet. 1:1, 10). Certainty of one's election is not a reality by some special revelation or mystical experience. One does not have it

---

7   Heidelberg Catechism Q 1, in Schaff, *Creeds of Christendom*, 3:307–8.

by peeking into the book of life in heaven. Nor does one obtain it by intense scrutiny of oneself, one's own spirituality, in a kind of spiritual "navel-gazing."

Certainty of election is the assuring work of the Holy Ghost by way of one's believing in Jesus Christ. By faith, and by faith alone, the child of God is saved, also regarding certainty of his election. As he is chosen "in Christ Jesus," so does he have assurance of salvation in Christ Jesus, by faith in him. One looks away from self to Jesus. This is faith. When Peter took his eyes off Jesus, he began to sink (see Matt. 14:28–31).

Calvin taught that the believer must find his election in Christ by describing Christ as the "mirror of election": "Christ, then, is the mirror wherein we must, and without self-deception may, contemplate our own election."[8]

In view of the controversy that has often racked the Reformed churches over the issue, it is worth noting that the article on predestination in the Confession does not address, much less decide, the in-house debate over infralapsarianism and supralapsarianism. This is a debate concerning the order of the eternal decrees of God. Specifically, the debate concerns the relationship of the decree of predestination to the decree of the fall of man. Infralapsarianism has God electing and reprobating humans after (infra-) the decree of the fall of the race in Adam. Predestination therefore is the election and reprobation of humans viewed by God as already fallen. Supralapsarianism has God predestinating humans before (supra-) the decree of the fall. The objects of predestination in God's eternal counsel therefore are humans viewed as unfallen.

---

8   Calvin, *Institutes*, 3.5, 2:970.

It is commonly thought that article 16 of the Belgic Confession adopts the infralapsarian position. But this is a mistake. The article does not teach that God elected and reprobated humans in the condition of perdition, that is, as already fallen. But it teaches that, in history, God saves from perdition all whom he eternally elected and leaves in perdition all whom he eternally reprobated. The order of the eternal decrees is left undecided. The confession only states that both salvation and non-salvation in time and history are determined by the eternal counsel of God, regardless of the order of the eternal decrees.

ELECTION ACCOMPANIED BY REPROBATION

The decree of election is accompanied by a decree of reprobation. Reprobation is the divine decree that appoints some humans to damnation, which damnation is on account of their unbelief and other sins. Or it is the decree determining that the eternal destiny of some humans will be their perishing in hell. Reprobation *rejects* these humans regarding salvation in Jesus Christ.

Reprobation is an element of the very same decree in which God chooses some to salvation. It is the element that consists of God's not choosing all, but passing some humans by with the decree of election, and thus appointing them to perish in their sin. There is one decree determining salvation and damnation. In this decree, God chooses some and rejects others. In Reformed theology, this decree is called predestination. The two elements of the one decree are election (unto salvation) and reprobation (unto damnation).

The Confession teaches reprobation in article 16, albeit very briefly. It teaches reprobation in the concluding line of its treatment of election: "Just, in leaving others in the fall and perdition wherein they have involved themselves." According to the Confession, God has not chosen all in Christ unto salvation. He leaves the others, whom he has not elected, in their perdition. Since God saves all whom he has chosen in eternity, he did not choose these others. His not choosing them was his appointment of them to damnation.

Brief as this reference to reprobation is, the description of it by the Confession, in connection with the decree of election, makes known the fundamental truth of the doctrine.[9] Reprobation is an eternal decree, indeed, part and parcel of the decree that elected. Inasmuch as God did not elect all but passed some by with the electing decree, in the same eternal decree in which he elected he also reprobated. One cannot therefore deny reprobation without at

---

9   The Reformed churches make a fuller confession of reprobation in the Canons of Dordt in response to the assault on it by the Arminian heresy. See Canons 1.15, in Schaff, *Creeds of Christendom*, 3:584. Also significant is that this creedal statement on reprobation insists that reprobation be considered only in closest connection with election. The article begins: "What peculiarly tends to illustrate and recommend to us the eternal and unmerited grace of election." See also the rejection of errors section of the first head of doctrine of the Canons, in *Confessions and Church Order*, 159–62. It is especially the danger of treating reprobation apart from the decree of election, and unnecessarily roughly, against which the Canons warn in its Conclusion: "This Synod exhorts all their brethren in the gospel of Christ to conduct themselves piously and religiously in handling this doctrine...to direct it...to the glory of the Divine name, to holiness of life, and to the consolation of afflicted souls...and to abstain from all those phrases which exceed the limits necessary to be observed in ascertaining the genuine sense of the Holy Scriptures, and may furnish insolent sophists with a just pretext for violently assailing, or even vilifying, the doctrine of the Reformed Churches" (Canons of Dordt, Conclusion, in Schaff, *Creeds of Christendom*, 3:597).

the same time denying biblical and Reformed election. The election of *some* implies the reprobation of others.

Reprobation is the appointment unto damnation of a certain number of specific persons. The Confession describes them as "others." They are the specific persons and the definite number whom God determines to leave in the fall and perdition when he elects the specific, definite number of persons unto salvation. To deny reprobation as the rejection of a certain number of specific persons is the rejection of the biblical and Reformed doctrine of election.

Like election, reprobation is sovereign, unconditional, and unchangeable, as sovereign, unconditional, and unchangeable as is election, with which reprobation constitutes one decree determining the salvation and damnation of all humans. This one decree with its two constituent elements, Reformed theology calls predestination. Regardless whether the objects of the reprobating decree in the eternal counsel of God are viewed as fallen or unfallen, as already sinful by their own disobedience, or as about to become sinful by their own disobedience (and good Reformed believers defend both views), the decision of God to appoint them to destruction in the way of their unbelief and other sins is sovereign and unconditional, unless the decree to elect some is determined by something in the elect, and conditional. Even if the objects of reprobation (and election) appear in the mind of the electing and reprobating God as fallen into sin, the explanation of God's choosing some and rejecting the others is the sovereign good pleasure of the predestinating God.

It is especially the sovereignty of God in reprobation that is offensive to theologians and churches. The first response of the soundly Reformed church to these objectors to reprobation is that they revolt against the Reformed creeds, which determine biblical, Reformed orthodoxy and to which these theologians and churches have sworn allegiance. By their opposition to reprobation, and with this necessarily to the gospel of election, they manifest themselves as traitors in the camp, false swearers, fifth columnists, and heretical—heretical not only regarding reprobation, but also regarding election.

Second, the doctrine that so offends many nominally Reformed churches and theologians is biblical. Every passage in scripture that teaches that God has elected a definite number of specific persons unto salvation, which election assures final salvation, also teaches reprobation, by implication. Such a passage is Romans 8:29–30: "Whom he did foreknow, he also did predestinate to be conformed to the image of his Son, that he might be the firstborn among many brethren. Moreover whom he did predestinate, them he also called: and whom he called, them he also justified: and whom he justified, them he also glorified." If God does not justify and glorify all humans without exception, neither did he predestinate, or elect, all without exception. Those specific persons whom he does not justify and glorify, he did not elect, but reprobated.

In addition, a number of passages in scripture teach reprobation expressly. There is the bulk of the Old Testament. God's election for the most part was limited to the nation of Israel. With the rare exception, he reprobated the members of the other nations. "He sheweth his word unto Jacob, his statutes and his judgments unto Israel. He hath not dealt so with any nation" (Ps. 147:19–20). Unless there was salvation without God's word, his withholding of his word from the nations carried out his reprobation of the members of the nations.

Romans 9:6–33 is the *locus classicus* on the eternal decree of reprobation, significantly in inseparable connection with the decree of election. Truly, it is the biblical stone of stumbling and rock of offense to the enemies of predestination without and within the Reformed churches. God reprobated Esau in his hatred of that son of believing Jacob and Rachel while the boy was yet unborn and had as yet done no evil (vv. 10–16).

God has "mercy on whom he will have mercy, and whom he will he hardeneth" (v. 18). The will to have mercy is eternal election; the will to harden is eternal reprobation. Both "wills" have a definite number of specific individuals as objects. Both "wills" determine the spiritual and everlasting destiny of the objects. And both "wills" are sovereign: "whom he will."

First Peter 2:8 teaches that Christ is a stone of stumbling and a rock of offence to some, who stumble at the word of the gospel in their unbelief. They are disobedient to the call of the gospel to believe in Christ Jesus. The sin is their own. At the same time, the apostle accounts for this disobedience, in distinction from the obedience of others: "whereunto they were appointed." The appointment unto disobedience, which disobedience is their spiritual and eternal perishing, is God's appointment of them in the decree of reprobation. Apparently this description of the decree of reprobation is stronger than that of article 16 of the Confession, which speaks only of leaving some in their perdition. But the difference is only apparent. The decree to leave sinners in their sin is, in fact, an appointment of them unto damnation. Noteworthy is the close connection of reprobation in 1 Peter 2 with election. In chapter 1, the apostle has explained the obedience of the believers to the word of the gospel by their being "elect according to the foreknowledge of God the Father" (1 Pet. 1:2).

The main heresies in the twenty-first century regarding predestination include the teaching that God has elected all and that all will therefore be saved. This is sheer universalism. For all its learned ingenuity and complicated nuancing, this is, in the end, the doctrine of election of Karl Barth. Another heresy is the teaching that God has elected all, but that he has done so *conditionally*, so that the salvation of those who eventually are saved depends on their fulfilling the condition, whether the condition be responding rightly to the revelation of God in nature or the revelation of God in the preaching of the gospel. This is the denial of the grace of election and therefore the grace of salvation.

Yet another heresy, which is popular in Reformed churches, has God offering salvation to all humans, or at least all those who come under the gospel, with the gracious desire (will) that all respond positively and thus be saved. This is the false doctrine that calls itself the well-meant offer (of salvation). The theology of the well-meant offer of salvation, which has God sincerely desiring the salvation of all humans, at least all humans to whom the gospel comes, and with this gracious desire offering salvation, is plain contradiction (disguised as "paradox") of the truth of predestination as taught in article 16 of the Confession. Invariably, the theology of the well-meant offer of salvation soon silences all confession of reprobation and then produces the message of universal, conditional election, which election is expressed in a universal, ineffectual atonement.

All of these false doctrines concerning predestination share the error of denying the Confession's teaching that God's merciful will of salvation (election) is the choice of some fallen sinners only and that this will infallibly effects the salvation of all who are its objects. Apart from universalism, these false doctrines also imply that the eventual salvation of those who are elected conditionally and of those who respond favorably to the well-meant offer, which is made to all humans alike, is due to their own fulfillment of the condition, or their acceptance of the offered Christ. This contradicts the Confession's teaching that election is "without any respect to...works." According to these teachings, it is not the merciful will of God, but the will of the sinner himself that delivers from perdition.

The heresies also obviously deny reprobation. Choosing all conditionally, or well-meaningly offering salvation to all, is not the divine justice that leaves some sinners in the fall and perdition wherein they have involved themselves. It is not the sovereign counsel of God that has mercy on whom he wills to have mercy and hardens whom he wills to harden. The denial of reprobation is necessarily also the denial of election.

THE RELATIONSHIP OF ELECTION AND SALVATION IN JESUS CHRIST

The relationship of article 17 to article 16 is that election is the source of Jesus Christ, of the promise of the gospel, and of all of the salvation of fallen mankind. Article 17 confesses the "most gracious God," who in his grace seeks and comforts "miserable" man and who does this by the gospel-promise of "his Son," Jesus Christ. This revelation of the grace of God to miserable sinners, the comfort, the gospel promise, and Jesus Christ himself are born from the womb of eternal election.

Article 17 has in view the historical event recorded in Genesis 3 and the promise of God in verse 15. God sought out disobedient man, not in wrath to punish him, but in grace to "comfort him when he trembling fled from his presence." The comfort was the promise of God's Son, Jesus the Christ, who would "bruise the head of the serpent" and make miserable man "happy" by redeeming him from sin and death and establishing with him the covenant of grace, of which the covenant that Adam broke was the divinely appointed figure, or type.

The promise of God to which the Confession refers, and which it quotes in part, is Genesis 3:15. In God's word to the serpent, that is, to the devil, who had used the serpent, was the gracious promise of God to miserable man: "I will put enmity between thee and the woman, and between thy seed and her seed; it shall bruise thy head, and thou shalt bruise his heel." According to the Reformed confession, the seed of the woman who would accomplish the utter defeat of the devil and all his works and thus save the woman and all her seed is God's "Son, who should *be made of a woman*," that is, Jesus Christ. This promise indicates that the saving work of the Son of God would be accomplished by means of the bruising of the Savior's heel. Thus is described the atoning lifelong suffering of Jesus Christ, culminating in his death by crucifixion.

This promise of the gospel is the source of the coming into the world of the eternal Son of God in the incarnation and of all his saving work, which are the subjects of the articles in the Confession that immediately follow. The promise of Genesis 3:15 is therefore known as the mother promise. But the mother promise itself originates from God's decree of election, so that Jesus himself, the seed of the woman, and all his saving work, the bruising of the head of the serpent, have their source and explanation in God's election of grace.

Thus the article confesses all of salvation to be gracious. None of it is the work of the sinner himself. None of it is deserved, merited, or due to a condition fulfilled by the sinner himself. Any such doctrine is exposed and condemned by the Reformed Confession in article 17. The salvation of the sinner is the work of the Seed of the woman, consisting of the bruising of the serpent's head. The sinner has nothing to do with this saving act. Besides, the One who accomplishes salvation is the "Son [of God], who should be made of a woman." No sinner possesses this marvelous qualification, this awesome power.

Further, the Savior proceeds from the promise of God in Genesis 3:15. This promise was a wholly gracious promise to "wholly miserable" man, who was so far from making himself a worthy object of the promise that, on the contrary, he "trembling fled from his [the promising God's] presence." It was a promise made to man who "had… thrown himself into temporal and spiritual death." The ultimate source of the promise, of the Savior, and of all his saving work of making man "happy" is God's merciful decree of election. According to this decree, God *gives* his Son: "he would *give* his Son."

Already before the Confession comes to treat of the work of salvation in detail, it has the Reformed Christian confessing salvation by grace alone by Christ alone.

The "admirable wisdom and goodness" of God, of which the Confession speaks, is the wisdom and goodness that provides the Savior that fallen man needs. It is also the wisdom and goodness that provides a Savior and that gives a salvation that glorifies God, rather than the sinner himself. The incarnate Son of God is the one and only Savior who can and will deliver miserable man from the guilt, depravity, and death of his fall and who will make man truly and supremely happy. The gracious gospel promise of salvation in this Son of God and of the great mercy of God in him is the one and only means of comforting fearful and trembling sinners, inclined to flee from God in the twenty-first century in civilized America as once in the Garden of Eden at the beginning of history.

The admirable wisdom and goodness of God are also displayed by his plan to save sinners and to glorify himself to the uttermost in the way of the redemption of fallen humans by the Savior, Jesus Christ, rather than in the way of an obedient Adam. His wisdom is the ability to attain the highest and best end by means of the disobedience and fall of man. His goodness is not only his mercy to fallen man, but also his government of all things, including the disobedience of Adam, on behalf of the achievement of the highest end, namely, his own glory in the salvation of the church by Jesus Christ. This the Reformed Christian believes, when he can neither comprehend nor feel. For what the Confession declared in article 13 concerning divine providence is true: "Nothing happens in this world without his appointment."

That "man" is the object of God's gracious attitude, of his promise, and of his saving work in Jesus Christ in article 17 is not to be understood as though God is gracious to all humans, graciously promises salvation to all alike, and accomplishes salvation for all humans without exception, at least regarding God's desire. This doctrine would have the Confession forgetting everything that it has just taught in article 16 concerning election and reprobation.

"Man" in article 17 is, first, Adam, the historical Adam, who by his disobedience threw himself into death; who trembling fled from God in the garden; whom God comforted with the mother promise; and to whom, with Eve, God promised the Seed of the woman. For Reformed Christianity, uncorrupted by the unbelief of the apostasy of modernism, or liberalism, this Adam was a real, historical person. All that is recorded of him in the opening chapters of the Bible is historical reality. To deny his historicity is to negate everything that is taught in article 17 of the Belgic Confession, including the mother promise and therefore the reality of Jesus Christ and of the bruising of the head of the serpent, and the genuine happiness of believing members of the church.

But man is more than the individual, Adam. It is significant that, whereas articles 15 and 16 speak of Adam, article 17 speaks of "man." Man fell into sin and death. God comforted man with the promise of the gospel. God would make man happy by the Seed of the woman. Man in the article is the human race, the race of which Adam the first was created the covenantal head. The object of the saving grace of God, of the saving promise of the gospel, and of the saving purpose and work of the Son of God is the human race.

But the human race that is the object of the saving grace of God in Jesus Christ in article 17, as in scripture, is not all humans without exception. Article 16 of the Belgic Confession has made this perfectly clear. God's saving grace, which is indubitably the subject of article 17, has for its object "all whom he, in his eternal and unchangeable counsel, of mere goodness hath elected in Christ Jesus our Lord," and them only. The "others" he has determined to "leave... in the fall and perdition wherein they have involved themselves." A Confession that has confessed predestination in article 16 will not in the very next article confess that God seeks and comforts every human without exception, that God promises (or well-meaningly offers) his Son and salvation to every human, and that God will in the bruising of this Son accomplish redemption for every human, in order to make every human blessed with the bliss of salvation. There may be theologians who are so illogical and whose theology is thus absurd, not to say heretical, but this is not true of Reformed theology, and certainly not of the Reformed confessions.

By "man" in article 17, the Confession refers to the human race. But the human race is all nations and peoples as determined by the headship of Jesus Christ, the individual members of which are all who belong to Jesus Christ by a true and living faith. Jesus Christ is the second Adam (1 Cor. 15:45). In Christ, God saves not alone some, or even many, individuals out of the race, but the race itself—mankind. But the race—mankind—is not all humans. Rather, it is made up of all those who are in Christ, the head of the race, by faith (Gal. 3:16, 26–29). As the preceding article of the Confession has stated, those who are in Christ and are saved in him are all those in all nations whom God has elected in grace. The church of the elect is the new human race. It is the object of the saving grace, saving promise, and saving work of God in the seed of the woman in article 17.

They and they alone are "happy."

Chapter Thirteen

THE INCARNATION OF
THE SON OF GOD

(ARTICLE 18)

ART. XVIII. OF THE INCARNATION OF JESUS CHRIST.

We confess, therefore, that God did fulfill the promise which he made to the fathers by the mouth of his holy prophets when he sent into the world, at the time appointed by him, his own only-begotten and eternal Son, who took upon him the form of a servant, and became like unto men, really assuming the true human nature, with all its infirmities, sin excepted, being conceived in the womb of the blessed Virgin Mary, by the power of the Holy Ghost, without the means of man; and did not only assume human nature as to the body, but also a true human soul, that he might be a real man. For since the soul was lost as well as the body, it was necessary that he should take both upon him, to save both. Therefore we confess (in opposition to the heresy of the Anabaptists, who deny that Christ assumed human flesh of his mother) that Christ is become a partaker of the flesh and blood of the children; that he is a fruit of the loins of David after the flesh; made of the seed of David according to the flesh; a fruit of the womb of the Virgin Mary; made of a woman; a branch of David; a shoot of the root of Jesse; sprung from the tribe of Judah; descended from the Jews according to the flesh: of the seed of Abraham, since he took upon him the seed of Abraham, and became like unto his brethren in all things, sin excepted; so that in truth he is our IMMANUEL, that is to say, God with us.

INTRODUCTION

With the following two articles, article 18 forms a distinct section of the Belgic Confession. The subject of the three articles is the coming into our world of the eternal Son of God as Jesus Christ: the incarnation. Article 18 describes the incarnation itself—what it was. Article 19 explains who Jesus is by virtue of the incarnation. Article 20 declares the purpose of God with the incarnation.

The subject of the section is that of Anselm's classic book *Cur Deus Homo* (*Why God [became] Man*).

The relationship of article 18 to the preceding article is that the incarnation was God's fulfillment of the promise that he had made first to Adam and Eve in paradise. Article 17 has Reformed believers confessing that God promised fallen, guilty man that God would give his Son, who should be made of a woman, to bruise the head of the serpent, and would make him happy. This is the promise of Genesis 3:15. This promise was wholly gracious. It had its origin not in any claim that man had on God, but in God's free election (art. 16). The content of the promise was Christ, the Seed of the woman.

This original, or mother, promise, God repeated "to the fathers by the mouth of his holy prophets," as article 18 puts it, many times throughout the Old Testament. Although the repetition of the promise took many forms, always the content was Christ and his coming.

The incarnation, which is the subject of article 18, was the fulfillment of the promise: "We confess, therefore," that is, because God had earlier promised to give his Son, "that God did fulfill the promise...when he sent into the world... his own only-begotten and eternal Son."

WHAT THE INCARNATION WAS

Even though the word does not occur in the article, or in the two articles that follow, the subject of article 18 and of the two articles that follow is the truth of the incarnation. "Incarnation" is a word that derives from the Latin *carnis* and means "infleshing" or "become flesh." The word refers to the act of the eternal Son of God of becoming flesh in Jesus, as we read in John 1:14: "And the Word was made flesh." The Word became incarnate. This act was the incarnation of the Word, or Son of God.

The incarnation of the Word, or Son, was the wonderful work of the triune God by which the eternal Son of God, the second person of the Trinity, became a man—a full, genuine human. "Flesh" in John 1:14, as in article 18 of the Confession, means human nature, that is, a man. The Son of God assumed, or united to himself, or took on, a human nature, while continuing to be God. He did not change into a man, thus ceasing to be God. Before the incarnation, the eternal Son was God; in the incarnation he becomes also a man. This is the clear explanation of the incarnation by the Confession: "[The] eternal Son...*took upon him the form of a servant, and became like unto men,* really assuming the true human nature."

In support of this understanding and confession of the incarnation, the Confession quotes or alludes to several passages of scripture. Concerning the origin and nature of Jesus Christ, John 1:14 states that "the Word was made flesh." Philippians 2:7 teaches that in Jesus Christ the Son of God "took upon him the form of a servant, and was made in the likeness of men." That "Christ is become *a partaker of the flesh and blood of the children*" is the message of Hebrews 2:14.

The incarnation was the work of the triune God, even though primarily it concerned the Son. The eternal Son himself acted to assume the human nature: "[The Son]... took upon him the form of a servant" (see Phil. 2:5–7). God the Father acted in sending forth his Son, "made of a woman, made under the law" (Gal. 4:4). The Confession calls attention to this sending by the Father: "God...sent into the world...his own only-begotten Son." God the Holy Ghost acted in that he was the power who accomplished the amazing union of the eternal Son with the human nature in Mary's womb (Luke 1:35). To this incarnating power of the Spirit, the Confession refers when it states that the Son was "conceived in the womb of the blessed Virgin Mary, by the power of the Holy Ghost."

The incarnation of God the Son was a work of the greatest power, as was acknowledged by the angel at the annunciation: "For with God nothing shall be impossible" (v. 37). If God can and will perform the incarnation on behalf of the salvation of the elect church, he can and will perform everything that is necessary for her salvation. Nothing that belongs to her salvation is more demanding of God's love and power than the incarnation.

It was a work of marvelous grace and goodness. The Confession accounts for the incarnation in God's purpose of the full salvation of elect sinners: "to save both [soul and body]." This salvation will be explained more fully in article 20 of the Confession.

The incarnation was God's greatest work. It was the central wonder of both creation and salvation. With a view to it, God created in the beginning. For the cross, it was the indispensable reality. The incarnation is incomprehensible in power: God thus closely united with humanity. It is astounding in love. God did so love sinful humans, on their part his enemies, that he incarnated his only begotten Son, as the gracious act of Father, Son, and Holy Ghost. Only faith knows and confesses the mystery of the incarnation: "Great is the mystery of godliness: God was manifest in the flesh" (1 Tim. 3:15).

THE NECESSARY MEANS OF THE INCARNATION

The necessary means of the incarnation was the conception of Jesus in, and the birth of Jesus from, the virgin. The Confession indicates this necessary means: "being conceived in the womb of the blessed Virgin Mary."

It is historical fact that Jesus was conceived in Mary, his mother, "without the means of man." No human father begot him. Rather, the Holy Ghost worked conception in Mary's womb. This was the prophecy of Isaiah 7:14: "The Lord himself shall give you a sign; Behold, a virgin shall conceive, and bear a son, and shall call his name Immanuel." This prophecy of virgin conception and virgin birth was fulfilled in the conception and birth of Jesus, as Matthew 1:18–25 and Luke 1:26–38 reveal. To Mary's response to the angel's announcement that she would have a child,

THE BELGIC CONFESSION: A COMMENTARY

"How shall this be, seeing I know not a man?" the angel replied: "The Holy Ghost shall come upon thee, and the power of the Highest shall overshadow thee: therefore also that holy thing which shall be born of thee shall be called the Son of God" (Luke 1:34–35).

Not only was the virgin conception and birth a sign of the hidden wonder of the incarnation, but also it was the necessary means by which the incarnation took place. Only if an earthly father is excluded can the Holy Ghost unite a sinless human nature to the person of the eternal Son of God. A human father would exclude the person of the Son of God. Even if somehow the resulting child could be freed from the sin of Adam and the depravity of the race, he would not be a divine person but a human person. This would render him incapable of the great work of salvation. Virgin conception was necessary if the Savior was to be the eternal Son of God as to his person, that is, virgin conception was necessary for the incarnation.

The angel taught the necessity of the virgin birth for the incarnation in the announcement of her conception to Mary. He announced her conception as a virgin in the words: "The Holy Ghost shall come upon thee, and the power of the Highest shall overshadow thee." Because of this miraculous conception, "*therefore,*" her child would be the Son of God: "therefore also that holy thing which shall be born of thee shall be called the Son of God" (v. 35).

Denial of the virgin birth is, by virtue of this fact, denial of the incarnation. Denial of the incarnation is denial of the Christian religion, as of all possibility of salvation.

Mary's place in the incarnation is obviously important. But that place is not that of a co-worker with God in providing the Savior. Rather, she is the privileged means whom

God uses to bring his Christ into the world. The Confession proves that Reformed believers are not averse to calling Mary "the blessed virgin." This was the address of the angel to Mary: "Blessed art thou among women" (v. 28). She is blessed in the sense that God graciously privileged her to bring into the world and rear to manhood his Son, the Savior. She is the *recipient* of God's blessing. She is not blessed in the sense that she herself has some inherent goodness that qualifies her to be the mother of the Savior and thus cooperate with God in the work of bringing the Savior and his salvation into the world. Mary is not the *subject* of her own blessedness.

Rome's doctrine and practice regarding Mary are idolatry: a creature cooperates with God in the work of salvation and is worshiped. Mary is co-mediator ("mediatrix") with Jesus. Through her, sitting bodily at Jesus' side in heaven, according to Roman Catholic mythology, sinners come to God. To her, Roman Catholics offer worship, regardless what play upon words is used to defend the practice when it is challenged. Regardless that it is not yet official Roman Catholic doctrine, it is the fault of Roman Catholic theology and practice concerning Mary that some esteem her as a fourth member of the Godhead, so that the Trinity becomes a Quaternity: Father, Son, Holy Ghost, and Virgin Mary.

The biblical account in Luke 1 of the announcement to Mary of her virgin conception exposes the Roman Catholic basis of its Mariolatry as false. Mary's honor as the mother of Christ is not due to any worthiness of her own. But God freely favors her or is gracious to her: She is "highly favored" (v. 28); she "found favor with God" (v. 30). As grace alone saves unworthy sinners, so also grace alone appoints this Jewish maid mother of the Christ. This grace of God makes

Mary willing to fulfill the office to which God calls her. Mary submits to the will of God for her: "Behold the handmaid of the Lord; be it unto me according to thy word" (v. 38). The mighty grace of God makes her willing. In view of the fact that being the mother of the Christ would mean for her that a sword would pierce her soul (2:35), the grace that makes Mary willing to conceive and bear the Messiah was great grace. But it was grace, and grace only.

Mary herself acknowledges that her blessedness is the gracious will and work of God. It is nothing of herself. Her song confesses her own natural lowliness: "the low estate of his handmaiden" (v. 48). Her blessedness as the mother of Christ is the grace of God toward her: "He that is mighty hath done to me great things" (v. 49). Therefore, Mary herself does not magnify herself, as Rome magnifies Mary, but "My soul doth magnify the Lord" (v. 46). Mary's is a Protestant response to the virgin conception.

"A REAL MAN"

The Confession ignores this controversy of the Reformed faith with the Roman Catholic Church regarding the "blessed Virgin Mary." It does engage in a lengthy controversy with the "heresy of the Anabaptists." The entire second half of the article is devoted to this controversy. The purpose of this controversy is to defend the truth that in the incarnation the Son of God became a "real man." This is to defend the incarnation itself. If the Son of God did not become a real man, there was no incarnation.

The Anabaptists denied, and still today deny, that the Son of God became a real human. At the time of the Reformation in the sixteenth century, they were a party that left the Roman Catholic Church but rejected also both branches of the Reformation, Lutheran and Reformed. They established their own churches. The name "Anabaptist" refers to their insistence on baptizing again those who had been baptized as infants. They repudiated infant baptism. Thus they were the original Baptists. One of their leading figures was Menno Simons.

It is not their error concerning baptism that concerns article 18 of the Confession, but their grave error concerning the incarnation. The Anabaptists taught that the incarnation amounted to nothing more than this, that God specially created a human nature out of nothing and then placed this embryo in Mary's womb, there to develop of itself for nine months, in order to be born as the baby Jesus. In the words of the Confession, the heresy of the Anabaptists was to "deny that Christ assumed human flesh of his mother." For nine months the unborn baby Jesus lay in Mary's womb as a piece of fruit lies in a basket. The fruit has no living connection with the basket. It does not develop from the basket. It certainly does not originate in any sense from the basket in which it lies. The basket is merely a storage unit for the fruit.

The argument that the Anabaptists gave for this denial of Jesus' truly being conceived in Mary's womb (Luke 1:31) and of Jesus' genuinely being born of Mary (v. 35), as really the son of Mary, was that a living, physical relationship of the baby with Mary would have meant the corruption of Jesus with the natural depravity of his mother. He would have inherited the sinfulness of the human race, which Mary shared. The solution for Anabaptism was to separate Jesus from the human race. Therein is found the heresy of Anabaptism, as the Confession exposes at length. One who is not a genuine member of the human race cannot be the Savior of humans. Being an alien to the human race, Anabaptism's "Jesus" cannot save humans. He may not represent them in his suffering and death, for God's justice requires that a human suffer the punishment that humans have incurred. He cannot infuse into humans his new life, for only the life of a human can be imparted to humans. In the language of scripture, which the Confession quotes, the Savior of humans must "become *a partaker of the flesh and blood of the children*" (see Heb. 2:14).

Although the Confession does not directly address the reason for Anabaptism's denial that Jesus is a "real man," it does indicate the response to Anabaptism's fear that a living, physical relationship of Jesus to Mary would have polluted the child. The Confession states that Jesus was "conceived in the womb of the blessed Virgin Mary, *by the power of the Holy Ghost.*" It was no minor aspect of his miraculous conception of the baby in Mary's womb that the Holy Ghost, while deriving the baby's human nature (that is, the *baby*) from his mother, sanctified that particular nature in the sense that he kept from it the natural depravity of the mother. By the work of the Holy Ghost in the conception of Jesus in Mary, Mary's depravity of nature did not pollute her son. The angel alluded to this aspect of the wonder of the incarnation when he said that the result of the work of the Holy Ghost in the conception of Jesus in Mary would be that the child would be "that holy thing" (Luke 1:35).

The deeper theological reason for Anabaptism's denial of the incarnation was that Anabaptism rejected the entire material world as evil. God can have nothing to do with the material world other than to destroy it. He certainly cannot unite with this material world, as he would have done if the eternal Son of God took to himself a human nature that was derived from Mary. Against this error of Anabaptism, the Reformed faith affirms the goodness of the material world by virtue of its creation by God. In the incarnation, God was not at work to create a new and different world, but to redeem and renew the original, now fallen, world. This demanded his intimate union with the world he had created by incarnation as a real man, a genuine member of the human race, although untainted by its sinfulness.

The controversy of the Reformed faith with Anabaptism over the nature of the incarnation is by no means a thing of the past. The Anabaptist heresy is perpetuated today by their theological and spiritual descendants, the Baptists. A representative is the well-known advocate of creation science Henry Morris. This president emeritus of the Institute for Creation Research has written concerning the conception and birth of Jesus that "the body of the second Adam must be formed directly by God and placed in a virgin's womb...This wonderful body would not... grow from a woman's egg, for...a sin-carrying...embryo would necessarily result. It must instead be a seed specially formed by the Creator Himself, then planted in the virgin's womb, where it forthwith would become His 'tabernacle.' The 'new thing' in the chosen woman must be '*created.*'" All of this denial of the truth that Jesus was conceived and born of Mary, as a member of the human race, is in order that Jesus might have a "body unmarred...by inherent sin spiritually."[1]

In reality, Morris' doctrine of the conception and birth of Jesus is a denial of the incarnation. The incarnation

---

1   Henry M. Morris, "When God Became Man" (Santee, CA: Institute for Creation Research, n.d.).

was not the use of Mary's womb as a storage unit for nine months of the eternal Son of God united to a specially created human embryo. It was the becoming flesh—the genuine human nature created by God in the beginning and passed on to Jesus from his mother—of the eternal Son of God. The man Jesus is not a marvelous Alien among us, but one of us, sharing our nature, like us in all things, except sin. He is our brother: "*like unto his brethren.*" Mary was not a storage unit of the baby Jesus. She was his mother, his flesh-and-blood mother.

The Confession condemns the doctrine of the incarnation of Henry Morris and the Anabaptists, past and present, as heresy: "the heresy of the Anabaptists, who deny that Christ assumed human flesh of his mother." The heresy is nothing less than a denial of the incarnation. According to the Anabaptist heresy, God did not really become a man, a member of the human race, a descendant of father Adam. According to the Anabaptist heresy, Jesus Christ could not redeem and save humans. Only one who shares their nature can save humans.

Against the Anabaptist heresy, the Reformed Confession teaches that the Son of God assumed a human nature *derived from Mary*, so that Jesus has his body and soul *from Mary*, who therefore is truly his mother, as Jesus called her more than once in the Bible. She was his mother, not merely a human basket containing divine/human fruit. The Confession calls Jesus "*a fruit* of *the womb of the Virgin Mary.*" It applies to the conception of Jesus the words of Galatians 4:4: "made of a woman," where the preposition "of" is the Greek word *ek*, which means "out of," as of source. Thus, and only thus, as the Confession indicates, is Jesus a genuine descendant of David, Abraham, and Adam.

The heavy emphasis of the Reformed confession on the reality of Jesus' human nature in view of a heresy that denies the real humanity of Jesus is a biblical emphasis, and for the same reason. Already in the earliest days of the apostolic church, a heresy appeared that denied the reality of Jesus' human nature. The heresy taught that Jesus merely *seemed* to be a human. The heresy is known as "docetism," from the Greek word *dokeoo* that means "seeming" or "apparent." Against the heresy of docetism, the apostle John inveighs in 1 John 4:2, 3: "Hereby know ye the Spirit of God: Every spirit that confesseth that Jesus Christ is come in the flesh is of God: And every spirit that confesseth not that Jesus Christ is come in the flesh is not of God: and this is that spirit of antichrist, whereof ye have heard that it should come; and even now already is it in the world."[2]

With appeal to scripture, the Confession affirms the essential characteristics of the human nature that the Son of God assumed from Mary in the incarnation and therefore the characteristics of the human nature of Jesus the Savior. It is a *real* human nature, as opposed to a "docetic" human nature: "a real man." It is a *complete* human nature: soul as well as body. Here the doctrinal principle is stated that Jesus must be whatever of us is in need of redemption by him: "Since the soul was lost as well as the body, it was necessary that he should take both upon him, to save both." By affirming that Jesus was human regarding his soul as well as regarding his body, the Confession repudiates the ancient heresy concerning the incarnation that taught that

---

2   The church historian Eusebius informs us of the opposition to the apostle John at Ephesus by the Docetist heretic Cerinthus.

Jesus was human as to his body, but that the Godhead took the place of the soul in him.

The human nature that the Son assumed in the conception of Jesus was a weakened human nature: "the true human nature, with all its infirmities." It tired; it suffered pain of soul and of body; it felt the misery of ridicule, hatred, and opposition; it needed sleep; it could and did weep; it was not only susceptible to the last enemy, death, but it could and did die; indeed, it underwent the fearful experience of dying from the moment of birth; it agonized in the consciousness of abandonment by God. The Confession has in mind Hebrews 4:15: "We have not an high priest which cannot be touched with the feeling of our infirmities; but was in all points tempted like as we are." All of this "infirmity" of the human nature, and more, was the effect and suffering of exposure to the wrath and curse of an offended, holy God upon the human nature who was the substitute for guilty sinners.

A weakened human nature, with all its infirmities, the Confession declares, "sin excepted." This is the exception stated in Hebrews 4:15: "yet without sin." Sinlessness was necessary, if he is to save others. In the act of conceiving Jesus, the Holy Ghost purified the nature of Mary that becomes the human, Jesus. Jesus was free of the depravity of human nature. Soul and body, he was perfectly holy. As a divine (and not a human) *Person*, Jesus bore no responsibility for the disobedience of Adam. Therefore, Jesus was free from both original guilt and original corruption. He came into the world sinless. He was both innocent and holy.

In addition, he never sinned, whether in thought, will, word, or deed. He lived a perfectly obedient life. He asserted this perfection of life in a rhetorical question to his adversaries: "Which of you convinceth me of sin?" (John 8:46). All his life, he obeyed the will of God. Not only did he obey extensively, that is, regarding every aspect of the will of God for him, but he also obeyed intensively, that is, taking human obedience to its deepest depths of doing the will of God. Paul has this in mind in Philippians 2:8: "He humbled himself, and became obedient unto death, even the death of the cross." Jesus plumbed the depths of obedience. Obedience itself was amazed at what it found out about itself in the obedience of Jesus.

What is not expressly stated in the Confession about the human nature of Jesus, although it is plainly indicated, is that it is a human nature that came down in the line of the covenant. It is a covenantal human nature. Mary was a daughter of David, so that Jesus is a "branch of David." David was of the tribe of Judah, so that Jesus is "sprung from the tribe of Judah." Judah was a father of the Jews, so that Jesus is "descended from the Jews according to the flesh." The Jews arise from Abraham, so that Jesus is "of the seed of Abraham."

The family in history of which Jesus is the descendant is the covenantal family by the promise of God. To this family, God promised the Savior, not only of that family, but of all nations. From this family, God promised to bring forth the Savior. With this family, God had fellowship throughout the old dispensation, which fellowship was this family's salvation. In Jesus, the incarnate Son of God, who is the head of the covenant of grace, the covenant of God with men is fulfilled.

Indeed, this Jesus is, in himself, the realization of the covenant as God's fellowship, or communion, with man. This, his God-given name indicates: "Immanuel" (Isa. 7:14;

Matt. 1:23), for the name means "God with us." In Jesus personally, God is with man in that the divine nature and the human nature are intimately united in the person of the eternal Son of God. Jesus himself personally is the Friendship of God with man. By the saving work of Jesus, God is with elect men and women in the union of the bond of faith. By the union of elect men and women with him by faith, Jesus unites them with God in the friendship of the covenant.

The incarnation and therefore the realizing of the covenant and the full salvation that the covenant accomplishes are not the work of man, not whatsoever. In the incarnation of Jesus Christ, man is wholly excluded: "without the means of man," the Confession states. It is precisely the source of Rome's heresy of synergism, that is, its doctrine of man's cooperating with God in the work of salvation, that Rome has Mary cooperating with God in the conception of Jesus, that is, in the incarnation. But Protestantism errs similarly when it teaches that the covenant and its salvation are conditional, that is, dependent upon the will and work of the sinner. Thus Protestantism shows that it has never understood, or has forgotten, the truth of the incarnation of him whose name is Immanuel: "without the means of man."

In the incarnation of Jesus Christ, the Reformed Protestantism of article 18 of the Belgic Confession confesses *grace,* grace *only.*

Chapter Fourteen

THE UNION AND DISTINCTION OF THE TWO NATURES IN THE PERSON OF CHRIST AND GOD HATH MANIFESTED HIS JUSTICE AND MERCY IN CHRIST

(ARTICLES 19 AND 20)

ART. XIX. OF THE UNION AND DISTINCTION OF THE TWO NATURES IN THE PERSON OF CHRIST.

We believe that by this conception the person of the Son is inseparably united and connected with the human nature; so that there are not two Sons of God, nor two persons, but two natures united in one single person; yet each nature retains its own distinct properties. As then the divine nature hath always remained uncreated, without beginning of days or end of life, filling heaven and earth, so also hath the human nature not lost its properties, but remained a creature, having beginning of days, being a finite nature, and retaining all the properties of a real body. And though he hath by his resurrection given immortality to the same, nevertheless he hath not changed the reality of his human nature; forasmuch as our salvation and resurrection also depend on the reality of his body. But these two natures are so closely united in one person, that they were not separated even by his death. Therefore that which he, when dying, commended into the hands of his Father, was a real human spirit, departing from his body. But in the mean time the divine nature always remained united with the human, even when he lay in the grave; and the Godhead did not cease to be in him, any more than it did when he was an infant, though it did not so clearly manifest itself for a while.

Wherefore we confess that he is VERY GOD and VERY MAN: very God by his power to conquer death, and very man that he might die for us according to the infirmity of his flesh.

ART. XX. GOD HATH MANIFESTED HIS JUSTICE AND MERCY IN CHRIST.

We believe that God, who is perfectly merciful and also perfectly just, sent his Son to assume that nature in which the disobedience was committed, to make satisfaction in the same, and to bear the punishment of sin by his most bitter passion and death. God therefore manifested his justice against his Son when he laid our iniquities upon him, and poured forth his mercy and goodness on us, who were guilty and worthy of damnation, out of mere and perfect love, giving his Son unto death for us, and raising him for our justification, that through him we might obtain immortality and life eternal.

INTRODUCTION

Following hard on the explanation of the incarnation in article 18, the question is, "Who and what is this Jesus Christ as the incarnate one?" The incarnation took place in the conception of a child in the womb of Mary. Who and what is that child who was conceived by the Holy Ghost in the virgin? The great question that article 19 answers is, "Who is Jesus?"

The Reformed answer to the question, describing Jesus as one divine person in two natures, is the same as that which was given by the early church in the Symbol of Chalcedon (AD 451).

> One and the same Son, our Lord Jesus Christ, the same perfect in Godhead and also perfect in manhood; truly God and truly man, of a reasonable soul and body; consubstantial with the Father according to the Godhead, and consubstantial with us according to the Manhood.[1]

The Confession demonstrates that the Reformed churches are one with the early church in the faith concerning Jesus Christ as true God and true man.

Although the truth about Jesus both in the Symbol of Chalcedon and in article 19 of the Confession is carefully formulated by means of certain, definite, fixed theological terms, particularly "person" and "natures," the Christian church confesses truth about Jesus that is simple. There is one Jesus, but this one Jesus is both God and man. As the Belgic Confession states at the end of article 19, "He [that is, the one Jesus] is very God and very man."

---

1 Symbol of Chalcedon, in Schaff, *Creeds of Christendom*, 2:62.

This simple truth, every believer plainly sees when he reads the Bible, especially the gospels. Jesus is a man—a *true* man. He is conceived; he is born; the infant becomes a child; he grows into manhood; he eats and sleeps; he suffers; he cries; he dies; and then he rises from the dead in his (human) body.

He is also more and other than a man. He is true God. He lives eternally before he was born; he commands the wind and the waves, which obey him as their creator; he forgives sins; he raises the dead; his is one with the Father; his name is "I am."

PERSON AND NATURES

"Person" and "natures" are important terms by which the church confesses who and what Jesus is. They are important terms in article 19 of the Confession. Reformed believers must grasp their meaning and significance. They are not biblical terms, at least not with the sense that they have in the doctrine of the incarnation of Jesus. They are theological terms, but these doctrinal terms express biblical teaching. By them the church confesses and maintains the truth about Jesus revealed in scripture. The church confesses and maintains the truth about Jesus against heretics, who deny or corrupt not only the terms themselves, but also the fundamental doctrinal truths that the terms teach. Every aspect of the truth confessed at Chalcedon in the fifth century and by the Confession in the sixteenth century has been denied by heretics. Some taught that Jesus is two persons. Others taught that Jesus is one nature.

By "person" in Christian orthodoxy concerning Jesus is meant that in Jesus that says, "I." The traditional definition is: "an individual subsistence in a rational-moral nature."[2] A person is an individual, but an individual who thinks and wills. A person knows, or comes to know, the difference between good and evil. An angel is a person. A devil is a person. A human is a person. The three individuals in the being of God are persons. An animal, a tree, and the earth are not persons.

An important characteristic of a person is that he or she is conscious of others, including God, and of oneself.

The person in us, to speak this way, is that which is the unchanging subject of all our life. It is the same when one is seventy as it was when he was an infant. It will be the same everlastingly in heaven as it was when one lived his earthly life.

Jesus has (is) a "person." He says, "I."

By "nature" is meant the sum total of the qualities that make someone who and what he is. Nature is what someone is in the totality of his being. The nature of God is all the attributes that make up, or belong to, Deity, or Godhead.

The natures of Jesus are what he is.

JESUS' PERSON

Jesus' person is the second person of the Trinity. It is the person of the eternal Son of God. When Jesus says "I," this "I" is the "I" of God the Son. Jesus revealed this as his person in John 8:58: "Before Abraham was, I am." His claim to be the person of God the Son does not only consist of his assertion to be eternal. But it is also his identification of himself as Jehovah, the "I am." Affirming that his person is

---

2   Herman Hoeksema, *Reformed Dogmatics* (Grand Rapids, MI: Reformed Free Publishing Association, 1966), 359.

the person of the eternal Son of God, Jesus declared, "I and my Father are one" (John 10:30).

This divine person is the subject of all his life—his birth, his words, his deeds, his suffering, his death. The eternal Son of God was born, spoke, acted, suffered, and died—in the man Jesus.

Jesus has (or is) one, and only one, person. The Confession denies that there are "two persons." That Jesus is two persons was the teaching of an ancient heretic, Nestorius. Against this heresy, the Symbol of Chalcedon pronounced that Jesus is "one Person and one Subsistence, not parted or divided into two persons, but one and the same Son, and only begotten, God the Word."[3]

Jesus is not a human person. He does not have a human person. He can be, and is, a real, complete human *being* without a human *person*.

The oneness of Jesus' person establishes the unity of Jesus himself and the unity of his life and work. It also establishes the *value*, or *worth*, of all his life and labor: his is the life and labor of God.

JESUS' NATURES

Jesus has two natures. Because his person is the eternal Son of God, he has a divine nature: he is God. All the attributes that make up the Godhead are his. The Confession alludes to two of the attributes, or qualities, of Godhead that Jesus possesses: eternality and immensity. According to his divine nature, Jesus is "uncreated, without beginning of days or end of life, filling heaven and earth."

Because he was truly conceived in and born of Mary,

---

3 Symbol of Chalcedon, in ibid.

Jesus has a human nature: he is a real man, with all the properties, or qualities, of humanity. The Confession mentions his having a beginning; his being finite, or limited; his having a real body.

These two natures, Jesus retains in and after his resurrection. He did not cease being a man in the resurrection, as some have supposed. Rather, the resurrection glorified his human nature. It is no longer the humiliated human nature with which he was born, under the law, subject to the wrath of God, the man of sorrows, because of the Lord's laying on him the iniquity of us all (Isa. 53). The human nature of Jesus was raised in glory and power (1 Cor. 15:43). God highly exalted the human nature of Jesus (Phil. 2:9). Indeed, the very quality of Jesus' body was changed for the better, without affecting the essential humanity of the body. The resurrection body of Jesus is spiritual, not natural (1 Cor. 15:44). Literally, the text calls Jesus' resurrection body a "spiritual body" in distinction from its previous condition of having been "soulish." This is a higher degree of bodily perfection.

In this respect, the resurrection body of Jesus is superior to that of unfallen Adam in paradise. In every respect, the life of the risen Jesus is higher, better, more glorious than the life of Adam in paradise. Jesus does not recover and restore to his people the life of Adam. He creates for himself and for all who believe in him a human life that is far better, far more glorious, than the life of Adam was or could ever have become. The Confession points to the exaltation of the human nature of Jesus in the resurrection, above that of unfallen Adam, when it states that in his resurrection Jesus has "given immortality" to human nature. For all his glory, Adam never possessed immortality. Adam could die.

The Confession is concerned to establish that, although Jesus exalted his human nature in his resurrection, he "hath not changed the reality of his human nature." He remains a real human, both in body and in soul. Indeed, he remains the same human nature—the same man—that he had always had, or been. He proved this during the forty days between the resurrection and the ascension. His body was the same body that had been laid in the grave—the grave was empty after three days of burial. His resurrection body was pierced with the holes of the nails that had fastened him to the cross. His body could be handled. It was flesh and bones. He ate food. Although his body was spiritual, Jesus was not a spirit (Luke 24:36–43; Matt. 28:9). Regarding his human soul, the risen Jesus thought and willed as a human (John 20:11–18). To his disciples, the risen Jesus was not only their God, but also their (human) brother (Matt. 28:10).

In order to know the truth of Jesus, that is, to know Jesus himself, according to the scriptural revelation of him, it is necessary clearly and sharply to distinguish his two natures. He was born, grew, showed ignorance of certain things, for example, the day of his second coming, suffered, and died *in his human nature, as a man.* Although, as the Confession states, the divine nature "remained united with the human" in all these human experiences and activities, none of these characteristically human experiences and activities was that of the divine nature. For instance, the divine nature of Jesus—his Godhead—did not die on the cross.

The importance of distinguishing the divine and human natures of Jesus is evident in two seemingly contradictory statements that Jesus himself makes about himself regarding his relationship to God. In John 5:17–18, Jesus claims equality with the Father. In John 14:28, he confesses that "my Father is greater than I." There is no contradiction. In John 5, Jesus speaks of himself according to his divine nature. In John 14, he speaks of himself regarding his human nature.

UNION OF THE NATURES

There is and must be a union of the two natures. In the language of the Confession, the divine nature must be "united and connected with the human nature." The two natures must be "closely united."

The union is personal. The two natures are united and connected in the one person of Jesus: "two natures united in one single person." No closer union is possible. This union happened in the incarnation. The person of the eternal Son of God took a human nature from Mary in the conception of Jesus in and from Mary into such union with himself that the divine nature upholds and gives infinite value to all that is done in the human nature. Close as the union of the two natures in the one person is, it does not consist of a mixing, or confusion, of the divine and the human. The divine nature remains divine, possessing only the attributes of the Godhead. The human nature remains human, possessing only the qualities of humanity. As the Confession states, "Each nature retains its own distinct properties." To all eternity, God is God, and man is man. The union, the *sole* union, of God and man is their personal union in the incarnation of the Son of God, not a confusion of being.

In its insistence that "each nature retains its own distinct properties," the Confession not only does justice to the truth of the incarnation, but also distinguishes the

Reformed faith from the Lutheran faith. Lutheran theology teaches that the incarnation comes to consist of the sharing of certain divine qualities, or perfections, by the human nature. Especially does the human nature share the divine perfection of omnipresence. Lutheranism is forced to teach this by its doctrine of the Lord's supper. According to the Lutheran doctrine of the supper, the body and blood of Jesus are physically present in the bread and wine of the supper so that every participant everywhere in the world eats and drinks the body and blood with his mouth. This is possible, declares Lutheranism, because of the "ubiquity," or omnipresence, of Jesus' human nature after his resurrection.

In addition to the error of this teaching regarding the doctrine of the Lord's supper, as though the presence of Jesus in the supper is physical rather than spiritual, the Lutheran doctrine confuses the two natures of Jesus Christ. It denies that "each nature retains its own distinct properties." It sins against Chalcedon's confession that Christ is to be "acknowledged in two natures, *inconfusedly*."[4] It is therefore a grievous false doctrine concerning the incarnation.

To avoid this confusion, it is the part of wisdom to avoid describing Jesus as the "God-man," as is commonly done in Reformed theology. Jesus is God and man. He is God become man. But he is not a "God-man," as though he were a mixture of divinity and humanity.

Implied is that a human's union with God is not, and can never be, his proud ascendancy unto Godhead, as will be the effort and claim of antichrist, but spiritual union with God by faith in Jesus Christ.

---

4 Symbol of Chalcedon, in Schaff, *Creeds of Christendom*, 2:62.

Concerning the relationship and reality of the two natures of Christ, Chalcedon confessed that Christ is to be "acknowledged in two natures, *inconfusedly, unchangeably, indivisibly, inseparably*; the distinction of natures being by no means taken away by the union, but rather the property of each nature being preserved, and concurring in one Person."[5]

Such was the close and permanent union of the divine and human natures in the incarnation that it is never broken, indeed, *cannot* be broken, not even at Jesus' death. On behalf of the intimacy and permanency of the incarnation, the Confession makes the strong, even startling, statement: "These two natures are so closely united in one person, that they were not separated even by his death...The divine nature always remained united with the human, even when he lay in the grave; and the Godhead did not cease to be in him, any more than it did when he was an infant." Since Jesus commended his spirit into the hands of God at his death (Luke 23:46), the Confession affirms that the divine nature remained united with Jesus' body in the grave. The Godhead was with and in the dead body of Jesus in the grave. This union of the divine nature with the humanity of Jesus in the grave is the reason why the Messiah was confident that God would not leave his soul in the realm of the dead or suffer his Holy One "to see corruption" in the grave (Ps. 16:10).

The Confession asserts the continuing union of the Godhead and Jesus in Jesus' dead body in the grave to emphasize the close and inseparable character of the union of the two natures in the incarnation. It also magnifies the

---

5   Symbol of Chalcedon, in ibid.

love of God. How great is the love of God for Jesus, his Son in human flesh! How great is the love of God for all the members of Jesus' body, the church! The Godhead was willing to descend into and cleave to the man Jesus in the dark, lowly chambers of the dead. "Low in the grave he lay!" Not only the man Jesus in his dead body! But also God the eternal Son in the bodily aspect of the human nature of Jesus Christ!

NECESSITY OF THE INCARNATION

The necessity of the incarnation, as it is the answer to the implied question of Anselm's great book, *Cur Deus Homo* (*Why God [became] Man*), is the salvation of elect humanity. The Confession concludes its treatment of the incarnation in article 19 with the expression of this necessity: "very God by his power to conquer death, and very man that he might die for us according to the infirmity of his flesh."

Anselm had written:

> The restoring of mankind ought not to take place, and could not, without man paid the debt which he owed God for his sin. And this debt was so great that, while none but man must solve the debt, none but God was able to do it; so that he who does it must be both God and man. And hence arises a necessity that God should take man into unity with his own person; so that he who in his own nature was bound to pay the debt, but could not, might be able to do it in the person of God.[6]

---

6 Anselm, "Cur Deus Homo," in *St. Anselm: Basic Writings*, trans. S. N. Deane (La Salle, IL: Open Court Publishing Company, 2nd ed. 1962), 293.

The salvation of sinful humans requires that Jesus have two natures; that they be divine and human; that they be united; and that they be united in the one person of the eternal Son of God.

This necessity of the incarnation, and the purpose of God with the incarnation of the eternal Son, are the confession of the Reformed faith in article 20 of the Confession: "God hath Manifested his Justice and Mercy in Christ."

THE PURPOSE OF THE INCARNATION

The purpose of the incarnation, the answer to the question, why did God become man in Jesus, was the salvation of sinners, to whom article 20 of the Confession consistently refers by the first-person plural: "us," "our," and "we." This salvation consisted primarily of "satisfaction." "God...sent his Son" in the incarnation "to make satisfaction." Since this satisfaction was the manifestation of God's justice, it is evident that the purpose of the incarnation, according to confessional Reformed orthodoxy, was Jesus' satisfying the justice of God. He did this by "bear[ing] the punishment of sin by his most bitter passion and death." In his justice, God "laid our iniquities upon him [Jesus]."

Although the suffering and death of Jesus Christ as satisfaction are more fully explained and grounded in holy scripture in the following article, already article 20 confesses the suffering and death of Jesus Christ as substitutionary satisfaction of the justice of God. Jesus suffered fully the punishment of sin as required by the justice of God in the place, or stead, of guilty sinners. Since God's justice demands damnation of the sinner, Jesus suffered damnation. He suffered damnation under the judgment of God. Bearing, or suffering, the full and awful punishment that disobedience to the holy God deserves and demands, and doing so in perfect love for the God whose damning punishment he suffered, Jesus satisfied divine justice.

At the end of Jesus' life of humiliation, climaxing in his death by crucifixion, divine justice said, "Enough; justice has no further demand; the full punishment due to sin against me has been borne, and borne away." Justice, with its rigorous, exacting, uncompromising demand, is satisfied. No smidgen of guilt remains. No drop of righteous punishment is left over. All justice in the case of Jesus the Christ has been "manifested," that is, inflicted and endured. Iniquities were so laid upon Christ that no iniquity remains to be laid upon those who committed them. In the word of Jesus himself, "It is finished" (John 19:30).

Inasmuch as the suffering and death of Christ were satisfaction of the justice of God, according to the Reformed creed, the death of Christ was substitutionary. This comes out clearly in the Confession, although the word itself is not used: "laid our iniquities upon him...[our iniquities] who were guilty and worthy of damnation." In his suffering, Christ was the substitute for others, referred to in the Confession as "us." Not only has the Confession, in article 16, identified "us" as "all whom he [God]...hath elected in Christ Jesus," but also it clearly teaches that those for whom Christ became incarnate and died are not all humans without exception by explaining Christ's suffering and death as satisfaction in article 20.

Christ's death did not merely make salvation, specifically satisfaction of God's justice, possible for humans. But it *was* satisfaction of the justice of God. It *was* the bearing of the punishment of sin. Unless all humans without exception are saved, the suffering and death of Jesus were particular, not universal. Since all are alike sinners, it is not the will of the sinners themselves that determines their salvation, but the electing will of God. The only way to deny limited, or particular, or definite, atonement is by denying that the cross of Christ was satisfaction of the justice of God on behalf of and as the substitute for sinners. Every form of the theory of universal atonement embraces the denial of substitutionary satisfaction.

The suffering and death of Christ were the great substitutionary transaction: justice against the Son of God; mercy and goodness on us. For the Son of God, who was innocent, "death"; for us, "who were guilty and worthy of damnation...immortality and life eternal."

This saving work of Jesus Christ explains the purpose of the incarnation. Man must make satisfaction. The justice of God demands that "that nature in which the disobedience was committed...make satisfaction." The Savior therefore must be a real man, sharing the nature of Adam and his children. Only God can make this satisfaction. But God must make this satisfaction in the human nature that disobeyed. Therefore, the Savior must be God and man, united in the personal union of the person of God the Son.

The incarnation accomplishes God's purpose of the salvation of guilty, damnworthy sinners. In Jesus, the human nature that sinned bears the punishment of sin. In Jesus, the divine nature upholds the human nature in the suffering and gives the suffering and death of Jesus infinite worth and value. There is the union of the two natures in the one person of the eternal Son of God.

Thus the incarnation reveals God's justice and his mercy. Justice is manifested against Jesus. Mercy is poured forth on us. In this respect also, the substitutionary nature of the incarnation is expressed.

By faith alone in Jesus, the elect receive both this justice and this mercy of God. They are justified. To them is imputed the justice, or righteousness, of God worked out in the suffering and death of Jesus as their very own. Thus they are assured of their immortality and eternal life. Since this righteousness is the obedience of Jesus Christ for them and in their stead by the mercy and goodness of God, with this justification come to them the experience and assurance of the mercy of God toward them.

From this article of the Confession, the Reformed believer carries away the conviction that his misery of the guilt of sin is great, if what was necessary for his salvation was the wonder of the incarnation of the Son of God. If the incarnation of the Son of God—the becoming flesh of God the Son—was necessary for the salvation of humans, Jesus is the only Savior, with none beside, including the sinner himself. And how adorable is the love of God, which is the ultimate source of the incarnation and its salvation: "out of mere and perfect love, giving his Son unto death for us."

Without denying the truth of the statement, one may dissent from the Confession's allusion to Romans 4:25 as though the text were teaching that Jesus was raised in order that he might justify us. The text teaches that as Jesus was delivered *on account of* our offences, so he was raised again *on account of* our justification. Our offences brought him to the cross. Our justification by his full satisfaction of the justice of God on the cross was the judicial ground of God's raising him.

Chapter Fifteen

THE SATISFACTION OF CHRIST, OUR ONLY HIGH PRIEST, FOR US

(ARTICLE 21)

ART. XXI. OF THE SATISFACTION OF CHRIST, OUR ONLY HIGH-PRIEST, FOR US.

We believe that Jesus Christ is ordained with an oath to be an everlasting High-Priest, after the order of Melchisedec: who hath presented himself in our behalf before his Father, to appease his wrath by his full satisfaction, by offering himself on the tree of the cross, and pouring out his precious blood to purge away our sins; as the prophets had foretold. For it is written, He was wounded for our transgressions, he was bruised for our iniquities: the chastisement of our peace was upon him, and with his stripes we are healed; he was brought as a lamb to the slaughter, and numbered with the transgressors; and condemned by Pontius Pilate as a malefactor, though he had first declared him innocent. Therefore, he restored that which he took not away, and suffered the just for the unjust, as well in his body as in his soul, feeling the terrible punishment which our sins had merited; insomuch that his sweat became like unto drops of blood falling on the ground. He called out, My God, my God, why hast thou forsaken me? And hath suffered all this for the remission of our sins. Wherefore we justly say with the Apostle Paul, that we know nothing but Jesus Christ, and him crucified; we count all things but loss and dung for the excellency of the knowledge of Christ Jesus our Lord: in whose wounds we find all manner of consolation. Neither is it necessary to seek or invent any other means of being reconciled to God, than this only sacrifice, once offered, by which believers are made perfect forever. This is also the reason why he was called by the angel of God, Jesus, that is to say, Saviour, because he should save his people from their sins.

INTRODUCTION

The place of article 21 in the Confession is that it continues the section on Christology, that is, the Confession's doctrine of Christ. This section began in article 18 with the truth of the incarnation. Article 21 concludes the section that treats of the doctrine of Christ. Article 22 begins the section of the Confession on the doctrine of salvation, known in theology as soteriology.

It is striking that of the entire ministry of Jesus only one work of the Savior is confessed and explained by the Confession, namely, the death of Jesus. After the Confession has explained his conception, birth, and natures, it moves at once to his death. There is nothing of his miracles; nothing of his ministry of teaching; nothing of his encounters and controversies, although later the Confession will explain his work of intercession and his conducting of the final judgment. Only his death!

The explanation is that his death was the main saving work of Jesus the Christ. All his earthly ministry centered on and moved toward his death as its goal. In its treatment of the earthly ministry of Jesus Christ, the Confession is faithful to the word of the apostle, which the article also quotes: "I determined not to know any thing among you, save Jesus Christ, and him crucified" (1 Cor. 2:2).

The preceding article confessed that this death of Christ was the purpose of the incarnation of the eternal Son of God: "God...sent his Son...to make satisfaction...and to bear the punishment of sin by his most bitter passion and death." As was demonstrated earlier, the satisfactory death of Jesus Christ was the reason why he must be true God and true man in the unity of one, divine person.

Just as the wonder of the incarnation was a mystery, so also was the atoning death of the incarnate Son of God a "great mystery," according to article 22 of the Confession. Reverently, we seek to know it insofar as the death of the Son of God is made known to us in holy scripture.

SATISFACTION

The truth that reveals the mystery of the cross and death of Jesus Christ, as it is the main truth of article 21 of the Confession, is "satisfaction." In his death, Christ appeased the wrath of God "by his full satisfaction." Christ's death was satisfaction. Although the word itself is not used in scripture for the death of Christ, it does express the biblical idea and truth of his death. Indeed, "satisfaction" describes the fundamental nature of the suffering and death of Jesus Christ. Therefore, the truth of satisfaction is one of the main doctrines in all of scripture. It is basic to the gospel of grace. Loss or denial of the truth of the satisfactory nature of the death of Jesus Christ is the loss or denial of Christianity.

Because of its fundamental importance for the gospel, the truth of satisfaction is always and in all kinds of ways under attack by heretics and heresies. Theological modernism attacks satisfaction by the theory that the death of Christ was nothing more than an example, mainly of love, that serves to improve humanity morally. The Roman Catholic Church denies that the death of Christ was "full satisfaction" by its teaching that the sacrifice of Christ on the cross must be repeated for the salvation of sinners and by its doctrine that the sinner himself must pay for his sins in part by the suffering of the pains of purgatory. All Protestant churches and theologians that teach universal atonement, that is, that Christ died for all humans, necessarily deny satisfaction: if Christ died for all, but not all are saved (as is evident), his death was not satisfaction, unless God is unjust, demanding payment for sin both from Christ and from the sinners for whom Christ died.

This is necessarily the heresy of all Arminian churches and theologians. Universal atonement is a cardinal doctrine of these churches and theologians. Inasmuch as their universal atonement fails to save many, as they themselves acknowledge, the death of Christ in their theology was not satisfaction. Thus they deny the cross and death of Jesus.[1]

---

1 See the entire rejection of errors section of the second head of doctrine of the Canons of Dordt, in *Confessions and Church Order*, 164–66. Particularly error 3 exposes and condemns the Arminian denial of the death of Christ as satisfaction: "Who teach that Christ, by His satisfaction, merited neither salvation itself for anyone, nor

Today, the attack on satisfaction is found in evangelical and Presbyterian churches with a history of or a reputation for orthodoxy. These are the churches that are influenced by a movement that calls itself the new perspective on Paul. The heretic who is most responsible for introducing the denial of satisfaction into these churches is the Anglican bishop N. T. Wright. The new perspective rejects the gospel truth of justification by faith alone. Wright denies that biblical justification is God's imputation of the righteousness of Christ to the believing sinner. Fundamental to this denial is Wright's denial that the cross of Christ was God's imputation of the guilt of sinners to Jesus Christ. This is the denial of satisfaction.[2]

Reformed churches openly reject the doctrine that the death of Christ was satisfaction of the justice of God for the sins of those on behalf of whom Christ died. C. J. den Heyer, a seminary professor of the Reformed Churches in the Netherlands (GKN), has written that "the classic doctrine of atonement does not appear in the New Testament." Den Heyer rejected "the idea that Christ's death once for all removed the guilt for human sin." Thus he denied the Belgic Confession's teaching in article 21, which is the creed of his churches, that the death of Christ was "full satisfaction" for the sins of all humans for whom he died. The

---

faith, whereby this satisfaction of Christ unto salvation is effectually appropriated." The error rejected is the denial that the cross was satisfaction.

2 For Wright's denial that the cross of Christ was satisfaction in closest connection with Wright's affirmation of universal "atonement," cf. N. T. Wright, *The Climax of the Covenant: Christ and the Law in Pauline Theology* (Minneapolis, MN: Fortress Press, 1991), 213, 196, 150; *What Saint Paul Really Said: Was Paul of Tarsus the Real Founder of Christianity?* (Grand Rapids, MI: Eerdmans, 1997), 110; and *Justification: God's Plan & Paul's Vision* (Downers Grove, IL: IVP Academic, 2009), 228, 232, 188.

synod of the GKN approved den Heyer's heretical denial of satisfaction.[3]

Satisfaction was Christ's act in suffering and dying of paying to God the debt that Christ's elect people owed to the just God. Literally, the word means "doing enough." Christ did enough to meet the demands and claims of the justice of God against guilty sinners. The debt that the people for whom Christ died owed to God on account of their sins and sinfulness was the suffering of God's wrath in all its killing, cursing, damning reality. The lifelong suffering and the death by crucifixion of Jesus Christ were his payment of that debt. Especially the cross was payment of that debt to the justice of God. It was punishment. Jesus *felt* that punishment in both body and soul, according to the Confession: "[He] *suffered the just for the unjust*, as well in his body as in his soul, feeling the terrible punishment which our sins had merited." Payment of the debt of the guilt of his people's sins meant for him his blood, in death: "pouring out his precious blood to purge away our sins."

But satisfaction was more than only payment and punishment. It was active payment and suffering of punishment on the part of Jesus *in love for God*. The damned in hell, who are compelled to suffer for their sins, do not satisfy, not

---

3   The quotations are the (accurate) analysis of den Heyer's rejection of the atonement in his book *Jesus and the Doctrine of the Atonement* (Harrisburg, PA: Trinity Press International, 1998). The book was translated from the Dutch by John Bowden. The analysis appears in *Christian Observer*, February 1998, 6. Den Heyer, who is a theologian in the Reformed Churches in the Netherlands—the denomination of Abraham Kuyper and Herman Bavinck—denies that "the death of Jesus was a 'payment' to God which assuaged God's wrath" (53). What offends den Heyer is this doctrine's affirmation of God's justice (133). Rather than having been atonement, "Jesus' life and death had an 'exemplary' character" (134).

to all eternity. Here Christ's activity in suffering and dying must be noted, as the Confession does indeed notice: he "hath presented himself in our behalf before his Father"; "offering himself on the tree of the cross, and pouring out his precious blood." Basic to satisfaction was that it be obedient, and obedience for the great High Priest was that he offer the atoning sacrifice in the willingness of love for God, whose justice had been offended. Not simply the suffering of the punishment, but the offering of it in love for God, that God might be just in justifying him who believes in Jesus (Rom. 3:26), was the sweet-smelling incense in the nostrils of God.

ASPECTS OF CHRIST'S DEATH AS SATISFACTION

These are the outstanding aspects of the death of Christ as satisfaction. First, the necessity of satisfaction is God's righteousness, or justice. Ultimately, this is the glory of God as good. All theories of the death of Christ that deny satisfaction are denials that God is righteous. If he is not righteous, he is unrighteous. And an unrighteous God is not God, but the devil. This at bottom is the quarrel that the Reformed faith has with liberal Protestantism, with Rome, with Arminianism, with the new perspective on Paul, with the federal vision, and with C. J. den Heyer and his GKN.

Second, an outstanding aspect of the death of Christ as satisfaction is the seriousness of sin as disobedience to God and thus the assault upon his righteousness. Such is the seriousness of sin that by it there is hell to pay. "By the offence of one judgment came upon all men to condemnation" (Rom. 5:18).

Third, inasmuch as the death of Christ was satisfaction, the manner of his death was important: "the tree of the cross," as the Confession describes it. The significance is not so much that the Romans employed this shameful mode of execution for the worst of criminals, or that it was an extraordinarily painful form of death. But by the effective word of God in Deuteronomy 21:23, hanging on a tree was an accursed death. To this truth about the manner of Christ's death, Galatians 3:13 appeals in support of its contention in slightly different words that Christ's death was satisfaction of the justice of God on behalf of all those for whom Christ died: "Christ hath redeemed us from the curse of the law, being made a curse for us: for it is written, Cursed is every one that hangeth on a tree." The dying Christ was cursed of God, as he made plain in his cry of dereliction, "Why hast thou forsaken me?" (Matt. 27:46). The effect of the divine curse is damnation in hell. This was the debt owed to God.

Fourth, as satisfaction Christ's death was substitutionary: he paid the debt for others, by taking their place. The substitutionary nature of the death of Christ is clear in the lengthy quotation of Isaiah 53 by the Confession: "*wounded for our transgressions...bruised for our iniquities: the chastisement of our peace was upon him, and with his stripes we are healed.*" The truth of substitution is affirmed throughout this article of the Confession: "presented himself in our behalf"; "pouring out his precious blood to purge away our sins"; ""*suffered the just for the unjust*"; "feeling the terrible punishment which our sins had merited"; "suffered all this for the remission of our sins"; "in whose wounds we find all manner of consolation"; "this only sacrifice, once offered, by which believers are made perfect forever."

The substitution that is fundamental to satisfaction is also the significance of the Confession's reference to

Christ's condemnation by judge Pontius Pilate: "condemned by Pontius Pilate as a malefactor, though he had first declared him innocent." As an earthly judge condemned the innocent Jesus to death, so the heavenly Judge condemned the innocent Jesus to death in the place of and on behalf of a guilty people for whom Jesus was the substitute, making satisfaction for them. Indeed, *by* the condemnation of Pilate God condemned Jesus to the death of the cross as the substitute of the people for whom Jesus was making satisfaction. This, ultimately, was the reason why Jesus never raised a complaint against his condemnation by Pilate. As the substitute making satisfaction for a guilty people, he was guilty and worthy of condemnation, even the accursed death of hanging on a tree. He accepted this guilt. "But Jesus yet answered nothing; so that Pilate marveled" (Mark 15:5).

Fifth, as satisfaction the death of Jesus was the one and only, complete, and perfect payment for sin and earning of salvation for all for whom he suffered and died. The Reformed creed calls the death of Christ a "full satisfaction." Nothing of the debt to the justice of God remains to be paid. No punishment for sin is left for the sinners themselves. The wrath of God is fully appeased. It burned itself out, regarding all those for whom Christ died, in Jesus Christ. Upon the death of Jesus, all those for whom he died have full and unchallengeable right to all of salvation. The Confession goes on to affirm the fullness of the satisfaction of the death of Christ in different words: "this only sacrifice, once offered, by which believers are made perfect forever."

The conclusion that the Confession draws from the complete and perfect satisfaction that is the death of Jesus is that it is not "necessary to seek or invent any other means of being reconciled to God, than this only sacrifice." This is the Reformed, biblical condemnation of the Roman Catholic mass, which claims to repeat the sacrifice of the cross, albeit in an unbloody manner. It is the condemnation, as well, of all human works that are intended to add to Christ's work, as conditions unto salvation. All such works pretend, in fact, to be means of being reconciled to God. Every such theology of the works of humans denies the satisfaction of the cross.

BIBLICAL BASIS

The passages of scripture adduced by the Confession are both the authoritative basis of the Confession's doctrine of satisfaction and biblical explanation of the nature of satisfaction. Prominent is Isaiah 53, as it is one of the outstanding passages in all scripture on the nature of the suffering and death of the Messiah: "He was wounded for our transgressions," and what follows (v. 5). The passage prophesied the suffering of the Messiah as satisfying the justice of God for the sins of the people of God: "All we like sheep have gone astray...and the LORD hath laid on him the iniquity of us all" (v. 6). In his suffering the Messiah would be the substitute for others: "bruised for our iniquities" (v. 5). His suffering and death would be sufficient for the reconciliation to God and salvation of the people: "With his stripes we are healed" (v. 5).

Psalm 69:4 foretold the full satisfaction of the righteousness of God on behalf of a guilty people by the innocent substitute: "Then I restored that which I took not away."

First Peter 3:18 emphasizes the substitutionary nature of the death of Christ: "the just for the unjust." What follows in the text teaches that this substitutionary death was full satisfaction of God's justice, for it accomplished the reconciliation of the elect to God: "that he might bring us to God."

The spiritual effect of this satisfaction upon the believing church is gloriously expressed in the words of 1 Corinthians 2:2 and Philippians 3:8, as expressed by the Confession: "We know nothing but Jesus Christ, and him crucified; we count all things but loss and dung for the excellency of the knowledge of Christ Jesus our Lord."

CHRIST JESUS OUR HIGH PRIEST

The Confession directs Reformed believers to view Christ's great work of satisfaction as his exercise of his office of high priest. Such is the opening line of article 21: "We believe that Jesus Christ is ordained with an oath to be an everlasting High-Priest." As high priest, he presented himself to God in making satisfaction. The cross, then, was the high priest's solemnly stepping up to the great altar of burnt offering, to slay and burn the Lamb—himself. In keeping with this view of the suffering Jesus as high priest, the article uses appropriate language: "offering"; "pouring out his precious blood"; and "sacrifice, once offered."

As the reference to the Old Testament high priest Melchisedec indicates, the instruction of article 21 of the Confession bases itself largely on the epistle to the Hebrews. That is the great epistle on Jesus' high priestly office and on his work of satisfaction by sacrifice (see especially Heb. 4:14; 10:39).

Generally, the work of the high priest was to consecrate the people to God. It was covenantal work. He accomplished the fellowship of God's sinful people with the righteous God. Although the high priest had compassion on the people, his work was God-ward. According to Hebrews 5:1, "Every high priest...is ordained for men in things pertaining to God." The Confession therefore describes the main work of Christ as high priest as reconciliation. The saving effect of his satisfaction is his people's "being reconciled to God."

The work of the high priest in the Old Testament was twofold. He made the sacrifice for sins that satisfied the righteousness of the offended God. Then, on the basis of the sacrifice, he interceded for the people with God.

Jesus Christ is the true and real high priest, of whom the Old Testament high priests, especially Melchisedec (see Gen. 14:18–20; Ps. 110:4), were foreshadowing types. "Jesus Christ is ordained with an oath [by God] to be an everlasting High-Priest" (see Heb. 7:21). God ordained Jesus as high priest in the decree of the covenant, in which God elected Jesus Christ head and mediator of the church. Therefore, first, Christ's work, particularly making satisfaction, is official work, authorized work, work that God recognizes and accepts as valid and effectual.

That Jesus is the high priest ordained by God means, in the second place, that Christ's work of satisfaction is God's own work by means of Jesus Christ. God is not changed by Christ's death from hatred to love, from a determination to damn to a determination to forgive and bless. But God himself, in his eternal love for his elect,[4] made satisfaction to himself through the High Priest whom he appointed.

The work of Christ as high priest was satisfaction of the righteousness of God for the sins of the people: "to appease

4 See article 16 of the Belgic Confession.

his wrath by his full satisfaction." This Christ did by offering the sacrifice to God that suffered the punishment due to the guilty people of God. The sacrifice was the High Priest himself. Sacrificing Priest and sacrificial offering were one and the same. This work of the High Priest has been accomplished! This is finished! This sacrifice was perfect! This atoning sacrifice is unrepeated and unrepeatable! The Confession gives expression to this Reformed orthodoxy in the words "this only sacrifice, once offered, by which believers are made perfect forever."

The work of Christ as high priest continues in the activity of intercession. This aspect of the high priestly office of Christ is set forth at some length in article 26 of the Confession. It consists of Christ's pleading with God that the people for whom Christ died may enjoy the benefits of his death, on the basis of the satisfaction of justice by his death.

That Christ is high priest "after the order of Melchisedec" legitimizes the priesthood of Christ, who was not from the tribe of Levi but from the tribe of Judah, "of which tribe Moses spake nothing concerning priesthood" (Heb. 7:14). It also magnifies the priesthood of Christ as better than the Old Testament priesthood of Aaron (Heb. 7). Christ's priesthood was the reality of Old Testamental typical priesthood. It took away sin once for all, and it effectually reconciles the people to God. In addition, like the priesthood of Melchisedec, Christ's priesthood combines the priestly office with the kingly office, a thing prohibited to the Aaronitic priesthood. And the priesthood of Christ is everlasting, without "beginning of days, nor end of life... [He] abideth a priest continually" (v. 3).

FOR WHOM THE HIGH PRIEST SATISFIED

The Confession does not sharply and explicitly address the question, for whom did Christ offer the sacrifice that satisfied the justice of God, that is, for whom did Christ die? No doubt, the explanation is in part that this question was not an issue in the Reformed churches at the time of the writing of the Belgic Confession. The later Arminian controversy made necessary the explicit confession of Christ's death for the elect alone and the explicit denial of the doctrine of Christ's death for all humans. The Reformed churches made this fuller and explicit confession of Christ's particular death for the elect only in the Canons of Dordt, 1618–19:

> This was the sovereign counsel and most gracious will and purpose of God the Father, that the quickening and saving efficacy of the most precious death of his Son should extend to all the elect…that is, it was the will of God, that Christ by the blood of the cross…should effectually redeem out of every people…all those, and those only, who were from eternity chosen to salvation, and given to him by the Father.[5]

Not content to confess the truth of the particular, or definite, or limited atonement of Christ positively, the Canons adds the condemnation of the heretical theory of universal atonement:

> The Synod [of Dordt] rejects the errors of those… Who teach that Christ, by His satisfaction, merited neither salvation itself for anyone, nor faith, whereby

---

5 Canons of Dordt 2.8, in Schaff, *Creeds of Christendom*, 3:587.

this satisfaction of Christ unto salvation is effectually appropriated; but that He merited for the Father only the authority of the perfect will to deal again with man, and to prescribe new conditions as He might desire, obedience to which, however, depended on the free will of man.[6]

This theory of universal atonement, the Canons condemns as "the Pelagian error out of hell."[7]

Brief and implicit as it may be on the issue of the extent of the atonement of the cross, the Confession nevertheless makes clear that it is the Reformed faith that Christ died only for the elect, not for all humans without exception. First, the Confession speaks of the High Priest's presentation of himself as sacrifice for sin "in *our* behalf"; of Christ's "offering himself...and pouring out his precious blood to purge away *our* sins"; of his "feeling the terrible punishment which *our* sins had merited"; and of his suffering "all this for the remission of *our* sins." The Confession identifies these "our" as "believers": "by which [sacrifice] believers are made perfect forever."

Second, the Confession includes two passages of scripture that are clear and powerful in teaching definite, particular redemption, namely, Isaiah 53 and Matthew 1:21. The latter text is quoted by the Confession at the very end of its exposition of Christ's satisfaction: "SAVIOUR, because he should save his people from their sins." The very name of the savior, "Jesus," that is, "Jehovah Salvation," is the revelation not only that he saves "*his people*," but also that he "*saves.*" The heresy of Arminianism is not only that Jesus is

---

6 Canons of Dordt 2 error 3, in *Confessions and Church Order*, 165.
7 Ibid.

a (would-be) savior of all humans without exception. But its false doctrine is that Jesus does not *save*. He merely makes salvation possible. The reality of salvation is the act of sinners themselves (supposedly by their free will).

Third, the Confession teaches definite, particular, limited atonement by its very doctrine of satisfaction. Inasmuch as Christ's death was satisfaction of the righteousness of God, all for whom he died are and must be saved. The justice of God requires this. God's wrath regarding those for whom Christ died is appeased. For them Christ made "full satisfaction." His blood purged away their sins.

If Christ died for all, but some yet perish, unsaved, the death of Christ was not satisfaction as the Confession affirms that it was and as the abundant scripture adduced by article 21 reveals it to have been. Herman Hoeksema is right: "The Arminian, who, because of his denial of limited atonement, cannot and does not maintain the truth of satisfaction."[8] Thus the Arminian denies the cross! He does so as really as does the Roman Catholic.

PRACTICAL IMPLICATIONS

The Confession itself draws out of its (Reformed) doctrine of the death of Christ as satisfaction the practical implications of the doctrine for the church and for the individual believer. Both church and believer know, proclaim, and confess only Jesus Christ and him crucified. Indeed, they count all else, particularly all doctrine and religious activity pertaining to salvation that competes with the cross of Christ, that compromises the cross of Christ, or that adds

8 Herman Hoeksema, *The Triple Knowledge: An Exposition of the Heidelberg Catechism* (Grand Rapids, MI: Reformed Free Publishing Association, 1970), 1:243.

to the cross of Christ ("other means of being reconciled to God") as "dung." The Reformed faith concerning the cross and death of Christ renounces and repudiates all human worth, all human will, and all human work that conditions reconciliation and salvation. Its confession is "Christ Jesus alone!"

The practical implication is also that the Reformed believer finds in Christ's wounds, as present in the gospel, "all manner of consolation." This is consolation of the deep sorrow of sin. There is forgiveness. It is also the consolation of all the sorrows of the Reformed believer, including sickness, death, and every form of adversity. He satisfied! God is now for us! Who or what can be against us?

ABOUT THE AUTHOR

David J. Engelsma was ordained to the gospel ministry in 1963 and served as pastor of Protestant Reformed congregations for twenty-five years. For twenty years he worked as professor of theology in the Theological School of the Protestant Reformed Churches. He became emeritus in 2008. For sixteen years he was editor of the Reformed semi-monthly magazine the *Standard Bearer*. He is the author of the following books published by the Reformed Free Publishing Association:

Battle for Sovereign Grace in the Covenant: The Declaration of Principles

Better to Marry: Sex and Marriage in 1 Corinthians 6 and 7

Bound to Join: Letters on Church Membership

Christianizing the World: Reformed Calling or Ecclesiastical Suicide?

Common Grace Revisited: A Response to Richard J. Mouw's He Shines in All That's Fair

Covenant and Election in the Reformed Tradition

The Covenant of God and the Children of Believers: Sovereign Grace in the Covenant

A Defense of the Church Institute: Response to the Critics of Bound to Join

Federal Vision: Heresy at the Root

Gospel Truth of Justification: Proclaimed, Defended, Developed

Hyper-Calvinism and the Call of the Gospel: An Examination of the Well-Meant Offer of the Gospel

Marriage: The Mystery of Christ and the Church

Prosperous Wicked and Plagued Saints: An Exposition of Psalm 73

Reformed Education: The Christian School as Demand of the Covenant

The Reformed Faith of John Calvin: The Institutes in Summary

Reformed Worship (coauthor with Barrett Gritters and Charles Terpstra)

Trinity and Covenant: God as Holy Family

Unfolding Covenant History: Judges and Ruth

David J. Engelsma has also edited the following publications of the Reformed Free Publishing Association:

All Glory to the Only Good God: Reformed Spirituality

Always Reforming: Continuation of the Sixteenth-Century Reformation

Communion with God: Reformed Spirituality

Peace for the Troubled Heart: Reformed Spirituality

Righteous by Faith Alone: A Devotional Commentary on Romans

The Sixteenth-Century Reformation of the Church

The Reformed Baptism Form: A Commentary

The Rock Whence We Are Hewn: God, Grace, and Covenant

www.ingramcontent.com/pod-product-compliance
Lightning Source LLC
Chambersburg PA
CBHW060653150426
42813CB00053B/809